KEN HAEDRICH

Apple Pie *Perfect*

100 Delicious and Decidedly

Different Recipes for America's Favorite Pie

The Harvard Common Press • Boston, Massachusetts

The Harvard Common Press
535 Albany Street
Boston, Massachusetts 02118
www.harvardcommonpress.com

©2002 by Ken Haedrich
Photographs ©2002 by Eric Roth Photography
Illustrations ©2002 by Linda Hillel

Printed in the United States of America

Printed on acid-free paper

Library of Congress Cataloging-in-Publication Data
Haedrich, Ken.
    Apple pie perfect : 100 delicious and decidedly different recipes for America's favorite pie / Ken Haedrich.
        p. cm.
    ISBN 1-55832-224-8 (cloth : alk. paper)—ISBN 1-55832-225-6 (pbk. : alk. paper)
        1. Pies. 2. Cookery (Apples) I. Title.

TX773.H218 2002
641.8'652—dc21

2002017262

Special bulk-order discounts are available on this and other Harvard Common Press books. Companies and organizations may purchase books for premiums or resale, or may arrange a custom edition, by contacting the Marketing Director at the address above.

10 9 8 7 6 5 4 3 2 1

Cover and interior design by Night & Day Design
All photographs (except for that of author's parents) by Eric Roth Photography
Food styling by Mary Bandereck
Illustrations by Linda Hillel

For reasons I've tried to make clear in the introduction—among many other reasons—this book is dedicated, with love and appreciation, to my parents, Warren and Muriel Haedrich. This is their wedding picture, taken in Indiana shortly before my dad shipped out for combat duty in World War II. Notice the calm, content expression of a young couple blissfully ignorant of the challenges of raising a child, let alone seven of them, as they would so valiantly do. That was 58 years ago, and I'm happy to say that they're still sitting arm in arm, looking every bit as happy and young at heart as they do here.

Contents

9

APPLE PIE ON THE FRINGES 193

10

A FEW FOR THE KIDS 209

11

APPLE PIE IN A JIFFY 223

Acknowledgments

I seem to thank a lot of the same people from book to book—some simply for putting up with me, others whom I have had the ongoing pleasure of working with on a regular basis for many years, and still others who have been particularly helpful in the evolution of the book in question. For this book they include:

Nancy Wall Hopkins, Karen Pollock, and Anna Anderson at *Better Homes and Gardens.*

Kristine Kidd, Barbara Fairchild, Sarah Tenaglia, Anthony Head, Katie O'Kennedy, and Victoria von Biel at *Bon Appétit.*

Cindy Littlefield at *Family Fun*; working with you is always a pleasure.

David Sokol at *Disney Magazine*; I'm ready for another trip to Florida anytime you are.

Georgia Orcutt, formerly of *Yankee.*

Susan Peery at *digitalhearth.com.*

Sheila Buckmaster, Jayne Wise, and my other friends at *National Geographic Traveler.*

Kathy Farrell Kingsley at *Vegetarian Times.*

Patsy Jamieson, once and now again at *Eating Well.*

For her wonderful apples and time on the phone I thank Betsy King of Michigan's King Orchards. Similarly, I'd like to thank Bob and Susan Jasse of New Hampshire's Alyson's Apple Orchard for the generosity of their delicious apples. And a tip of my hat to my old friends Mike and Nancy Phillips for the great apple and elderberry pie recipe you'll find on page 66.

Early in my writing career, Marion Cunningham—you know her better as the Fannie Farmer cook—was uncommonly generous with her kind words, encouragement, and telephone calls. Thanks so much.

 In addition, I want to thank my agent, Meg Ruley, and Don Cleary, both of the Jane Rotrosen Agency, for more of their usual fine work on my behalf.

 Large slices of gratitude to Bruce Shaw, Pam Hoenig, Valerie Cimino, and the staff of the Harvard Common Press for really getting behind this book; I think it looks wonderful.

 My children—Ben, Tess, Ali, and Sam—have given my life purpose, direction, and more joy than they know. An occasional headache, too—but nothing personal, right? Thanks for never turning down yet another slice of apple pie.

 Love to Cindy C., Sam and Karen, Jonathan and Lauren for insisting I do a section on easy pies made with someone else's crust, and Dave, Laurie, Alexa, and Nick for the wonderful meals we've shared. Of course, love and gratitude to my siblings—Joe, Barb, Tom, Bill, Joanne, and Mary—for everything we've shared over the years. And to my wonderful parents, Warren and Muriel, to whom this book is dedicated.

 Lastly, love to Bev for sharing your life—and far too many apple pie calories—with me. But do explain: why is it that *my* slices of apple pie go right to my waist and *yours* are nowhere to be found? It's just not fair.

Introduction

Why a book of 100 apple pie recipes? That's a perfectly reasonable question, and I probably have as many answers for it as I do, well, recipes for apple pie. But I doubt I could say it better than the eminent horticulturist Liberty Hyde Bailey, who addressed the issue—if only by extension, and one step shy of the oven—in his 1922 book *The Apple Tree*:

> *Why do we need so many kinds of apples? Because there are so many folks. A person has a right to gratify his legitimate taste. If he wants twenty or forty kinds of apples for his personal use, running from Early Harvest to Roxbury Russet, he should be accorded the privilege.... There is merit in variety itself. It provides more contact with life, and leads away from uniformity and monotony.*

Which is to say that we need a book full of apple pie recipes because taste is indeed a very personal matter and variety is the spice of life. You may like a saucy apple pie with very little spice and a top crust. I, on the other hand, might prefer firmer apples, lots of spice, and a crumb topping. Is my pie better than yours? Certainly not—no more than my choice of religion or automobile or hometown is better than yours. Every apple pie has its merits, as the writer reminds us, and reflects a set of biases and circumstances unique to the pie maker himself. And if no collection of apple pie recipes could speak to all those biases and individual situations, it's certainly my hope—in casting the widest of nets over the subject of apple pie—that I've made America's favorite pie more accessible to a wide range of home cooks than anyone before me.

OKAY—YOU'VE MADE YOUR POINT, BUT I'M A BEGINNER. CAN I REALLY LEARN TO BAKE A GREAT APPLE PIE?

In a perfect world, all of us would have been blessed with good baking genes—and given the popularity of apple pie, those precise genes required to roll out a respectable-looking pie pastry. Alas, as one who has spent a good part of his career writing books and articles devoted to the subject of baking and given numerous baking classes, workshops, and demonstrations, I'm here to tell you that there are many among us who believe that making an apple pie they can be proud of requires a set of skills that's beyond their reach. To which I say, that's a lot of hooey.

Put another way, making a gorgeous, delicious apple pie is one of the easiest tricks in the home cook's bag of kitchen skills. Loan me any 10-year-old for a couple of hours, and I'll teach him to make an apple pie—not because I'm such a great teacher, but because there's nothing to it: you mix a pastry, roll the pastry, prepare the filling, put it in the pie shell, and bake it. In one session, you can master 90 percent of what you need to know. Beyond that, it's just a matter of refining the basic steps, like rolling the pastry nice and round and knowing when your pie is baked to perfection. You may be surprised at how quickly these skills can be acquired, especially when you're new to pie baking and able to build rapidly on the lessons you learn. Just imagine, if you bake one apple pie a week, or two a month, that's 25 or 50 pies you will make in the coming year. At the end of the year, I guarantee you'll be the best apple pie maker on your block—and you'll have more friends than you'll know what to do with.

Once you've mastered the mechanics of making apple pie—or perhaps while you're mastering them—you may notice a change in your approach. With the basic techniques under your belt, you'll probably start paying more attention to your ingredients, particularly your apples. At the risk of stating the obvious, good apples are essential to a good apple pie—and the better the apples, generally speaking, the better the pie.

Which apples make the best pie? I can't answer that question unequivocally, although I try to steer you in the right direction in the apple guide starting on page xv. The thing is, the best pie apple is a matter of personal preference and a reflection of the quality of a given apple at a given time of the year. And it's a moving target. The Northern Spy apples in your neck of the woods might be super one year, the Jonathan apples a little better the following year. The Golden Delicious apples you find in your supermarket could be great this week, not so great a month from now. Part of the challenge of making a good

apple pie is to find good apples, make notes of their suitability in pie, and incorporate that knowledge into your pie-baking life. And don't forget to share that information with fellow apple pie makers you meet along the way.

AFTER ALL, APPLE PIE IS ABOUT SHARING AND CARING, NOW MORE THAN EVER

I'm a cook, not a social scientist, so I can't really tell you what it is that makes people weak in the knees and wax patriotic when it comes to apple pie. Certainly, the flavor and aroma are part of the allure: nothing smells as good as apple pie in the oven or tastes as good as warm apple pie. But if I had to venture a guess, I would say that apple pie is an American favorite because we associate it with our youth, when life seemed so much simpler than it does today. That's certainly the case with me.

I'm one of seven children of Warren and Muriel—to whom this book is dedicated, for reasons that will become obvious in a moment. She's a homemaker; he's a jack of many trades and retired printer. As with many men of the "Greatest Generation," my dad's place was in the workplace, not in the kitchen. There were exceptions, certainly. Dad carved the Thanksgiving turkey and all other Significant Holiday Roasts. And he held court with his Sunday pancake breakfasts. But his role in the kitchen was pretty much in keeping with the narrowly defined norms of the day.

Except for one thing, and that was his apple pies. I call them *his* apple pies, but in fact my mom and dad worked on these pies together (see page 24 for their pie recipe). It's just that my mental photo album of these times contains more images of my dad than of my mom, probably because she stood out less than he did against the backdrop where I was accustomed to her presence. In any event, I will always remember coming in from mowing the lawn or playing baseball with my friends to find Mom preparing the filling and Dad wearing one of mom's aprons, deftly and meticulously rolling out a circle of pastry, a smear of Pillsbury flour floating across his bald spot like a lazy cloud.

It seems like such a small and simple thing—a married couple making apple pie together. But in that simple act was the expression of so many things a child should experience to feel safe, secure, and grounded in this world: cooperation, the joy of shared effort, tactile engagement, love, and playfulness.

My theory, then, is that we love apple pie because so many of us have a story like mine—a story in which we watched or even helped a favorite grandma make apple pie, or in which a fragrant apple pie was always waiting, steam still pouring from the little top vents, when we arrived for dinner at an aunt's house. When we were young, we never gave it much thought: those apple pies were just something great to eat. Now that we're older and wiser, we realize that apple pie connects us to our past and the people we care about most. None other than Bob Hope said, "When we recall the past, we usually find that it is the simplest things—not the great occasions—that in retrospect give off the greatest glow of happiness." I believe apple pie is, for many of us, that simple thing.

So do this: proceed confidently, learn to make the best apple pie you can, and be quick to share your skills and the fruits of your labor with others. Here's hoping that you'll find much happiness, for you and yours, in this collection of apple pie recipes I've had the pleasure of making over many years.

A Pie Maker's Guide to Apple Varieties

I'm less convinced than I once was that pie makers need to worry about the ideal of "the perfect pie apple." Clearly, there are superior varieties of apples whose tartness, flavor, and texture render them excellent for making pies. Some of these are widely available on a seasonal basis, and some are harder-to-find antique varieties. But there are also many good pie apples to be had right at your local supermarket and farm stand—apples, for the most part, that account for most of the pies baked in this country. Think of it this way: if apples were books of fiction, antique apples would be literary fiction, and standard market apples would be popular fiction. And who says we can't enjoy a good Stephen King thriller as much as a Richard Ford novel? We can relish both, when the situation warrants.

Besides, apple people will tell you it's often less the apple than it is the condition and age of the apple that matters most. I think this accounts for the fact that, in consulting multiple sources, it wasn't unusual for me to find one that would

FOOD WRITER JOHN THORNE ON APPLES

"The best rule here, I guess, is to pick your apple tree and stick with it. My mother makes a great pie from the Wolf River apples that grow (and grew long before they ever got there) in the pasture of their old Maine farm. Hardly any source mentions the Wolf River; it is not so much rare as deliberately obscure, being not an immediately attractive apple. But it's there, fresh and free, so my mother has taken its measure, upping sugar and baking time when it's fresh and tart, and lowering both later, when it is neither. She knows that apple; this, not the apple, makes the difference....

"Not having a tree, the next best policy is to pay careful attention when buying them: apples should be unblemished and feel heavy for their size, resisting a gentle push with the thumb. Buy a few extra so you can discard the proverbial bad one. After that, find a favorite and stick with it. Famous for pies are Granny Smiths, Gravensteins (fresh!), Jonathans, Northern Spies, and Baldwins. All have juice and flavor and hold their shape when baked. Personally, I think McIntosh is better for sauce than pies. Golden Delicious has fans; not me. The important thing is to find *your* apple. If you love even the Red Delicious enough, you can learn to make a pie from it."
—*Simple Cooking* (Viking Penguin, Inc., 1989)

rate a given apple "fair" for making pie, another that would judge it "good," and yet another that would consider it "excellent." Any such rating system is also rife with individual subjectivity and personal taste. The truth is, I believe, that almost any fresh, crisp, juicy apple—regardless of variety—is going to make a pie superior to one made with the best antique apple that's been stored for too long.

How can you tell if the apple is fresh, crisp, and juicy? There are telltale signs: firmness, absence of dents and bruises, and a fair heft in proportion to size. And the season, of course: almost any domestically grown apple you buy in March has spent a fair amount of time in storage and will have lost some of its youthful luster. But the very best way to judge is to take a bite before you buy and see what you think. I embarrass my kids whenever I do this in a store—and draw the disapproving stares of other shoppers as well, especially when I put the apple back in the pile. (Only kidding; I always buy the sample apple.) But it is the acid test of apple quality. And I salute those rare markets—like the Fresh Fields store where I shop in Annapolis, Maryland—that have the savvy to know this and will happily cut up samples for their shoppers to nibble on.

So let me echo the opinion of John Thorne (see page xv), who says essentially this: Don't worry so much about variety. Just get to know your apples and start making pies. The fact is, I've met very few apples in my lifetime that I couldn't make into a respectable pie. My advice— no matter where you shop—is to try different apples, take notes in the margins of recipes, and find one or two you're crazy for in pies. Then stick with them when you can. Stay amenable to trying new apples, but know that you can fall back on your favorites when you need to.

That said, here's a rundown of popular apples with some comments that you might find useful when choosing a pie apple.

Baldwin: The Baldwin is grown widely in New England and New York State. It's an all-purpose red-skinned apple with a mild, sweet-tart flavor and crisp texture. It was once grown more commonly than it is now, having fallen out of favor due to the fact that the fruit is prone to cold injury and the trees bear fruit only every other year. But old-timers love it for its ability to store well in root cellars. An aromatic apple with a firm texture, the Baldwin makes a commendable pie.

Braeburn: Discovered in New Zealand in 1952, the Braeburn varies in color from greenish gold to red with yellow markings. The Braeburn has a smooth, juicy, crisp flesh and excellent flavor. Its sweet juiciness and fine aroma make it a good choice for pie.

Cortland: The Cortland is grown extensively in the northeastern part of the United States; it's one of the leading Vermont apples. The peel is a deep red, often with yellow-green striping, and the flesh is very white. The Cortland is said to be a good storage apple, although I believe that this is probably truer of the early crop than the later ones. Generally speaking, I think early Cortland apples are better for pie because they're tarter than later ones, which tend to be fairly sweet.

Fuji: The Fuji apple hasn't been around all that long in the American market, but it is quickly gaining fans here. The Fuji is a cross between a Red Delicious and a Ralls Janet and is said to be the best-selling apple in Japan, where it was first bred at the Tohuku Research Station. It's considered less of a baking or pie apple than it is a dessert apple—one that's best eaten out of hand—but I think that its excellent, almost spicy flavor and consistent juiciness make it more than suitable for pies. I have read several times that the flavor of the Fuji apple improves with age, and indeed it might; I just haven't noticed.

Gala: Sometimes called Royal Gala, this apple has many of the same fine characteristics as the Fuji: crisp, aromatic flesh, sweet flavor, and lots of juice. It is said to descend from the Cox's Orange Pippin (see page 56), which partly explains, to my mind, why it makes a fine pie apple—though, again, it is more widely considered a snacking apple.

Golden Delicious: The Golden Delicious, sometimes called the Yellow Delicious, is considered a good all-purpose apple, but it has a fair number of detractors who consider it insipid and unexciting—which it can be at its worst. It's a medium-size to large apple with pale yellow or yellow-green skin. The skin is more tender than most, so if I'm making a Golden Delicious apple pie, I'm often a little lazy about getting off all the peel, considering a little of the peel in the pie a quaint, healthy touch. (Incidentally, you can spot an old Golden Delicious from a mile away because the skin tends to shrivel with age.) On the upside, the apple is sweet, and its slices hold their shape in pies. On the downside, the flavor can be bland and lacking in tartness. So use plenty of lemon juice with this apple.

Granny Smith: Granny Smith is widely thought to be one of the better pie apples: it has good flavor, juiciness, and a firm texture. But despite all this, it isn't universally loved, since so many of the Granny Smith apples we eat are imported from the Southern Hemisphere. It belies the sentiment "as American as apple pie," you know. (Some states, I understand, will not even allow them in their state fair apple pie contests.) Call me unpatriotic, but I like a Granny Smith pie. Indeed, I have an all-Granny pie on page 40 and it is one of the most popular pies I make. The flavor is pleasing, the aroma is enticing, and there's just the right amount of texture (for my taste) in a Granny pie.

Gravenstein: The Gravenstein apple originated in Germany and arrived in the United States in the 1700s. It doesn't grow well in warm, dry areas, but it has flourished in parts of California, including the Sonoma Valley, and in the Annapolis Valley in Nova Scotia. It's thought to be one of the best early apples for pie makers, ripening in late August. The Gravenstein has creamy, tart-sweet flesh, and the skin typically has a greenish yellow background with broad red stripes.

Ida Red: A cross between a Jonathan and a Wagener, the Ida Red was introduced in 1942, the result of research performed at the Idaho Agricultural Experiment Station. Grown widely in the Northeast and upper Midwest, has bright red skin and firm white flesh tinged with green. It is one of the better keeping apples, and some say the flavor improves with age. I think the Ida Red makes a superior pie.

Jonagold: The Jonagold is one of the darling apples of the last few years, highly valued as a snacking and processing fruit. It's a cross between a Jonathan and a Golden Delicious, developed at the New York State Agricultural Experiment Station at Geneva in 1943 and introduced commercially in 1968. It's a pretty apple—

AN EXPERT'S NOTES ON ANTIQUE APPLES

[I spent countless hours surfing the Web while researching this book, and by far the most fetching and useful apple Web site I found in my searches was www.applejournal.com. Apple Journal is the brainchild of Mike Berst, a veritable encyclopedia of all things apple. He's particularly passionate about antique apples, so I thought I'd give him an opportunity to say a few words on the subject.]

Modern shoppers would find it hard to imagine the diversity of apple varieties that once was available. The U.S. Government publication "Nomenclature of the Apple" (circa 1905) listed the names of some 17,000 apple varieties that had been identified in nineteenth-century America. Many factors have contributed to the dramatic decline in these numbers as centralized distribution systems for agricultural produce have resulted in only the few varieties that bear up well to the rigors of packing, shipping, and long-term storage. We have a paucity of regional selections—apples that are considered indigenous to a particular section of the country— nor is there a ready availability of those apples that are best suited to specific uses, such as those once cultivated for cider, drying, or baking. Americans no longer have any sense of "seasonal varieties,"

those delightful cultivars that were harvested during different times of the year. The old heirloom varieties, which have disappeared from market, are now called "antique apples."

The apple is one of the oldest of all cultivated crops. It is the most familiar and widely grown of any temperate-climate fruits. The first true apples were grown in Kazakhstan and the Caucasus region in Central Asia. Their cultivation spread during prehistoric times, and carbonized apples have been found among the remains of those prehistoric tribes that lived in Western Europe. We know from the writings of Homer, Cato, and Pliny that apple cultivation was important in early Greek and Roman cultures. One variety occasionally still found in American orchards, the lady apple, is thought to have originated with the Romans. Fruit historians in the United Kingdom have determined the precise variety that grew in Sir Isaac Newton's mother's garden. When an apple fell from one of those trees in 1665, the story goes, this event led to Newton's development of the theories that formed the foundation of modern physics. This tale inspired James Lovell to secretly obtain some seeds from this Flower-of-Kent apple, which he smuggled aboard the Apollo spacecraft in a fountain pen in order to greenish yellow with mottled red striping—and has sweet, creamy, juicy flesh. The Jonagold doesn't store particularly well, but if you buy the apples early and use them quickly, they make a very good pie.

Jonathan: Echoing what I said at the beginning of this section, the Jonathan encompasses many of the conflicting opinions one finds on the subject of pie apples—and why you should take everything you read on the subject, here and elsewhere, with a grain of salt. In one tasting I read about, a group of gourmets rated the

honor the Father of Modern Physics.

When the colonists came to the New World, they brought with them their love of apples, especially in the form of cider. Trees and branches were both difficult and expensive to bring across the ocean, however, and this meant that the familiar European varieties were not available in the colonies. Seeds were much easier to transport. This copious importation of apple seeds resulted in what some have called the greatest agricultural experiment in history. American colonists planted thousands of new orchards from seed. Since apples do not grow true to variety from seed, and because specific varieties can only be propagated by grafting, the product of these new orchards were thousands of new, hitherto unknown apple varieties. Most have deservedly disappeared, but many were found to be of high quality and/or superbly adapted to a particular use or climate. From these colonial orchards came some of the best-known, best-loved American varieties, among them Rhode Island Greening, Jonathan, Northern Spy, Golden Russet, Westfield-Seek-No-Further, Roxbury Russet, and many others.

Some of these antique cultivars are closely associated with historical people or events. The Newtown Pippin, discovered as a chance seedling on Long Island in the early 1700s, is the subject of a narrative concerning Benjamin Franklin. He brought samples of this variety to the royal court in England in 1759, which led to the first export trade in American apples. The Spitzenburg, discovered in Ulster County, New York, in the mid-1700s, was a favorite of Thomas Jefferson and was grown extensively in his orchards at Monticello.

As so often happens in American culture, the tide of standardization in apple varieties has created a small but growing riptide of interest in these older American cultivars—as well as interest in the many historical varieties from Europe. Orchards offering two hundred or more old varieties can now be found here and there across the country. Part of the attraction is the romance and history of these apples, which have evocative names such as Maiden Blush, Winter Banana, Opalescent, Snow Apple, Sheepnose, and Hubbardston Nonesuch. Americans accustomed to or familiar with modern offerings are surprised to see such diversity in the shapes, sizes, and colors of these antique varieties. The most important reason to seek out this fascinating part of our heritage is one we have not mentioned yet: the quest for superior and distinctive flavor. Those who are tired of the increasingly bland and uniform American diet will find that the taste of these gems is as diverse and as interesting as their appearance.

Jonathan as rather disappointing as a pie apple. But many rank the Jonathan up there with the Northern Spy as one of the best for pies. A certain book I consulted called it an "excellent" pie apple; other sources say it's much better as a snacking apple and for sauce. In any event, the Jonathan originated in Woodstock, New York—a place not unfamiliar to my fellow baby boomers—around 1826. It has soft, fine-textured flesh with a spicy, tangy flavor that's worth trying in your apple pies.

Macoun: A cross between a McIntosh and a Jersey Black, the Macoun was developed in New York State. It has attractive red skin with green to wine-colored streaking. The buzz is that if you like the McIntosh in a pie, you should try the Macoun, even though it is generally considered a dessert apple. I'm very fond of the flavor of the Macoun, and I make several all-Macoun pies every fall when I'm lucky enough to find these apples in the market.

McIntosh: Said to have originated as a chance seedling in the orchard of one John McIntosh in Ontario, Canada, the McIntosh apple is a hero to some pie makers and a villain to others. The controversy centers on its white, finely textured flesh, which becomes very soft in the baking—the sort of mushy soft that some people adore and others despise. If you like McIntosh apples, watch for the Early McIntosh, available in mid- to late August, which tends to be sweeter, firmer, and generally more distinctive than later ones. Much as I like it, it's not my first choice for an apple pie, but I will often add one or two Macs to

a pie for the softness they provide.

Mutsu: Also known as a Crispin, this is one of the largest apples you'll find in the market. As I note in my recipe for Crispin Apple Lemonade Pie (page 228), you could well make a nine-inch pie with three good-size specimens. The Mutsu/Crispin looks a little like an overgrown Golden Delicious, from which it descends, but the flesh tends to be firmer, crisper, and juicier—which is why, when I can find these apples, I nearly always choose them for a pie over the Golden Delicious, even though the flesh doesn't hold its shape quite as well in the baking.

Northern Spy: Widely regarded as one of the best pie apples, the Northern Spy is a firm apple with white, fine-textured flesh and an excellent balance of sweetness and tartness when the fruit is at its best. These large apples aren't usually found in supermarkets, except in parts of New England and Michigan, where the apples prosper. The Northern Spy is prone to easy bruising, so select fruits carefully when purchasing them.

Paula Red: You'll see the first Paula Red apples coming to market by late summer, which is why I often make a pie using them and blueberries, blackberries, peaches, or other summer fruits. The Paula Red won't be to everyone's taste as a pie apple, in part because it bakes up rather soft, like the McIntosh. And, in fact, it doesn't have nearly the allure of some of the later apples, such as the Mutsu/Crispin or Northern Spy. But it's not a bad choice for a pie, especially if you use the apples soon after they're purchased and don't try to store them.

Red Delicious: Pity the poor Red Delicious. In some ways, it represents the epitome of American apples: so shapely, firm, and perfectly red. Yet in others, it represents one of our greatest agricultural failings, in that American agri-biz so often puts appearance before taste and texture—which is to say that the Red Delicious often has a lackluster flavor, a cottony texture, and little personality. Is it a good pie apple? So-so. Frankly, I don't have much experience baking with the Red Delicious, which is considered more of a snacking apple. I wouldn't write it off as a pie apple, but I'd consider my options carefully before I made a Red Delicious pie.

Rome Beauty: The Rome Beauty is a large, globe-shaped apple with bright red skin. Considered a fine pie apple because its slices hold their shape well, the Rome Beauty has a tough skin and a dryish, somewhat coarse, firm flesh. The flavor of the Rome Beauty is very good; some maintain that it actually improves in the baking.

Winesap: This is an excellent, late-ripening apple with sweet-tart, winy, juicy flesh and one of the oldest apples still in commercial production. Cider makers have considered the Winesap one of the prime cider apples for more than 200 years. You'll be lucky to find Winesap apples in the supermarket, but they're worth seeking out at farm stands and from specialty growers. If you find them, buy a bushel: they're excellent keepers, and make one of the best apple pies you'll ever eat.

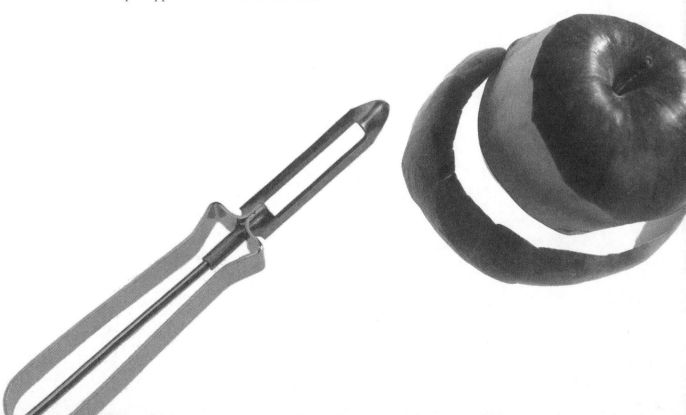

CHAPTER 1

Pastries for Your Apple Pies

With apple pie, as with much of life—marriages, business relationships, and movies—those who play supporting roles can mean the difference between a mediocre product and a stellar one. Frankly, it's almost impossible to make a bad apple pie using good ingredients. But to make a great one, you need to start with a pastry that's capable of greatness. I like to think you'll find a number of such pastries here.

Making pie pastry seems to be one of those cook's tasks that strike fear in the hearts of many, and I speak from experience. I have given quite a few cooking demonstrations over the years to live crowds, and by far the best attended have been those on the subject of pie and pie-crust making. At one such event in Nashua, New Hampshire, 300 people showed up to learn about the basics of making pie crust. About halfway into the two-hour demonstration, as I was rolling out yet another perfectly round piece of dough, I told the crowd that it sometimes helps if you visualize something round as you roll out the dough—like the globe, I said. With that, an older woman in the back of the crowd shouted out, just as sassy as can be, "I've tried that, and my pie crust just looks like part of the globe: Florida!"

Alas, if you've had your own share of Florida-looking pie crusts, forget about the past. Now is the time to start fresh, with a clean slate. It's not difficult to mix or roll out pie dough, but it does help if you know a few helpful tricks. Perhaps more than anything, I think most problems can be avoided by simply refrigerating the dough before you start rolling. Not only does chilling the dough give it time to relax, making it easier to roll, but it also stabilizes the fat in the dough, so it's less likely to stick to your rolling pin. Sticky dough is one of the most common complaints I hear from beginners.

So pick a pastry and proceed fearlessly into your apple pie adventure. Especially if you're new to this, don't rush: read the recipe through carefully before you begin, and try to create a mental image for each step of the process. Then, with any luck at all, your pie pastry won't come out looking like Florida.

All-American Double Crust

To my mind, an all-American crust should include butter, for great flavor; vegetable shortening, for tenderness and flakiness; and white flour, not whole wheat. The recipe also must be generous enough to make a top and bottom crust, because a big double-crust pie is what I believe most people envision when they think of the classic all-American apple pie. This recipe meets all of those criteria. You can make this pastry by hand (directions follow), but I nearly always make mine in a food processor. This is about as large a pastry recipe as I would recommend preparing in a food processor, for the simple reason that an overcrowded processor will not mix the pastry evenly, likely resulting in a tough crust. To prevent this from happening, whenever I stop the machine, I "fluff" the ingredients with a fork to loosen anything that may have begun to compact under the blade.

If you've made other pastry with vegetable shortening, you may have noticed that it doesn't firm up quite like a butter pastry does; it remains softer, which can make the pastry slightly more difficult to roll, especially in warmer weather. To counter this tendency, I like to put the fully refrigerated pastry in the freezer for about 10 minutes before I roll it. It makes a difference.

3 CUPS ALL-PURPOSE FLOUR

2 TABLESPOONS SUGAR

¾ TEASPOON SALT

¾ CUP (1½ STICKS) COLD UNSALTED
  BUTTER, CUT INTO ¼-INCH PIECES

¼ CUP COLD VEGETABLE SHORTENING, CUT
  INTO PIECES

½ CUP COLD WATER

1. Put the flour, sugar, and salt in a food processor; pulse several times to mix. Remove the lid and scatter the butter pieces over the dry ingredients. Pulse the machine 5 or 6 times to cut in the butter.

2. Remove the lid and fluff the mixture with a fork, lifting it up from the bottom of the bowl. Scatter the shortening pieces over the flour and pulse the machine 6 or 7 times. Remove the lid and fluff the mixture again.

3. Drizzle half of the water over the flour mixture and pulse the machine 5 or 6 times. Remove the lid, fluff the pastry, and sprinkle on the rest of the water. Pulse the machine 5 or 6 times more, until the pastry starts to form clumps. Overall, it will look like coarse crumbs.

Dump the contents of the processor bowl into a large mixing bowl.

4. Test the pastry by squeezing some of it between your fingertips. If it seems a little dry and not quite packable, drizzle a teaspoon or so of cold water over the pastry and work it in with your fingertips. Using your hands, pack the pastry into 2 balls, as you would pack a snowball. Make one ball slightly larger than the other; this will be your bottom crust. Knead each ball once or twice, then flatten the balls into ¾-inch-thick disks on a floured work surface. Wrap the disks in plastic wrap and refrigerate for at least 1 hour before rolling. About 10 minutes before rolling, transfer the pastry to the freezer to make it even firmer.

To mix by hand: Combine the flour, sugar, and salt in a large mixing bowl. Toss well, by hand, to mix. Scatter the butter over the dry ingredients; toss. Using a pastry blender or 2 knives, cut the butter into the flour until it is broken into pieces the size of split peas. Add the shortening and continue to cut until all of the fat is cut into small pieces. Sprinkle half of the water over the dry mixture; toss well with a fork to dampen the mixture. Add the remaining water, 1 tablespoon at a time, and continue to toss and mix, pulling the mixture up from the bottom of the bowl on the upstroke and gently pressing down on the downstroke. Pastry made by hand often needs a bit more water, so add it 1 to 2 teaspoons at a time—if it seems necessary—until the pastry can be packed. Form the pastry into balls, as instructed above, then shape and refrigerate as directed.

Makes enough pastry for one 9-inch deep-dish double-crust pie or two 9-inch deep-dish pie shells

---

ROSEMARY SEMOLINA DOUBLE CRUST

I love this pastry in mixed pear and apple pies, such as the one on page 30. The rosemary gives the crust a wonderful aroma and savory lift, and the semolina adds a bit of crunchy texture and relaxes the pastry, which bakes up very tender. Follow the directions above, substituting ⅓ cup fine semolina or fine yellow or white cornmeal for ⅓ cup of the flour. Add ½ teaspoon finely crushed dried rosemary to the dry ingredients and proceed as usual. Note that the pastry may require 1 to 2 tablespoons less water than the basic recipe.

Shortening Double Crust

For many pie bakers, there is only one kind of pie crust, and this is it. I think that this recipe makes a great pie crust—different from a butter pastry, most noticeably in flavor, but quite good nonetheless. Unlike the directions for the other pie pastries here, I don't even bother to give food processor instructions. Because shortening—even cold shortening—is so soft in texture, it doesn't make sense to mix it in a food processor when the hand method is so much simpler.

Some pie makers tell me they don't even bother to refrigerate the dough before rolling it. Still, whether your pastry is made from butter or shortening, I highly recommend chilling it first. You'll experience fewer problems with the dough sticking to the rolling pin and work surface.

Tip: Have a stack of paper towels at the ready as you mix this pastry so that you can wipe off your hands and your utensils before you wash them.

2¾ CUPS ALL-PURPOSE FLOUR

1 TABLESPOON SUGAR

1 TEASPOON SALT

1 CUP COLD VEGETABLE SHORTENING, CUT INTO PIECES

6 TO 8 TABLESPOONS COLD WATER, AS NEEDED

1. Put the flour in a large, wide mixing bowl—one that you'll have no problem getting both hands into as you mix the dough. Add the sugar and salt; mix well with a whisk or your hands.

2. Add the shortening to the dry mixture here and there, in big pieces. Using your hands, a pastry blender, or 2 knives, rub or cut the shortening into the dry ingredients until the mixture resembles a coarse, damp meal. You want to end up with both large and small clumps in the mixture.

3. With a fork in one hand and your water in the other, start adding water to the dough 1 to 2 tablespoons at a time—you needn't measure, you can just pour. As you add the water, mix the dough with the fork, sort of pulling up the dry ingredients from the bottom of the bowl and pushing down to mix everything well.

Continue adding water, more gradually as you progress, until the dough coheres. It should have a dampish feel, but it shouldn't feel wet; don't add more water than you need.

4. Dust your work surface with flour and turn the dough out onto it. Divide the dough into 2 pieces, one—the piece you'll use for the bottom pastry—somewhat larger than the other. Put the pieces on sheets of plastic wrap and flatten them into disks about ¾ inch thick. Wrap the pieces and refrigerate for 1 hour or more, if possible, before rolling.

Makes enough pastry for one 9-inch deep-dish double-crust pie or two 9-inch deep-dish pie shells

Note: If you're using this recipe to make 2 pie shells, divide the dough into equal halves.

HOW TO MEASURE SHORTENING

Unlike butter, which comes in nice, neat sticks, solid vegetable shortening from the can is icky stuff to measure. I've read any number of tricks that are supposed to make the process simpler or neater. There's the water displacement method, where you plop it into a measuring cup full of cold water; I thought that was cool for about a month—back in the late seventies, I think—before giving it up. Of course, there's the weigh-it-out method, advocated by food writers who seem intent on ignoring the fact that not one home cook in a hundred uses a kitchen scale.

My preferred method is neither sexy nor new: I just push it down into a dry measuring cup and level the top. I have learned that an ice cream spade—a wide spoon, not a scoop—is the perfect tool for spooning shortening out of the large container. I use the back of the spade to push down on the shortening—and you do have to push hard—to eliminate any air bubbles. Then I just spoon it out of the cup and into my dry ingredients. Simple as that.

Incidentally, you can also buy shortening in premeasured sticks. Each stick equals 1 cup and is marked in 1-tablespoon increments. Each package contains 3 sticks. You'll pay a little more for the sticks than you will for a can, but if you'd rather not fuss with the stuff, it's probably worth the extra money.

Whole Wheat Double Crust

Here's a whole wheat crust I like very much. It's not an all–whole wheat dough, which I think can be crumbly and frustrating to work with, but one that's made with half whole wheat flour and half all-purpose flour. I use whole wheat pastry flour—a soft, whole-grain wheat flour that makes a more tender, easier-to-roll pastry than the standard whole wheat flour you buy at the supermarket. (To find whole wheat pastry flour, visit the local health food store.) There's a little less fat and a little more water in this dough than in my other pastry doughs of this size. The reason is that the whole wheat flour absorbs more water than white flour, and the extra water helps keep the dough from drying out. If you like a whole wheat crust, you can use this dough for virtually any of the pies in this book, even if the recipe doesn't list it as an option.

1½ CUPS ALL-PURPOSE FLOUR

1½ CUPS WHOLE WHEAT PASTRY FLOUR

1 TABLESPOON SUGAR

¾ TEASPOON SALT

14 TABLESPOONS (1¾ STICKS) COLD UNSALTED BUTTER, CUT INTO ¼-INCH PIECES

½ CUP PLUS 2 TABLESPOONS COLD WATER

1. Put the flours, sugar, and salt in a food processor; pulse several times to mix. Remove the lid and scatter the butter pieces over the dry ingredients. Pulse the machine 6 or 7 times to cut in the butter.

2. Remove the lid and fluff the mixture with a fork, lifting it up from the bottom of the bowl. Drizzle half of the water over the flour mixture and pulse the machine 5 or 6 times. Remove the lid again, fluff the mixture, and sprinkle on the rest of the water. Pulse the machine again until the pastry starts to form coarse clumps. Dump the contents of the processor bowl into a large mixing bowl.

3. Packing the dough like a snowball, shape it into 2 balls, one—for the bottom pastry—a little larger than the other. (If the dough isn't packing easily, knead the dough several times, pressing the dough together with your palms.)

Flatten the balls into ¾-inch-thick disks on a floured work surface. Wrap the disks in large sheets of plastic wrap and refrigerate for about 1 hour before rolling.

To mix by hand: Combine the flour, sugar, and salt in a large mixing bowl. Toss well, by hand, to mix. Scatter the butter over the dry ingredients; toss well. Using a pastry blender or 2 knives, cut the butter into the dry mixture until the butter is broken into fine pieces no larger than split peas. Sprinkle half the water over the dry mixture; toss well with a fork.

Add the remaining water, a little at a time, continuing to toss and mix with the fork, pulling the dry stuff up from the bottom of the bowl on the upstroke and gently pressing down on the downstroke. Don't be surprised if the dough needs a little more water than you would use if making this in the food processor. Form the pastry into balls, as instructed above, then shape and refrigerate as directed.

Makes enough pastry for one 9-inch deep-dish double-crust pie or two 9-inch deep-dish pie shells

PIE CRUST "COOKIES"

Pie makers regularly face the issue of what to do with the leftover trimmings of pastry. When I'm making a double-crust pie and joining top pastry to bottom, there's inevitably a fair amount of bulk that needs to be trimmed.

May I suggest turning these little pieces into pie crust cookies? You can do this each time you make a pie; or toss your scraps into a plastic bag you keep in the freezer and make them once a month.

There are several ways you might make these cookies. The first and easiest is to simply reroll the trimmings and cut them into adjacent shapes, freehand, with a paring knife. (I prefer this to using a cookie cutter, because if you use a cutter, you'll only end up with more scraps to deal with.) If you're measuring, roll the dough about ⅛ inch thick. Once the shapes are cut, brush the pastry lightly with milk, then sprinkle with cinnamon sugar. Transfer to a lightly buttered baking sheet and bake in a preheated 350-degree oven until a light golden brown, 10 to 12 minutes.

If you have a big wad of trimmings, turn it into pinwheel cookies. Roll the dough into as big a circle as you can, making the dough slightly thinner than ⅛ inch. Spoon a very thin layer of fruit preserves over the dough, then sprinkle with cinnamon sugar. Cut the dough into 12 wedges, as you would a big pizza, then roll each wedge up, like a carpet, starting at the wide edge and rolling toward the point. Put these pinwheels on a lightly greased baking sheet, points facing down. Brush lightly with milk and sprinkle again with cinnamon sugar. Bake in a preheated 350-degree oven for about 20 minutes, until golden brown.

Kids are creative when it comes to this sort of thing. Hand over the ball of pastry scraps to them, and I promise they'll come up with more ideas than I've mentioned here. Some might not be edible, but they'll be creative nonetheless. And if you don't have kids, give me a call, and you can borrow mine for a while.

Best Butter Pie Pastry

This is the workhorse of my pie pastry repertoire. It has a great buttery flavor, it's easy to roll, and it holds up beautifully in the pan, remaining firm and distinct rather than turning into mush, as some pastries do. In short, I'm crazy about this pastry and almost reflexively refer to it when I'm going to make a single-crust pie. You can, if you like, make this pastry by hand, but if you have a food processor, I'm not sure why you'd want to. The most important thing to remember about this dough is not to overprocess it, or the butter will warm up and melt into the pastry, with less-than-desirable results.

1¾ CUPS ALL-PURPOSE FLOUR

1 TABLESPOON SUGAR

½ TEASPOON SALT

½ CUP (1 STICK) COLD UNSALTED BUTTER, CUT INTO ¼-INCH PIECES

1 LARGE EGG YOLK

ABOUT 3 TABLESPOONS COLD WATER

1. Put the flour, sugar, and salt in a food processor and pulse several times to mix. Remove the lid and scatter the butter pieces over the dry ingredients. Pulse the machine repeatedly—6 or 7 one-second bursts—until the butter is broken into very small pieces.

2. Place the egg yolk in a 1-cup glass measure and add just enough of the water to equal ¼ cup liquid. Using a fork, blend the water and yolk. Remove the lid of the processor and pour the liquid over the entire surface of the dry ingredients. Don't, in other words, pour it into one spot. Pulse the machine again, in short bursts, until the pastry starts to form large clumps. Don't overprocess, or the butter will start to melt rather than stay in small pieces. Tear off a sheet of plastic wrap about 14 inches long and place it nearby.

3. Empty the crumbs into a large mixing bowl. Using your hands, pack the dough as you would a snowball. Knead the dough 2 or 3 times, right in the bowl. Put the dough in the center of the plastic wrap and flatten it into a disk about ¾ inch thick. The edges will probably crack slightly; just pinch and mold them back into a smooth disk. Wrap the dough in the plastic and refrigerate until firm enough to roll, about 1 hour.

To mix by hand: Combine the flour, sugar, and salt in a large mixing bowl and mix well. Scatter the butter pieces over the dry ingredients and cut them in, using a pastry blender or 2 knives, until the butter is broken into very fine pieces; the mixture will not be quite as fine as with the processor. Blend the yolk and water as directed above. Sprinkle about half of the liquid over the flour, mixing it in with a fork. Lift the mixture up from the bottom of the bowl and press down on the downstroke. Add the remaining liquid a little at a time until the dough coheres. You may need 1 to 2 teaspoons more water.

Makes enough pastry for one 9-inch deep-dish pie shell

Is It Done?

If you're not an experienced apple pie baker, you may find yourself staring at your pie after about an hour wondering whether the blessed thing is done. Even if you are experienced, it might be useful to compare your own intuition on the subject with mine. So here's how I judge an apple pie for doneness.

By total elapsed time: With a few exceptions, most apple pies are fully baked in 1 to 1½ hours, unless your oven's thermostat is way out of whack. You will note that, for the most part, I start baking my pies at 400 degrees, then reduce the oven temperature to 375 degrees to finish the job. Why the higher temperature at first? First, the pie pan and pastry, and maybe even your apples, are cold, and you need more heat to accelerate the baking. Second, you're trying to "set" the crust—get it baking and browning before the moisture from the apples makes the pastry soggy—so you need the higher heat.

By sound: One sure sign that your pie is almost done is the sound of the juices bubbling up over the rim of the pan and onto the baking sheet. My experience is that until a pie's juices bubble, the thickening—be it flour, cornstarch, or tapioca—hasn't "taken" yet, which is to say, sufficiently swelled to thicken the juices. However, don't wait for the sound because your pie might bubble without actually bubbling over.

By sight: Elsewhere in this book, I have instructed you to make a couple of steam vents in the top pastry near the edge of the crust. Why? Because that's where you're most likely to see the juices bubbling from within. The same goes for crumb-topped pies, but steam vents aren't necessary because the juices will bubble up between the crumbs. In time you'll be able to distinguish between plain (thin) bubbling juice and thickened juices—similar to the textural difference between, say, water and light cream. There will be other visual clues as well. The bottom crust will be golden brown—here glass pans have a distinct advantage over metal—and the top crust or crumb topping will be golden brown as well. You have to be discerning in judging the latter, however, because if your oven is baking on the hot side, a crumb crust will overbrown before the pie is actually done. This propensity for overbrowning is one reason I generally cover my crumb pies with aluminum foil for the last 15 minutes or so of baking.

By smell: Smell is an indicator, but not always an accurate one. You're hoping for the smell of fresh-baked apple pie. But you're just as likely to get the burned smell of crumb topping or juices that have spilled over onto the baking sheet. Investigate, but don't let these smells trick you into removing the pie prematurely.

Three-Grain Butter Pastry

This was, back in my longhair grainy days, one of the few pie crusts I made. I loved then, and still do, the combination of cornmeal, oats, and white flour—the former two lending a wholesome, nutty flavor and nubby texture, and the latter adding the softness and fine texture necessary to hold a grainy pastry together. If you've shied away from whole-grain pastries in the past, don't let this one frighten you: it's very easy to roll. But note that it's best to let it chill for only about 45 minutes before you roll it. If the dough is too cold, the combination of the cold-firmness and the grain will make it a little crumbly.

This pastry is great for pie lovers of the healthy persuasion—those who like their apple pies sweetened with honey or maple syrup, and perhaps a granola crumb topping (see page 234).

⅓ CUP OLD-FASHIONED ROLLED OATS (NOT INSTANT)

¼ CUP FINE YELLOW CORNMEAL

1 TABLESPOON SUGAR

1⅓ CUPS ALL-PURPOSE FLOUR

¼ TEASPOON SALT

½ CUP (1 STICK) COLD UNSALTED BUTTER, CUT INTO ¼-INCH PIECES

1 LARGE EGG YOLK

ABOUT 3 TABLESPOONS COLD WATER

1. Put the oats, cornmeal, and sugar in a food processor and process until the mixture is very finely ground, 45 to 60 seconds. Add the flour and salt and pulse the machine several times to mix.

2. Remove the lid from the processor and scatter the butter pieces over the dry mixture. Pulse the machine 6 or 7 times, in short bursts, until the butter is broken into very small pieces.

3. Put the egg yolk in a 1-cup glass measure, adding just enough of the water to make ¼ cup liquid; blend with a fork. Remove the lid from the processor and add the liquid, distributing it over the entire mixture. Pulse the machine 3 times, then remove the lid and fluff the mixture with a fork. Pulse several more times, until the pastry forms large clumps. Dump the pastry onto a lightly floured work surface.

4. Pack the dough together like a snowball. Knead gently 2 or 3 times. Place the pastry on a large sheet of plastic wrap and flatten it into a disk about ¾ inch thick. Wrap the pastry in the plastic and refrigerate for about 45 minutes before rolling. The pastry will keep in the refrigerator for up to 48 hours. If you exceed much more than 45 minutes in the refrigerator, let the dough sit at room temperature for 5 to 10 minutes before rolling.

To mix by hand (though not entirely by hand, since you need to pulverize the oats in a blender): Put the oats and sugar in a blender and chop as finely as you can, periodically removing the blender from its base to "fluff" the oats with a fork. Combine the oats, corn-

meal, flour, and salt in a large mixing bowl and mix well. Scatter the butter pieces over the dry ingredients, cutting it in with a pastry blender or 2 knives to make medium-fine crumbs. Combine the yolk and water as instructed above. Sprinkle about half of it over the dry mixture, working it in with a fork. Add the remaining liquid about 2 teaspoons at a time, mixing until the dough coheres. You may need 1 to 2 teaspoons more water.

Makes enough pastry for one 9-inch deep-dish pie shell

FLOUR FOR PIE PASTRY: REGULAR ALL-PURPOSE OR UNBLEACHED?

Actually, I use both, depending on what's in the pantry. Regular all-purpose flour—such as Pillsbury, which I used to test many of the recipes in this book—is lower in gluten-forming proteins than unbleached all-purpose flour. Gluten, as you may know, gives dough its stretchability—something you'd rather avoid in a tender pie pastry. So here's a trick if you're using unbleached flour such as King Arthur, my favorite brand. For every 1 cup of flour you use, replace 1½ tablespoons of the flour with an equal amount of cornstarch. Just mix it right in with the flour. Cornstarch will counter unbleached flour's tendency to form gluten strands.

One other thing: pastry made with unbleached flour tends to take on a gray cast if it sits in the refrigerator overnight. This is a little unsightly, but any grayness pretty much bakes away and turns to golden brown in the oven. So don't worry about it.

Yeasted Butter Pastry

This pastry is a dream. I use it for a couple of my apple pies, notably Apple Pizza Pie (page 206). As I say in that recipe, you may like this pastry so much that you'll find many other uses for it, including actual pizza. This is made entirely in the food processor; hand-kneading isn't required. The finished texture is soft and bready, though somewhat short, like shortcake. Take care not to overknead it in the processor because the friction will melt the butter, and it won't be nearly as light and airy. I tend to make this pastry on weekends, when I seem to be in the kitchen all day turning out meals and snacks for my kids.

½ CUP LUKEWARM WATER

1 PACKAGE (ABOUT 2 TEASPOONS) ACTIVE DRY YEAST

2 CUPS UNBLEACHED ALL-PURPOSE FLOUR

1 ½ TABLESPOONS SUGAR

½ TEASPOON SALT

¼ CUP (½ STICK) COLD UNSALTED BUTTER, CUT INTO ¼-INCH PIECES

1 LARGE EGG YOLK

1. Measure the water in a 1-cup glass measure. Sprinkle the yeast over the water, mixing briefly with a fork. Set aside for 5 minutes to dissolve the yeast.

2. Meanwhile, put the flour, sugar, and salt in a food processor. Pulse several times to mix. Remove the lid and scatter the butter pieces over the dry mixture. Pulse the machine 7 or 8 times, until the butter is broken into very small pieces.

3. Add the egg yolk to the yeast water; blend with a fork. Remove the lid from the processor and add the liquid. Pulse the machine repeatedly, until the dough coheres, then run the machine nonstop for 8 to 10 seconds to knead the dough. Remove the dough and place it in a medium-size oiled bowl, rotating the dough to coat the entire surface.

4. Cover the bowl with plastic wrap and set aside to rise in a warmish spot for 1 hour. If for some reason you're called away and you need to delay the rising, simply put the dough in the refrigerator.

Makes enough pastry for 1 large pie

PASTRY ART: A CONFESSION

I am not, by my own admission, much of a pastry artist. I feel a little bit bad about this. When I see apple pies in cookbooks or magazines all decked out in intricate borders of hand-cut leaves, or with lattice tops woven from dozens of narrow pastry strips, or even with a still life of a New England apple-picking scene—well, it's enough to make an artistically challenged fellow like myself feel pretty inadequate.

But it's not just the lack of an artistic streak that's to blame; there are other considerations. I think having four kids has something to do with it. They're a little older now, but when they were young, it was all I could do to get a pie in the oven, let alone stand around carving up pastry. The trimmings were a great diversion for them, however. They loved to roll out the excess dough and cut it into shapes, which kept them busy while I was finishing my pie and cleaning up the mess.

Today there's a whole new climate of preparing food that's simple and hassle-free. My feeling is that, for most modern cooks, baking a pie is enough of a personal victory. We may admire the pastry art we see in the food magazines, but with careers and shuttling kids around, how many of us actually have the time to do it?

That said, I will—on occasion—take a stab at pastry decoration. All you really need are your pastry trimmings or a little dough you've saved. You simply roll the pastry on a floured surface, cut out the shapes you want for the top of the pie, brush the top pastry with milk, and lay the decorations in place. (For a couple of examples, see Valentine's Apple Pie for Two, page 106, or Harvest Pie with Autumn Leaves, page 34).

A couple of tips: Dough will cut more neatly if it is cold. I like to roll it onto a sheet of waxed paper and immediately put it in the freezer for 5 minutes. (Sometimes I will roll scraps ahead and store them in a plastic bag in the freezer.) Freehand cutting is fine for many occasions—like someone's name or birthday age—but small cookie cutters do a clean, good-looking job. The Valentine's pie, for example, looks very sweet with a border of tiny hearts.

Especially if you have kids, it's fun to suggest the contents of a pie through the pastry decorations on top, then see if they can guess what's inside (if the aroma hasn't already given it away). Such decorations might include different fruits, or a jar if you're using applesauce in the pie—that sort of thing.

So if you have the time and inclination to pursue pastry art, by all means do so. But if most of your pies—like most of mine—go into the oven minus an artistic flourish, don't you worry. Even a plain apple pie is a glorious work of art.

Flaky Cream Cheese Pastry

I love this fine, tender pastry. It's about the only pastry I use to make hand pies (turnovers), and it's the perfect choice for thin, delicate, double-crust pies, such as Apple Applesauce Cherry Pie (page 94). Unlike the other pastries in this collection, the fats are incorporated into the dough not by cutting them in, but by creaming them together, then blending them into the dry ingredients—a method that ensures even distribution.

One thing you should know about this crust is that a cream cheese dough, once you start to roll it, gets soft quicker than an all-butter pastry—so don't delay when you're working with this crust. For that reason, I prefer to make this pastry in the cooler months, not in the middle of summer. No matter when you make it, though, here's a little trick: if the dough starts to get soft and sticks to your rolling pin, simply slide the pastry—waxed paper and all—onto a baking sheet and put it in the fridge for 5 minutes. Then take it out and continue to roll. This recipe is written for a large stand-up mixer fitted with a flat beater. If you don't have one, use the hand method.

½ CUP (1 STICK) UNSALTED BUTTER, AT ROOM TEMPERATURE

4 OUNCES CREAM CHEESE, AT ROOM TEMPERATURE

1 CUP ALL-PURPOSE FLOUR

½ CUP CAKE FLOUR

2 TABLESPOONS CONFECTIONERS' SUGAR

1. Put the butter and cream cheese in the bowl of a large stand-up mixer fitted with the flat beater attachment. Blend for 30 to 45 seconds on medium-low speed.

2. Sift the flours and confectioners' sugar into a medium-size mixing bowl. With the mixer on low, add the dry mixture to the creamed mixture about ⅓ cup at a time, blending reasonably well after each addition. You don't have to wait until the previous addition has been entirely incorporated before adding the next, but do give it some time.

3. When all of the dry ingredients have been added and the dough starts to ball up around the beater, stop the machine. Remove the bowl and scrape the dough onto a lightly floured work surface. Knead the dough gently 3 or 4 times, then shape it into a ball. Place the ball on a lightly floured sheet of plastic wrap and flatten it into a disk about ¾ inch thick (unless the recipe instructs you to shape the dough into 2 balls for a double-crust pie). Wrap the disk in plastic and refrigerate for at least 1½ hours, until firm enough to roll.

To mix by hand: Using a wooden spoon, cream the butter and cream cheese together in a medium-size mixing bowl. Sift the dry ingredients together, as instructed above, then add them to the creamed mixture about ⅓ cup at a time, stirring well after each addition. When the dough coheres, proceed as directed above.

Makes enough pastry for one 9-inch deep-dish pie shell or one 9-inch thin-crusted double-crust pie

FREEZING PIE DOUGH

Pie dough freezes beautifully. I'll often plan to make a pie, prepare the pastry, and then, for one reason or another, not get to it for a few days. Sometimes—around Thanksgiving, for instance—I just want to get as much done in advance as I can, so I'll make my pastry and freeze it the week before.

To freeze your pastry, simply wrap it in plastic as usual, then slip it into a plastic food storage bag. The day before you plan to roll the pastry, transfer it to the refrigerator; it will be thawed and ready to roll in the morning. It's preferable to thaw the dough in the refrigerator, rather than at room temperature, because you'll end up with less moisture on the surface. And it thaws more evenly: you won't be fooled into thinking the dough is ready to be rolled while the interior is still hard.

I seldom keep dough in the freezer for more than a week or two, but it will stay frozen, in good condition, for at least a month.

Cheddar Cheese Pastry

Here's the pastry I use for Cheddar-Crusted Apple Pie (page 46). It has much in common with All-American Double Crust (page 2)—until you bake it, and the smell of toasted cheddar cheese starts to fill the house. For best results in texture and flavor, do use an extra-sharp cheddar cheese, not a mild one.

3 CUPS ALL-PURPOSE FLOUR

1 TABLESPOON SUGAR

½ TEASPOON SALT

¾ CUP (1½ STICKS) COLD UNSALTED BUTTER, CUT INTO ¼-INCH PIECES

2 TABLESPOONS COLD VEGETABLE SHORTENING, CUT INTO PIECES

1¼ CUPS GRATED EXTRA-SHARP CHEDDAR CHEESE

½ CUP PLUS 2 TABLESPOONS COLD WATER

1. Put the flour, sugar, and salt in a food processor; pulse several times to mix. Remove the lid and scatter the butter pieces over the dry ingredients. Pulse the machine 5 or 6 times to cut in the butter.

2. Remove the lid and fluff the mixture with a fork, lifting it up from the bottom of the bowl. Scatter the shortening pieces and cheese over the flour and pulse the machine 5 or 6 times. Remove the lid and fluff the mixture again.

3. Drizzle half of the water over the flour mixture and pulse the machine 5 or 6 times. Remove the lid, fluff the pastry, and sprinkle on the remaining water. Pulse the machine 5 or 6 times more, until the pastry starts to form clumps. Overall, it will look like coarse crumbs. Dump the contents of the processor bowl into a large mixing bowl.

4. Test the pastry by squeezing some of it between your fingertips. If it seems a little dry and not quite packable, drizzle a teaspoon or so of cold water over the pastry and work it in with your fingertips. Using your hands, pack the pastry into 2 balls, as you would pack a snowball. Make one ball slightly larger than the other; this will be your bottom crust. Knead each ball once or twice, then flatten the balls into ¾-inch-thick disks on a floured work surface. Wrap the disks in plastic wrap and refrigerate for about 1 hour before rolling.

To mix by hand: Combine the flour, sugar, and salt in a large mixing bowl. Toss well to mix. Scatter the butter over the dry ingredients; toss. Using a pastry blender or 2 knives, cut the butter into the flour until it is broken into pieces the size of split peas. Add the shortening and continue to cut until all of the fat is cut into small pieces. Sprinkle on the cheese and

cut briefly. Sprinkle about half of the water over the dry mixture; toss well with a fork to dampen the mixture. Add the remaining water and continue to toss and mix, pulling the mixture up from the bottom of the bowl on the upstroke and gently pressing down on the downstroke. Add more water, if necessary, by the teaspoon to make a dough that coheres. Form the pastry into balls, as directed above, and shape and refrigerate as instructed.

Makes enough pastry for one 9-inch deep-dish double-crust pie or two 9-inch deep-dish pie shells

---

Rack Matters: Is Your Pie in the Right Position?

Throughout this collection, I tell you to bake your pie on the center oven rack, or shelf, and that's a good place to start. But not all ovens bake the same or are designed the same, and your pies might do better in another position.

If your pies are consistently too dark on top, consider starting them one shelf lower. Since most ovens are hotter at the bottom than they are at the top, this may help. The advantage of using a low rack at the beginning is that the intense lower heat helps to "set" the crust quickly, so it browns nicely and keeps its shape and flakiness.

Small ovens are a special challenge. One of my New Hampshire ovens is very small; when I bake my pies on the center rack, the pie is too close to the top

of the oven, so I use a lower rack. And to keep the bottom of my pie from getting too dark, I lay a large sheet of aluminum foil on the rack directly under the pie, shiny side down, to deflect some of the heat coming from the bottom of the oven. I have a much larger, more modern oven in my Annapolis home; the pies that I bake there do beautifully on the center rack.

So keep an eye on those pies, and if common sense tells you to experiment with different rack positions, by all means do so. Incidentally, this is all par for the course. I've worked with any number of professional bakers who constantly juggle breads and pies in their ovens so that their products turn out perfectly.

Wheaten Oil Pastry

It's possible to make a very good oil pastry, but such a pastry will not have the same flaky tenderness as a butter or shortening crust. Nonetheless, this oil pastry has features to recommend it, namely good taste, a wholesome profile, and a grainy personality. I like to prepare this in the food processor, which makes for easy and thorough blending of the flour and oil. (Because of the bulk, if I need a double crust, I will make it twice rather than trying to double the recipe.) I suggest reading this recipe through before proceeding to familiarize yourself with the technique. It's particularly important with this dough to stop the machine and fluff it with a fork as you proceed, because the processor tends to pack the dough in the bottom of the bowl. (Note that for every tablespoon of liquid you add, you pulse the machine for 1 second.)

1¼ CUPS ALL-PURPOSE FLOUR

½ CUP WHOLE WHEAT PASTRY FLOUR

1½ TABLESPOONS SUGAR

SCANT ½ TEASPOON SALT

5 TABLESPOONS NONASSERTIVE OLIVE OIL OR CANOLA OIL

5 TABLESPOONS COLD WATER

1. Put the flours, sugar, and salt in a food processor; pulse several times to mix. With the machine running, add the oil in a stream through the feed tube; this should take about 5 seconds. Remove the lid and fluff the mixture with a fork, then pulse again for 1 or 2 seconds.

2. Pour the water into a measuring cup. With the machine running, add 3 tablespoons of the water through the feed tube in a 3-second stream. Stop the machine, remove the lid, and fluff again. Add the remaining 2 tablespoons water in a 2-second pulse of the machine. The pastry should resemble large crumbs.

3. Turn the pastry out onto a floured work surface, scraping the bowl thoroughly. Gently knead 2 or 3 times, then form into a ball. Place the dough on a large sheet of plastic wrap and pat it into a ¾-inch-thick disk. Smooth the cracks along the edges. Wrap the dough in the plastic and refrigerate for about 1 hour. It won't get very firm; this is primarily a rest to let the dough relax and become easy to roll.

4. To roll the dough, place it on a large sheet of floured waxed paper. Lightly flour the top of the pastry. Place a second sheet of waxed paper on top of the pastry and roll the dough into a circle; the recipe will specify the size. To get the pastry into the pan, peel off the top sheet of waxed paper. Invert the pastry over a lightly oiled pie pan, center it, and peel off the other sheet of waxed paper. Then tuck the pastry into the pan and proceed as directed.

Makes enough pastry for one 9-inch deep-dish pie shell

How to Prebake a Pie Shell

There are times when you'll need to partially—or fully, in rare cases—prebake a pie shell. Here's what you do.

First, freeze the pie shell until it is good and firm. Then tear off a long sheet of aluminum foil and press it into the pastry until it fits like a second skin. Arrange the excess foil on either side so it sort of points out like a pair of wings. This gives you something to grab when you remove the foil later. Don't bunch the foil around the pan, or it will deflect the heat. Fill the foil with about 1½ pounds of dried beans, pushing them up the sides a little to keep the pastry snug against the pan.

Bake the pie shell on the center rack of a preheated 400-degree oven for 20 minutes. Remove from the oven. Using potholders, grasp the foil on either side and slowly lift the beans out of the shell.

Using a fork, poke the bottom of the pastry 5 or 6 times, twisting the fork slightly to enlarge the holes, so steam can escape. This will prevent the pastry from puffing up.

Put the pie shell back in the oven and bake for another 7 to 8 minutes for a partially prebaked shell, or bake for about 15 minutes for a fully prebaked shell. The bottom of the former will be light golden in color; the latter will be a bit darker. Let cool on a wire rack for at least 15 minutes before filling.

If your filling is on the soupy side, you might want to fill in those little fork holes in the bottom of the shell to keep the liquid from running out. I make a small amount of flour-and-water paste, starting with 1 tablespoon each of flour and water. Then I dab the tiniest bit of paste into each hole. You'll never be able to detect the paste in the final analysis.

Graham Cracker Crust

Here is the recipe for graham cracker crust that I've been using for years. For best results, press this into your pan right after you make it: it behaves and stays in place best when everything is newly dampened. If it seems a tad dry, just sprinkle a teaspoon of water over the crumbs and rub it with your fingers.

10 WHOLE PLAIN OR CINNAMON GRAHAM CRACKERS

¼ CUP FIRMLY PACKED LIGHT BROWN SUGAR

¼ TEASPOON GROUND CINNAMON (OMIT IF USING CINNAMON GRAHAM CRACKERS)

BIG PINCH OF SALT

5 TABLESPOONS UNSALTED BUTTER, MELTED

1. Preheat the oven to 350 degrees and lightly butter your pie pan.

2. Break up the crackers coarsely with your hands, dropping them into a food processor. Add the brown sugar and process into a fine meal. Transfer the meal to a large mixing bowl and add the cinnamon, if using, and salt. Add the melted butter and incorporate well: mix first with a fork, then switch to your hands and rub everything together thoroughly to form evenly dampened crumbs.

3. Spread the crumbs evenly and loosely in the pan, then press the mixture into the bottom and up the sides. Don't worry about getting them too high up the sides—three-quarters of the way is fine. Bake on the center oven rack for 8 to 10 minutes. Let cool on a wire rack before filling.

Makes one 9-inch deep-dish pie shell

THE REAL MOCK APPLE PIE

It's not an easy task to piece together the historical crumbs of the mock apple pie—that is, an "apple" pie made with broken-up crackers instead of apples. Doubtless, inventive cooks have toyed with the idea during times of scarcity, such as the Great Depression, for many years.

But the idea really took off when Nabisco started printing the recipe for its Ritz Mock Apple Pie on the box during the Second World War. The Ritz cracker was introduced during the Depression, and it quickly became a national sensation. Ritz crackers were served on the *Queen Mary* ocean liner and at the Waldorf-Astoria hotel. In their first year of production, 1935, five billion Ritz crackers were sold. Apparently, Americans were ready for a cracker with a richer, more buttery flavor and a flakier texture than your average saltine.

The mock apple pie made with Ritz crackers became the gold standard of the genre and is by far Nabisco's most requested recipe of all time. Does it taste like a real apple pie? All we can say is that there are many who swear by it—so perhaps you should decide for yourself. Here's the original recipe.

PASTRY FOR DOUBLE-CRUST 9-INCH PIE

36 RITZ CRACKERS, COARSELY BROKEN (ABOUT 1¾ CUPS CRUMBS)

1¾ CUPS WATER

2 CUPS SUGAR

2 TEASPOONS CREAM OF TARTAR

2 TABLESPOONS LEMON JUICE

GRATED PEEL OF 1 LEMON

2 TABLESPOONS MARGARINE OR BUTTER

½ TEASPOON GROUND CINNAMON

1. Roll out half the pastry and line a 9-inch pie plate. Place cracker crumbs in prepared crust; set aside.

2. Heat water, sugar, and cream of tartar to a boil in saucepan over high heat; simmer for 15 minutes. Add lemon juice and peel; cool.

3. Pour syrup over cracker crumbs. Dot with margarine or butter; sprinkle with cinnamon. Roll out remaining pastry; place over pie. Trim, seal, and flute edges. Slit top crust to allow steam to escape.

4. Bake at 425 degrees for 30 to 35 minutes, until crust is crisp and golden. Cool completely.

Makes 8 servings

CHAPTER 2

Apple Pies of Fall and Winter

It's not by coincidence that this chapter of classic pies appears at the beginning of this collection. Here are apple pies steeped in tradition, the ones we might think of first—if not by their exact names, at least by association—when we hear the words "apple pie." I refer to them as classics not only because of their solid grounding in apple season and the months just beyond, but also because these recipes have withstood the test of time.

Classic apple pies are careful about the company they keep. These aren't pies that mix it up with tropical fruits or chocolate chips. They like to travel with a small circle of seasonal friends—cranberries, pears, green tomatoes—and keep the party from getting too crowded. They realize that when someone bakes a classic apple pie, they want to taste apples mainly, and understandably so, since the apples of fall are apples at their best.

So if you're looking for an apple pie with across-the-board appeal, and one that will best capture the flavor of apple season, this is a good place to start.

My Mom and Dad's Brown Sugar Apple Pie

This is the way my dad and mom always made apple pie and still—on occasion—make it today. If anything inspired me to become a pie baker myself, and ultimately nudged me toward a career as a food writer, it was the sight of the two of them happily, purposefully engaged in the simple art of making an apple pie. This pie reminds me that small things can make a big difference in an apple pie. For years, as an adult, I tried to make a pie like the one my parents made, and over the years, I must have made hundreds of them. It wasn't until I asked them to tell me, point by point, how they actually made their pie that I was able to replicate it to my satisfaction. (Don't ask me why I didn't ask them sooner.) I should mention that my father is adamant about not using any thickener in his pie; I prefer some myself.

1 RECIPE ALL-AMERICAN DOUBLE CRUST (PAGE 2), REFRIGERATED

FILLING:

8 CUPS PEELED, CORED, AND SLICED MCINTOSH APPLES

½ CUP FIRMLY PACKED LIGHT BROWN SUGAR

1 TABLESPOON FRESH LEMON JUICE

½ TEASPOON GROUND CINNAMON

¼ TEASPOON GROUND NUTMEG

2 TABLESPOONS COLD UNSALTED BUTTER, CUT INTO SMALL PIECES

GLAZE:

MILK

GRANULATED SUGAR

1. If you haven't already, prepare the pastry and refrigerate it for at least 1 hour, until firm enough to roll.

2. On a sheet of lightly floured waxed paper, roll the larger portion of pastry into a 13½-inch circle with a floured rolling pin. Invert the pastry over a 9-inch deep-dish pie pan. Center it, then peel off the paper. Gently tuck the pastry into the pan, without stretching it, and let the overhang drape over the edge of the pan. Refrigerate. Preheat the oven to 400 degrees.

3. While the pie shell chills, make the filling. Combine the apples, brown sugar, lemon juice, cinnamon, and nutmeg in a large mixing bowl; toss well. Set aside while you roll the top pastry.

4. On another sheet of lightly floured waxed paper, roll the other half of the pastry into an

11½-inch circle. Turn the filling into the refrigerated pie shell, smoothing the apples with your hands. Dot the top of the pie with the butter, dropping pieces here and there over the apples.

5. Lightly moisten the rim of the pie shell with a wet finger or pastry brush. Invert the top pastry over the filling, center it, and peel off the paper. Press the top and bottom pastries together along the dampened edge. Trim the pastry with scissors or a paring knife, leaving a ½-inch overhang all around, then sculpt the overhang into an upstanding ridge. Make 2-inch-long slits in the top pastry at the 12, 3, 6, and 9 o'clock positions; the bottom of each slit should just reach the edge of the pie. Lightly brush the top pastry with milk and sprinkle with granulated sugar.

6. Place the pie directly on the center oven rack and bake for 30 minutes. Remove the pie from the oven and place it on a large, dark baking sheet covered with aluminum foil. Reduce the oven temperature to 375 degrees. Put the pie on the baking sheet back in the oven and bake for an additional 30 minutes. When the pie is done, you should be able to see the juices bubbling up onto the crust.

7. Transfer the pie to a cooling rack and let cool for at least 1 hour before slicing. However, when one doesn't use any thickener in a pie, I think it's best to let the pie cool to room temperature before slicing. I realize that many people—those who like a juicy pie—don't agree with me on this point.

Makes 8 to 10 servings

My Dad, On Making Apple Pie

"I always started with flour, butter, and Crisco, plus a tin cup filled with cold water and a few ice cubes to keep it cold. I liked working on a large maple board, which I floured so all was ready when I mixed the butter—cut into little squares with several tablespoons of Crisco—into the flour with a wire pastry blender. I would mix this combination with enough cold water to easily handle everything, then make up 2 balls for chilling in the refrigerator.

"After that, I would help your mother core, peel, and slice the apples. We decided New York State McIntosh were our favorites. I don't remember how many we would cut up. I do remember that there were a lot of sliced apples and we never thought we could get that many in a 9-inch pie plate. We used a glass pie plate at one time, but at some point shifted to a shiny metal one. Those who ate the pie never seemed to mind.

"The apples got a coating of nutmeg (just a small amount) and some cinnamon (a larger amount), a heavy dusting of brown sugar, and the rest of the stick of butter I didn't use for the crust. Then I got busy rolling out the dough using waxed paper until it looked right but was thick enough to handle. I lined the pie plate with the dough, with an extra inch hanging over the edge, then we poured the apples onto the dough. We would put the top layer on, slit the top dough, brush it with milk, dust it with a small amount of sugar, and put it in the oven until it was done. We learned to put foil under the pie rack to catch the drippings. Altogether, it smelled wonderful and tasted even better."

Grated Apple Pie

I had been thinking about grating apples for one of my apple pies, curious as to what that would do to the texture of the pie, when I came across a grated apple pie in a book on Pennsylvania Dutch cooking. The recipe I found—*griene ebbelkuche*, or green apple pie—called for eggs, but I didn't want this to be a custard pie. So I skipped the eggs and added some cornstarch but otherwise kept it very simple. The grated apples pretty much disintegrate while the pie bakes, leaving essentially a thick layer of finely textured applesauce. I love the way it tastes. I'd proudly serve this at any gathering, and I think it might appeal to young kids, who are sometimes distrustful of anything with a chunky texture, even apple pie. The original Pennsylvania Dutch recipe calls for Winesap apples, but any firm, juicy, tart apple, including Granny Smith, will do.

1 RECIPE ALL-AMERICAN DOUBLE CRUST (PAGE 2), REFRIGERATED

FILLING:

5 LARGE APPLES, PEELED AND CORED

2 TABLESPOONS FRESH LEMON JUICE

½ CUP SUGAR

2½ TABLESPOONS CORNSTARCH

¼ TEASPOON GROUND CINNAMON

½ CUP RAISINS

GLAZE (OPTIONAL):

MILK

SUGAR

1. If you haven't already, prepare the pastry and refrigerate it until firm enough to roll, about 1 hour.

2. On a sheet of lightly floured waxed paper, roll the larger portion of the pastry into a 13½-inch circle with a floured rolling pin. Invert the pastry over a 9-inch deep-dish pie pan. Center it, then peel off the paper. Gently tuck the pastry into the pan, without stretching it, and let the overhang drape over the edge of the pan. Cover the pastry loosely with plastic wrap. Refrigerate. Preheat the oven to 400 degrees.

3. While the pie shell chills, make the filling. Using the large holes of a standard box grater, grate the apples into a large mixing bowl, making sure you catch all the juice. Add the lemon juice and stir well. Combine the sugar, cornstarch, and cinnamon in a small mixing bowl.

Add to the apples and toss well to mix; using your hands is the easiest way to do this. Mix in the raisins. Set aside.

4. On another sheet of lightly floured waxed paper, roll the other half of the pastry into an 11½-inch circle. Turn the filling into the refrigerated pie shell; I find it simpler just to lift in the grated apples with my hands, then pour the remaining liquid over the fruit. Smooth the top of the filling with your hands.

5. Lightly moisten the rim of the pie shell with a wet finger. Invert the top pastry over the filling, center it, and peel off the paper. Press the top and bottom pastries together along the dampened edge. Trim the pastry with scissors or a paring knife, leaving an even ½-inch overhang all around, then sculpt the overhang into an upstanding ridge. Poke several steam vents in the top of the pie with a fork or paring knife; put a couple of the vents near the edge of the crust, so you can check the juices there later. If you want to glaze the pie, brush it with a little milk and sprinkle it with sugar.

6. Put the pie directly on the center oven rack and bake for 30 minutes. Remove the pie from the oven and place it on a large, dark baking sheet covered with aluminum foil. Reduce the oven temperature to 375 degrees. Put the pie on the baking sheet back in the oven and bake until the top is golden brown and any juices—visible at the steam vents—bubble thickly, another 35 to 40 minutes.

7. Transfer the pie to a cooling rack and let cool for at least 1 hour before serving.

Makes 8 to 10 servings

PEELING OPTIONS

I like to use a swivel peeler on my apples, mainly because a good peeler removes the skin only, without hacking off the flesh underneath the way a knife will, even in deft hands. To streamline the operation, I first peel all the apples—rather than peel, slice, peel, slice, which wastes valuable time. After all, there are likely anxious pie eaters in your midst. I still play around with different ways to peel apples. I like to go round and round in circles, but this is always a little distracting because I inevitably end up playing the game with myself of trying to make one long continuous peel. Taking off long vertical sheets of skin is a good way to go, too. When all the apples are peeled, I dispose of the skins to keep my work area clean, then I section, core, and slice the apples with my favorite paring knife (see page 47).

Incidentally, if you've not replaced your swivel peeler in a few years, it's probably time. A peeler costs only a few bucks, and a sharp tool makes a world of difference in the peeling. Rather than buy the cheapest one you can find, I suggest spending a few extra dollars and buying one with a bulky, rubberized handle, available at any kitchenware store (a company named OXO makes a couple of nice ones).

Traditional Lattice-Top Apple Pie

This is the classic lattice-top apple pie that you'd expect to be served at a great country inn or New England diner: a basic apple pie—this one sweetened with brown sugar—decorated with wide strips of criss-crossing pastry that always make me think of a cozy quilt. If you've never made a lattice top before, this is a good one to start with, since it's not fussy. The wide strips are thick and easy to work with. And since there just aren't that many strips—three going one way and five going the other—you don't have to be an Eagle Scout to figure out how they overlap. Indeed, the simplicity of this lattice makes it an excellent pie to make with kids, who especially love making pies with a decorative top crust.

1 RECIPE ALL-AMERICAN DOUBLE CRUST
(PAGE 2), DIVIDED AS INSTRUCTED IN
STEP 1 AND REFRIGERATED

FILLING:

8 CUPS PEELED, CORED, AND SLICED
APPLES

½ CUP FIRMLY PACKED LIGHT BROWN SUGAR

2½ TABLESPOONS ALL-PURPOSE FLOUR

½ TEASPOON GROUND CINNAMON

3 TABLESPOONS FRESH LEMON JUICE

2 TABLESPOONS COLD UNSALTED BUTTER,
CUT INTO SMALL PIECES

GLAZE:

MILK

GRANULATED SUGAR

1. Prepare the pastry, dividing it into 2 pieces, making one piece slightly larger than the other. Form the larger piece into a disk, as usual. Form the other into the best rectangle that you can; both of these should be about ¾ inch thick. Wrap both pieces in plastic and refrigerate until firm enough to roll, about 1 hour.

2. On a sheet of lightly floured waxed paper, roll the disk into a 13½-inch circle with a floured rolling pin. Invert the pastry over a 9-inch deep-dish pie pan. Center it, then peel off the paper. Gently tuck the pastry into the pan, without stretching it, and sculpt the overhang into an upstanding ridge. Refrigerate.

3. While the pie shell chills, prepare the filling. Combine the apples, brown sugar, flour, cinnamon, and lemon juice in a large mixing bowl. Toss well to mix; set aside. Preheat the oven to 400 degrees.

4. On another lightly floured sheet of waxed paper, roll the other piece of dough into a rectangle about 12 inches long and 10 inches wide. Using a pizza cutter or knife, cut the pastry into lengthwise strips, each 1¼ inches wide. (Each strip, in other words, will be about 12 inches long by 1¼ inches wide.)

5. Turn the pie filling into the pie shell, taking care to smooth the top so no apple pieces jut up (which could potentially tear the lattice). Place the butter pieces here and there over the top of the apples.

6. Lay 5 pastry strips vertically across the pie, evenly spaced, as shown in figure 1. Fold back strips 2 and 4, then lay another strip directly across the center of the pie, as shown in figure 2.

7. Unfold the folded dough strips, then fold back strips 1, 3, and 5. Lay another perpendicular strip across the pie as shown in figure 3.

8. Unfold strips 1, 3, and 5, then fold them up the other way as shown in figure 4. Place another perpendicular strip across the pie, as shown in figure 4, then unfold strips 1, 3, and 5. Trim the strips, then pinch the ends into the edge of the pastry. Lightly brush the pastry strips with milk and sprinkle the top of the pie with granulated sugar.

9. Place the pie on a large, dark baking sheet covered with aluminum foil and bake on the center rack for 20 minutes. Reduce the oven temperature to 375 degrees and bake until the top of the pie is golden brown and any visible juices bubble thickly, another 45 to 50 minutes.

10. Transfer the pie to a cooling rack and let cool for at least 1 hour before slicing.

Makes 8 servings

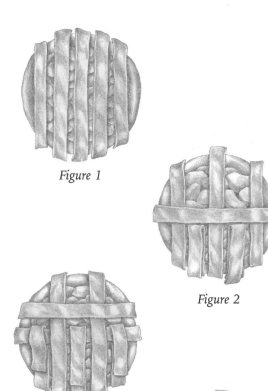

Figure 1

Figure 2

Figure 3

Figure 4

Apple Pear Crumb Pie

I'm always surprised when others are surprised that I like to mix pears and apples in the same pie. To some this seems just shy of genius—Wow! I never thought of that!—but to me nothing could be more natural, since the seasons for apples and pears essentially overlap and the flavors are perfectly harmonious. There's another, less obvious benefit to using them in combination, especially out of season: whereas the flesh of many storage apples can be rather dry, pears have a denser flesh and therefore retain more of their natural juices. This makes for a juicier pie and explains why a half-apple, half-pear pie like this one, made in March or April, may well taste more pear-like than apple-ish.

In addition to the fruit, the main flavor here is the ginger. I use fresh rather than dry because I like the big flavor of it. Feel free to use a top crust, but I prefer this crumb topping. Note that I often don't peel pears; unlike apples, the skins are, for the most part, quite soft. Also, there isn't as much crumb topping on this pie as there is on some of my others. If you like a thick coating of it, use almost any other crumb or streusel topping that calls for an entire stick of butter.

1 RECIPE BEST BUTTER PIE PASTRY (PAGE 8), REFRIGERATED

FILLING:

4 CUPS PEELED, CORED, AND SLICED APPLES (SUCH AS GRANNY SMITH OR NORTHERN SPY)

4 CUPS CORED AND SLICED RIPE PEARS

½ CUP GRANULATED SUGAR

1½ TABLESPOONS FRESH LEMON JUICE

1 TABLESPOON PEELED AND MINCED FRESH GINGER

PINCH OF GROUND NUTMEG

3 TABLESPOONS ALL-PURPOSE FLOUR

CINNAMON CRUMB TOPPING:

¾ CUP ALL-PURPOSE FLOUR

½ CUP FIRMLY PACKED LIGHT BROWN SUGAR

½ TEASPOON GROUND CINNAMON

¼ TEASPOON SALT

5 TABLESPOONS COLD UNSALTED BUTTER, CUT INTO ¼-INCH PIECES

1. If you haven't already, make the pastry and refrigerate it until firm enough to roll, about 1 hour.

2. On a sheet of lightly floured waxed paper, roll the pastry into a 13½-inch circle with a floured rolling pin. Invert the pastry over a 9-inch deep-dish pie pan. Center it, then peel off the paper. Tuck the pastry into the pan, without stretching it, and sculpt the edge into an upstanding ridge. Place the pie shell in the freezer for at least 30 minutes.

3. To make the filling, mix the apples, pears, granulated sugar, lemon juice, ginger, and nutmeg together in a large mixing bowl. Set aside for 10 minutes. Preheat the oven to 400 degrees.

4. Add the flour to the apples and toss well to mix. Turn the filling into the frozen crust, smoothing the top with your hands. Place the pie directly on the center oven rack and bake for 35 minutes.

5. While the pie bakes, make the topping. Put the flour, brown sugar, cinnamon, and salt in a food processor and pulse to mix. Remove the lid and scatter the butter over the surface. Pulse the machine, repeatedly, until the mixture resembles fine crumbs. Dump the crumbs into a large mixing bowl and rub between your fingers until the mixture forms large, buttery crumbs. Refrigerate.

6. After 35 minutes, reduce the oven temperature to 375 degrees. Remove the pie from the oven and place it on a large, dark baking sheet covered with aluminum foil. Carefully dump the crumbs in the center of the pie and spread them evenly over the surface with your hands. Tamp them down lightly. Put the pie on the baking sheet back in the oven and bake until you can see juices bubbling at the edge, another 30 to 35 minutes. If the top starts to get too brown, cover loosely with aluminum foil for the last 15 minutes.

7. Transfer the pie to a cooling rack and let cool at least somewhat before slicing.

Makes 8 to 10 servings

Baked Apple Dumpling Pie

If this pie sounds like a cross between baked apples and apple dumplings, well, it is. It's baked with a top pastry only, which molds itself around the apples so handsomely that I don't even bother to invert the pie, lest the pastry vanish beneath the apples. I use Golden Delicious apples here because they hold their shape well. They're halved, cored, and placed in the pan in a pool of melted butter, brown sugar, and raspberry preserves. A raisin–brown sugar–walnut mixture is spooned into the hollowed cores, à la baked apples, then the pastry is draped over the top, and the pie is baked. Since this bakes up in individual mounds, you don't slice it like a regular pie. Rather, you scoop out the mounds—which look like halved apple dumplings—and serve them with the pan juices. Excellent alone, but even better with chilled Vanilla Custard Sauce (page 33).

1 RECIPE BEST BUTTER PIE PASTRY
   (PAGE 8), REFRIGERATED

RAISIN WALNUT MIXTURE:

½ CUP RAISINS

½ CUP WALNUT PIECES

¼ CUP FIRMLY PACKED LIGHT BROWN SUGAR

¼ TEASPOON GROUND CINNAMON

FILLING:

3 TABLESPOONS UNSALTED BUTTER

¼ CUP FIRMLY PACKED LIGHT BROWN SUGAR

3 TABLESPOONS RASPBERRY PRESERVES

4 GOLDEN DELICIOUS APPLES

GLAZE:

LIGHT CREAM OR MILK

GRANULATED SUGAR

1. If you haven't already, prepare the pastry and refrigerate it until firm enough to roll, about 1 hour.

2. To make the raisin walnut mixture, combine all the ingredients in a food processor. Pulse repeatedly, until the mixture is finely ground. Set aside.

3. To make the filling, select an ovenproof skillet or sauté pan that measures 9 inches across the bottom and 11 to 12 inches across the top. Melt the butter in the skillet over medium heat, then stir in the brown sugar and preserves. When the mixture is bubbling evenly over the surface of the pan—30 seconds or so—remove from the heat.

4. Do not peel the apples; the peels will help them hold together. Do halve them, however, crosswise, and core each half. Place the apple halves in the pan, cut side down. You should be able to get 6 around the outside and 1 in the center. Finely dice the remaining apple half and scatter the pieces between the apples. Preheat the oven to 400 degrees.

5. Spoon some of the raisin walnut mixture into each apple half, compacting it with a finger. Sprinkle leftover mixture between the apples.

6. On a sheet of lightly floured waxed paper, roll the pastry into a 12-inch circle with a floured rolling pin. Invert the pastry over the apples, center it, and peel off the paper. Lifting the edge of the pastry, tuck the edge straight down along the inside of the pan. Poke several large vent holes in the pastry with a paring knife, twisting the knife to enlarge the holes.

7. Lightly brush the pastry with light cream and sprinkle with granulated sugar. Place the pie directly on the center oven rack and bake for 20 minutes. Reduce the oven temperature to 375 degrees and bake until the top crust is golden brown, another 25 minutes.

8. Transfer the pie to a cooling rack and let cool for at least 20 minutes before serving.

Makes 7 servings

VANILLA CUSTARD SAUCE

Ice cream is grand, whipped cream an ethereal dream, but there's almost nothing I'd rather serve with apple pie than vanilla custard sauce. For one, it's unexpected. It's hard to upstage an apple pie, but a little pitcher of this, pulled from the fridge at the last moment, can create quite a stir. It's different: a lot of people have never had it before. And it's delicious, like cool vanilla velvet on the tongue. Not only that, you can whip up a batch in less time than it takes to run to the store for a pint of vanilla ice cream. There's only one important rule to remember when preparing this sauce: don't boil it. Boiling will cause the yolks to curdle, leaving you with a pile of sweetened, semi-scrambled eggs. Here's how I make it.

6 LARGE EGG YOLKS

½ CUP SUGAR

2 CUPS LIGHT CREAM OR HALF-AND-HALF

¾ TEASPOON PURE VANILLA EXTRACT

1. Whisk the yolks and sugar together in a medium-size mixing bowl.

2. Bring the light cream to a simmer in a medium-size saucepan. Gradually whisk the hot cream into the yolks, adding ⅓ cup or so at a time. Return the mixture to the saucepan. Stir the custard over medium-low heat until it thickens enough to leave a path on the back of a wooden spoon when you draw a finger across it, about 5 minutes; do not boil.

3. Strain the sauce through a fine-mesh strainer into a small bowl and stir in the vanilla. Let cool to room temperature, then chill until cold. This will keep for 2 to 3 days.

Makes about 2½ cups

Harvest Pie with Autumn Leaves

Here's a pie I love to make when the leaves are turning, the pumpkins are crowding farm stand shelves, and the pie-baking bug has bitten me good. The filling is a real grab bag of fall favorites: sliced fresh apples and pears, diced pumpkin, and dried cranberries for extra sweetness and a splash of color. I use the pastry trimmings here to create a center spray of leaves. You can use a leaf cookie cutter, but even for someone as artistically challenged as myself, it's no trouble to cut a basic narrow leaf shape—something simple, like a birch leaf, not a maple—and make a few veins in it with the back of a paring knife. I put four of these on the top crust, stems ends in the middle with the leaves pointing out to the 12, 3, 6, and 9 o'clock positions.

This is the perfect pie for a fall outing or activity—a leaf-raking party or tailgate party, for instance. I love the juiciness of this pie, so I'd recommend serving it within an hour of baking. Do use a small sugar pie pumpkin, by the way—the larger ones tend to be too watery to use in a pie.

1 RECIPE ALL-AMERICAN DOUBLE CRUST (PAGE 2), REFRIGERATED

FILLING:

1 CUP FRESH APPLE CIDER

4 CUPS PEELED, CORED, AND SLICED APPLES

3 CUPS CORED AND SLICED RIPE PEARS

1½ CUPS PEELED AND SEEDED SUGAR PIE PUMPKIN CUT INTO ½-INCH CHUNKS

⅓ CUP DRIED CRANBERRIES

⅓ CUP GRANULATED SUGAR

2 TABLESPOONS CORNSTARCH

⅓ CUP FIRMLY PACKED LIGHT BROWN SUGAR

2 TABLESPOONS FRESH LEMON JUICE

GRATED ZEST OF 1 LEMON

¼ TEASPOON GROUND CINNAMON

⅛ TEASPOON GROUND CLOVES

GLAZE:

MILK

GRANULATED SUGAR

1. If you haven't already, prepare the pastry and refrigerate it until firm enough to roll, about 1 hour.

2. On a sheet of lightly floured waxed paper, roll the larger portion of the pastry into a 13½-inch circle with a floured rolling pin. Invert the pastry over a 9-inch deep-dish pie pan. Center it, then peel off the paper. Tuck the pastry into the pan, without stretching it, and let the edge of the pastry drape over the side of the pan. Refrigerate while you make the filling.

3. Put the cider in a small saucepan, bring to a boil, and let boil until it is reduced to ¼ to ⅓ cup; keep a heatproof measuring cup nearby to check it. Set aside. Put the apples, pears, pumpkin, and cranberries in a large mixing bowl. Add the reduced cider and granulated sugar and toss well to mix. Set aside for 10 minutes. Preheat the oven to 400 degrees.

4. In a small mixing bowl, combine the cornstarch and brown sugar. Add this to the fruit and mix again. Mix in the lemon juice, lemon zest, cinnamon, and cloves. Set aside.

5. On another sheet of floured waxed paper, roll the other half of the pastry into an 11½-inch circle. Moisten the rim of the pie shell with a damp pastry brush or finger. Turn the filling into the crust, smoothing the top with your hands. Invert the top pastry over the filling, center it, and peel off the paper. Press the pas-

tries together at the dampened edge, then trim the pastry flush to the edge of the pan with a paring knife. Using a fork or paring knife, poke several steam vents in the top pastry; put several of the vents near the edge of the pie, so you can check the juices there later.

6. Gather the pastry trimmings into a ball, then roll the dough about ⅛ inch thick on a sheet of floured waxed paper, flouring the dough as needed. Cut the dough into 4 leaves (see headnote), using the back of a paring knife to make a lengthwise vein down the center and smaller ones running diagonally to either side of the line. Lay the leaves on top of the pie with the stem ends in the center and the tips pointing out to the 12, 3, 6, and 9 o'clock positions. Brush the top of the pie lightly with milk and sprinkle with granulated sugar.

7. Place the pie directly on the center oven rack and bake for 30 minutes, then reduce the oven temperature to 375 degrees. Remove the pie from the oven and place it on a large, dark baking sheet covered with aluminum foil. Put the pie on the baking sheet back in the oven and bake until the juices bubble thickly at the edge, another 30 to 40 minutes.

8. Transfer the pie to a cooling rack and let cool for 30 to 60 minutes before serving.

Makes 8 to 10 servings

Smushy Paula Red Pie

Of the many things I learned about apple pie in the course of working on this book, one of the most notable is that not everyone's idea of the perfect baking apple is one that's firm and holds its shape in the oven. Indeed, I spoke to a number of people who much prefer an apple that bakes up soft, almost like applesauce. One such apple is the Paula Red. I use a lot of Paula Red apples because they're one of the first apples to hit the market in the fall and the flavor is good, both sweet and tart. It's hard for an apple pie maker to pass them by, waiting for the rest of the new crop to arrive. The "smushy" in this recipe's title comes from my daughter Alison, who, when she first tasted this, said, "I just love how smushy the apples are." Well put, I thought, so I borrowed the word for this pie. The filling is pretty basic, the way Alison likes it—just a little lemon juice, nutmeg, and sugar, and some flour to thicken it.

This pie is equally good with any crumb crust, but I've used a double crust because it traps the steam and makes the apples really soft, for all you lovers of soft apple pie.

1 RECIPE ALL-AMERICAN DOUBLE CRUST
  (PAGE 2), REFRIGERATED

FILLING:

9 TO 10 CUPS PEELED, CORED, AND SLICED
  PAULA RED APPLES

½ CUP SUGAR

2 TABLESPOONS FRESH LEMON JUICE

¼ TEASPOON GROUND NUTMEG

3 TABLESPOONS ALL-PURPOSE FLOUR

GRATED ZEST OF 1 LEMON

GLAZE:

MILK

SUGAR

1. If you haven't already, prepare the pastry and refrigerate it until firm enough to roll, about 1 hour.

2. On a sheet of lightly floured waxed paper, roll the larger portion of the pastry into a 13½-inch circle with a floured rolling pin. Invert the pastry over a 9-inch deep-dish pie pan. Center it, then peel off the paper. Gently tuck the pastry into the pan, without stretching it, and let the edge of the pastry drape over the side of the pan. Refrigerate for at least 15 minutes.

3. To make the filling, mix the apples, sugar, lemon juice, and nutmeg in a large mixing bowl. Set aside for 10 minutes. Preheat the oven to 400 degrees.

4. On another sheet of lightly floured waxed paper, roll the top pastry into an 11½-inch circle.

Sprinkle the flour and lemon zest over the fruit and mix well. Turn the filling into the refrigerated pie shell and smooth with your hands.

5. Lightly moisten the edge of the pie shell with a wet fingertip or pastry brush. Invert the top pastry over the filling, center it, and peel off the paper. Press the top and bottom pastries together along the dampened edge. Trim the pastry with scissors or a paring knife, leaving an even ½-inch overhang all around, then sculpt the overhang into an upstanding ridge. Poke several steam vents in the top of the pie with a fork or paring knife; put a couple of the vents near the edge of the crust, so you can check the juices there later. Brush the top of the pie with a little milk and sprinkle lightly with sugar.

6. Put the pie directly on the center oven rack and bake for 30 minutes. Remove the pie from the oven and place it on a large, dark baking sheet covered with aluminum foil. Reduce the oven temperature to 375 degrees. Put the pie on the baking sheet back in the oven and bake until any juices—visible at the steam vents—bubble thickly, another 30 to 40 minutes.

7. Transfer the pie to a cooling rack and let cool for at least 1 hour before slicing.

Makes 8 to 10 servings

MULLED CIDER

One of my favorite fall and winter drinks is mulled cider, or cider infused with the flavor of whole spices. It travels particularly well: bring it in a Thermos to fall football games, tailgate parties, apple-picking outings, pumpkin carvings, apple pie parties—you name it.

4 CLOVES

4 ALLSPICE BERRIES

4 WHOLE PIECES STAR ANISE, PLUS MORE FOR
  GARNISH

1 CINNAMON STICK

5 CUPS FRESH APPLE CIDER

3 CUPS CRANBERRY JUICE COCKTAIL

¼ CUP FIRMLY PACKED LIGHT BROWN SUGAR

1 SMALL NAVEL ORANGE, SLICED INTO ROUNDS

1. Tie the cloves, allspice, anise pods, and cinnamon stick in a cheesecloth bag. Combine the cider, cranberry juice, brown sugar, half of the orange slices, and spice bag in a large nonreactive saucepan. Bring to a gentle simmer, stirring occasionally. Simmer the cider (don't boil it), partially covered, for 10 minutes, then remove from the heat. Let stand for 30 minutes, then remove the orange slices and spice bag.

2. When you're ready to serve, reheat the cider nearly to a boil. Cut the remaining orange slices in half. Ladle the cider into mugs, adding a whole anise pod (omit if you're serving small children) and a half slice of orange for garnish.

Makes 8 to 10 servings

Peggy's Dutchess of Oldenburg Apple Pie

I first heard of the Dutchess of Oldenburg apple in my conversation with Susan Jasse of Alyson's Apple Orchard (see page 179), a conversation that led me to Peggy Pschirrer of East Haven, Connecticut. Peggy and her family have a country home in Walpole, New Hampshire, near Alyson's. A few years ago, Peggy—who has baked as many as 75 pies in one stretch for school fundraising events—entered an apple pie contest sponsored by Alyson's. She won top prize for a pie made with Dutchess of Oldenburg apples.

I tracked down Peggy, who told me that she and her family adore the apple, one of the finest pie apples you can find (if, indeed, you can find it; Alyson's grows some of these apples, but their season is short, and fans send for them from all over the country). Peggy compares it to a Rhode Island Greening, which itself isn't all that common. It's a smallish, quite tart apple with what she calls gorgeous white flesh and great flavor.

Like many apple pie bakers I spoke to, Peggy seldom measures ingredients for her pies, but she's made this one so many times now—using a formula she never deviates from—that she was able to recite the recipe from memory. Note that Peggy belongs to that corps of apple pie makers who don't use any thickener, so expect this to be a juicy pie. She does, however, like to add the sugar to her apples 15 minutes before baking, to let the apples juice. Depending on how much juice the apples put off, she may or may not use all of it in the pie.

Peggy always makes a shortening crust—no butter for her. Nor does she bother to chill the crust, even though I recommend it. I asked Peggy which apple she might recommend for those who can't find the two mentioned here. She said she likes the Jonathan, an apple she grew up with, and occasionally she'll use an early McIntosh, which will yield a much softer filling.

1 RECIPE SHORTENING DOUBLE CRUST (PAGE 4), REFRIGERATED

FILLING:

10 TO 12 SMALL DUTCHESS OF OLDENBURG APPLES, PEELED, CORED, AND THINLY SLICED (9 TO 10 CUPS)

SCANT 1 CUP SUGAR

1 TO 1½ TEASPOONS GROUND CINNAMON, TO YOUR TASTE

1 VERY GENEROUS TABLESPOON COLD UNSALTED BUTTER

GLAZE:

SUGAR

GROUND NUTMEG

1. If you haven't already, prepare the pastry. As I mentioned above, Peggy doesn't bother to refrigerate the pastry, even though I recommend it, especially for inexperienced bakers.

2. On a sheet of lightly floured waxed paper, roll the larger portion of the pastry very thinly into a 13½-inch circle with a floured rolling pin. Invert the pastry over a 9-inch deep-dish pie pan. Center it, then peel off the paper. Gently tuck the pastry into the pan, without stretching it, and let the edge of the pastry drape over the side of the pan. Refrigerate. Preheat the oven to 375 degrees.

3. To make the filling, put the apples in a large mixing bowl and add the sugar and cinnamon; mix well. Let the apples sit for 15 minutes. Meanwhile, roll the top pastry into an 11½-inch circle on another sheet of lightly floured waxed paper.

4. Tilt the bowl and look at the accumulated juice. If there's quite a bit of juice, you may not want to add all of it to the pie; that's up to you. Whatever you decide, turn the filling into the pie and smooth the top with your hands. Cut the butter in half and place the pieces near the center of the filling.

5. Moisten the rim of the pie shell with a pastry brush or wet fingertip. Invert the top pastry over the apples, center it, and peel off the paper. Press the top and bottom pastries together along the dampened edge. Trim the pastry, leaving a ½-inch overhang all around, then sculpt the overhang into an upstanding ridge. Poke several steam vents in the top of the pie with a fork or paring knife; put a couple of the vents near the edge, so you can check the juices there later. Sprinkle the top of the pie with a little sugar and nutmeg.

6. Put the pie on a large, dark baking sheet covered with aluminum foil and bake on the center oven rack for 1 hour. The juices will likely be bubbling up through the steam vents near the edge.

7. Transfer the pie to a cooling rack and let cool at least somewhat before slicing.

Makes 8 to 10 servings

All-Granny Pecan Crumb Crust Pie

There's much to be said for using just one type of apple in any given pie. You can, of course, use more than one, or even several, but then the individual personality of each apple tends to get lost among the whole. I call it the Family Reunion Syndrome. Every summer I attend our family reunion in the Adirondacks. There are a good 30 of us there from my immediate family and I always have a great time. But I never fail to come away feeling as if all my encounters with parents, siblings, nieces, and nephews have been too brief and too blurred by the magnitude of the event, and wishing I had been able to spend more time with each individual.

By extension, making a one-type-of-apple pie gives you a great taste of one individual—and since the Granny Smith is one of the most common and consistently good apples in the marketplace, it's a fine choice indeed. During my research for this book, perusing dozens and dozens of cookbooks, it came up time and again as a favorite for apple pie. In my version of an all-Granny pie, I keep the filling pretty simple. There's a little more flour than usual—¼ cup—because Granny Smith apples tend to be fairly juicy. Use a top crust if you want, but I like this pecan crumb topping. The earthiness of the nuts tastes great with the sweet-tartness of the apples.

1 RECIPE BEST BUTTER PIE PASTRY
(PAGE 8), REFRIGERATED

FILLING:

10 CUPS PEELED, CORED, AND SLICED
GRANNY SMITH APPLES

⅔ CUP GRANULATED SUGAR

2 TABLESPOONS FRESH LEMON JUICE

GRATED ZEST OF 1 LEMON

¼ CUP ALL-PURPOSE FLOUR

PECAN CRUMB TOPPING:

1 CUP PECAN HALVES OR COARSELY
CHOPPED PECANS

½ CUP GRANULATED SUGAR

¼ CUP FIRMLY PACKED LIGHT BROWN SUGAR

1 CUP ALL-PURPOSE FLOUR

¼ TEASPOON SALT

½ CUP (1 STICK) COLD UNSALTED BUTTER,
CUT INTO ¼-INCH PIECES

1. If you haven't already, prepare the pastry and refrigerate it until firm enough to roll, about 1 hour.

2. On a sheet of lightly floured waxed paper, roll the pastry into a 13½-inch circle with a floured rolling pin. Invert the pastry over a 9-inch deep-dish pie pan. Center it, then peel off the paper. Gently tuck the pastry into the pan, without stretching it, and sculpt the overhang into an upstanding ridge. Place the pie shell in the freezer for at least 30 minutes.

3. To make the filling, combine the apples, granulated sugar, lemon juice, and lemon zest in a large mixing bowl. Set aside for 10 minutes. Preheat the oven to 400 degrees.

4. Shake the flour over the filling and toss well to mix. Turn the filling into the frozen pie shell and smooth the surface of the filling with your hands. Place the pie directly on the center oven rack and bake for 35 minutes.

5. As the pie bakes, make the topping. Combine the pecans and sugars in a food processor and pulse several times to chop the nuts. Add the flour and salt and pulse again to combine. Remove the lid and scatter the butter over the dry ingredients. Pulse again repeatedly, until the mixture resembles medium-fine crumbs. Dump the crumbs into a large mixing bowl, rubbing the mixture gently between your fingers to make large, buttery crumbs. Refrigerate.

6. After 35 minutes, remove the pie from the oven and place it on a large, dark baking sheet covered with aluminum foil. Reduce the oven temperature to 375 degrees. Carefully dump the crumbs in the center of the pie, spreading them over the entire surface with your hands. Tamp down gently to compact the crumbs.

7. Put the pie on the baking sheet back in the oven and bake until any visible juices bubble thickly, another 35 to 40 minutes. If the topping starts to get too brown, loosely cover the pie with tented aluminum foil during the last 15 minutes of baking.

8. Transfer the pie to a cooling rack and let cool for at least 1 hour before serving.

Makes 8 to 10 servings

WHEN I SAY SLICED APPLES

In the recipes here, I'm talking about an average slice unless otherwise noted. What's an average slice? Assuming you've peeled, quartered, and cored your apples, an average slice is a generous ¼ inch thick on the outside, tapering to about half that on the edge closest to the core. Of course, I don't measure—this is a pie, not a model ship, for Pete's sake—so some of the slices are a little thicker, some a little thinner. This is a good thing, since a range of sizes gives your pie more variety of texture. Occasionally, if I want to use up extra apples in a pie or make a particularly full apple pie, I'll cut the slices crosswise and even dice up some of them. The smaller the pieces, the more apples you can fit in the pie.

Apple and Green Tomato Mock Mincemeat Pie

Old-fashioned mincemeat, like old-fashioned mincemeat pie, isn't something you hear much about anymore—a throwback to an earlier time in American cooking. One glance at my old copy of the *Joy of Cooking*, and it's easy to understand: beef suet and chopped ox heart aren't exactly in dietary vogue these days, especially when combined with copious amounts of sugar, dried fruit, candied citrus peels, a heavy hand with the baking spices, and sour cherries. I suppose that's why the nation's taste in mincemeat gradually shifted to a kinder, gentler mock version, like this one.

Here's a pie I like to make a few times a year, when the last of the green tomatoes are languishing in the kitchen. One needs an appropriate sendoff for these wannabes that never will, and this is just the pie. I use equal parts tomatoes and apples, along with a whole, ground orange, dried fruit, and lots of spices—these spiked with brandy and cider. If you have lots of green tomatoes, consider multiplying this recipe, assembling the pies, and freezing them. Sweet as it is, I like a top crust here, instead of a crumb crust. If you prefer, a lattice top looks good on this pie as well.

1 RECIPE ALL-AMERICAN DOUBLE CRUST (PAGE 2), REFRIGERATED

FILLING:

1 NAVEL ORANGE, WASHED

⅔ CUP SUGAR

2 LARGE TART APPLES, PEELED, CORED, AND FINELY CHOPPED

2 GREEN TOMATOES, CORED AND FINELY CHOPPED

½ CUP DRIED CURRANTS

¼ CUP DRIED CRANBERRIES

¼ CUP RUM OR BRANDY

¼ CUP FRESH APPLE CIDER

1 TABLESPOON UNSULFURED MOLASSES

½ TEASPOON GROUND CINNAMON

½ TEASPOON GROUND GINGER

¼ TEASPOON GROUND NUTMEG

¼ TEASPOON GROUND CLOVES

⅛ TEASPOON SALT

2 TABLESPOONS ALL-PURPOSE FLOUR

GLAZE:

MILK

SUGAR

1. If you haven't already, prepare the pastry and refrigerate it until firm enough to roll, about 1 hour.

2. While the pastry is chilling, make the filling. Cut the orange into large chunks and put them in a food processor with the sugar; process to a roughly textured puree. Scrape the puree into a large mixing bowl and add the remaining filling ingredients. Set aside for 1 hour, stirring occasionally.

3. While the filling sits, roll the larger portion of the pastry into a 13½-inch circle on a sheet of lightly floured waxed paper with a floured rolling pin. Invert the pastry over a 9-inch deep-dish pie pan. Center it, then peel off the paper. Gently tuck the pastry into the pan, without stretching it, and let the edge of the pastry drape over the side of the pan. Refrigerate for 15 minutes. Preheat the oven to 400 degrees.

4. On another sheet of lightly floured waxed paper, roll the top pastry into an 11½-inch circle. Turn the filling into the refrigerated pie shell and smooth the top with your hands. Lightly moisten the edge of the pie shell with a wet fingertip or pastry brush. Invert the top pastry over the filling, center it, and peel off the paper. Press the top and bottom pastries together along the dampened edge. Trim the pastry with scissors or a paring knife, leaving an even ½-inch overhang all around, then sculpt the overhang into an upstanding ridge. Poke several steam vents in the top of the pie with a fork or paring knife; put a couple of the vents near the edge of the crust, so you can check the juices there later. Brush the top of the pie with a little milk and sprinkle lightly with sugar.

5. Put the pie directly on the center oven rack and bake for 25 minutes. Remove the pie from the oven and place on a large, dark baking sheet covered with aluminum foil. Reduce the oven temperature to 350 degrees. Put the pie on the baking sheet back in the oven and bake for an additional 40 minutes. When the pie is done, you may or may not see juices bubble up onto the top crust from the vents; the juices are thick, and there's not as much as in other apple pies.

6. Transfer the pie to a cooling rack and let cool for at least 1 hour before slicing.

Makes 8 to 10 servings

Apple Cobbler Pie

People always ask me where I get ideas for my recipes. Here's a perfect example of how these things evolve.

I cannot tell you how many times my girlfriend, Bev, and I had the following conversation during the course of writing this book.

"Will you be putting apple cobbler in your book?" she would say in a tone that might best be described as equal parts question and direction.

"I'm sorry, sweetheart, I can't. A cobbler doesn't have a bottom crust," I would reply, at first believing that I had an airtight case.

"You have to put in a cobbler," she would lob back. "Cobblers taste so good!"

"So does asparagus risotto, but I'm not putting that in here. This is a book of apple pies." At which point she would let it drop for about a week before bringing it up again.

In the end, of course, a man's airtight case is no defense against a woman's formidable powers of persuasion. Thus was conceived Apple Cobbler Pie—the first apple cobbler, to my knowledge, with a pastry crust. Is it good? It's excellent. And this is one case where I break my own rule about letting apple pie cool before eating it. This one must be served while it's still hot, lest the juices all absorb into the biscuit-like cobbler topping. (Note that I don't use too much flour for thickening because the cobbler part should be fairly juicy.) You'll want to serve ice cream with this.

1 RECIPE BEST BUTTER PIE PASTRY (PAGE 8), REFRIGERATED

FILLING:

5 LARGE APPLES, PEELED, CORED, AND SLICED

½ CUP SUGAR

2 TABLESPOONS FRESH LEMON JUICE

GRATED ZEST OF 1 LEMON

1½ TABLESPOONS ALL-PURPOSE FLOUR

COBBLER TOPPING:

1⅔ CUPS ALL-PURPOSE FLOUR

3 TABLESPOONS SUGAR, PLUS MORE FOR SPRINKLING

2 TEASPOONS BAKING POWDER

¼ TEASPOON SALT

5 TABLESPOONS COLD UNSALTED BUTTER, CUT INTO ¼-INCH PIECES

½ CUP MILK

⅓ CUP PLAIN YOGURT OR SOUR CREAM

1 LARGE EGG, LIGHTLY BEATEN

½ TEASPOON PURE VANILLA EXTRACT

1. If you haven't already, prepare the pastry and refrigerate it until firm enough to roll, about 1 hour.

2. On a sheet of lightly floured waxed paper, roll the pastry into a 13½-inch circle with a floured rolling pin. Invert the pastry over a 9-inch deep-dish pie pan. Center it, then peel off the paper. Gently tuck the pastry down into the pan, without stretching it, and sculpt the edge into an upstanding ridge. Place the pie shell in the freezer for at least 30 minutes.

3. To make the filling, combine the apples, sugar, lemon juice, lemon zest, and flour in a large mixing bowl; toss to blend. Set aside for 10 minutes. Preheat the oven to 400 degrees.

4. Turn the filling into the frozen pie shell. Smooth the filling with your hands to even it out. Place the pie on a large, dark baking sheet covered with aluminum foil and set on the center oven rack. Bake for 45 minutes, covering it loosely with a sheet of aluminum foil for the second half of the baking.

5. Meanwhile, start making the cobbler topping. Sift the flour, 3 tablespoons sugar, baking powder, and salt together in a large mixing bowl. Add the butter and rub it into the dry mixture—or cut it in with a pastry blender—until the mixture resembles coarse crumbs. In a small mixing bowl, blend the milk, yogurt, egg, and vanilla. Don't combine the mixtures quite yet.

6. Just before the 45 minutes have elapsed, reduce the oven temperature to 375 degrees.

Then make a well in the dry ingredients, add the milk mixture, and stir with a wooden spoon just until the cobbler batter is uniformly blended.

7. Remove the pie and baking sheet from the oven. Using a large spoon, dollop the topping here and there over the apples in a random fashion. Keep it back just a little from the edge. Generously sprinkle the cobbler topping with sugar and bake until the topping is golden brown and the juices bubble up nicely around the edge, another 20 to 25 minutes.

8. Transfer the pie to a cooling rack and let cool for no more than 15 minutes before serving.

Makes 8 to 10 servings

JAMES BEARD ON APPLE PIE

"In early America and well up into the nineteenth century, pie was a standard breakfast dish. Since the men of rural families rose early and had an hour or more of outside chores before breakfast, there was time to make such treats. So common has apple pie always been in this country—although it did not originate here—that many old American cookbooks did not bother to give a recipe. It was taken for granted that every housewife had her own favorite."

—*James Beard's American Cookery* (Little, Brown and Company, 1972)

Cheddar-Crusted Apple Pie

New Englanders and others have known the gustatory pleasures of combining apple pie and cheddar cheese for a very long time—indeed, long enough to have generated more than a few opinions about how they should be eaten with each other. Some cooks like to include grated cheddar cheese in the filling itself. I've tried that, and not only does it look less than appetizing, but when the pie is cool and the cheese firms up, much of the appeal fades. Other cooks grate cheese over the top of the pie. Again, this is fine when the pie is warm but less so when it is cool because the cheese hardens. My favorite way is much simpler, and the way most old-timers do it. Take a thin slab of room temperature cheddar and lay it right up against the warm pie. Wait a few seconds for the cheese to soften, then eat your pie.

Still, I wanted way to integrate cheddar into the pie itself, so this is what I came up with: an apple pie with grated cheddar added to the crust. Putting the cheese in the crust avoids the textural problems I've just discussed while keeping the snappy cheddar flavor front and center. And one can still eat this the way we old timers do—with slabs of extra cheddar on the side. Generally speaking, I don't like eating hot pies, but this is one notable exception since the cheddar flavor is better that way.

1 RECIPE CHEDDAR CHEESE PASTRY (PAGE 16), REFRIGERATED

FILLING:

9 CUPS PEELED, CORED, AND SLICED GRANNY SMITH OR OTHER APPLES

½ CUP SUGAR

2 TABLESPOONS FRESH LEMON JUICE

½ CUP CHOPPED WALNUTS (OPTIONAL)

2½ TO 3 TABLESPOONS ALL-PURPOSE FLOUR

1. If you haven't already, prepare the pastry and refrigerate it until firm enough to roll, about 1 hour.

2. On a sheet of lightly floured waxed paper, roll the larger portion of the pastry into a 13½-inch circle with a floured rolling pin. Invert the pastry over a 9-inch deep-dish pie pan. Center it, then peel off the paper. Gently tuck the pastry into the pan, without stretching it, and let the overhang drape over the edge of the pan. Refrigerate.

3. While the pie shell chills, prepare the filling. Combine the apples, sugar, and lemon juice in a large mixing bowl. Set aside for 10 minutes. Preheat the oven to 400 degrees.

4. Stir the walnuts, if using, into the filling. Shake the flour over it and mix, using the larger amount of flour if the apples seem very juicy.

5. On another sheet of lightly floured waxed paper, roll the other half of the pastry into an 11½-inch circle. Turn the filling into the refrigerated pie shell and smooth the top with your hands. Lightly moisten the rim of the pie shell. Invert the top pastry over the filling, center it, and peel off the paper. Press the top and bottom pastries together along the dampened edge. Trim the pastry with scissors or a paring knife, leaving an even ½-inch overhang all around, then sculpt the overhang into an upstanding ridge. Poke several steam vents in the top of the pie with a fork or a paring knife; put a couple of the vents near the edge of the crust, so you can check the juices there later.

6. Put the pie directly on the center oven rack and bake for 25 minutes. Remove the pie from the oven and place on a large, dark baking sheet covered with aluminum foil. Reduce the oven temperature to 375 degrees. Put the pie on the baking sheet back in the oven and bake until the top is dark golden brown and any juices—visible at the steam vents—bubble thickly, another 40 to 45 minutes.

7. Transfer the pie to a cooling rack and let cool briefly before serving.

Makes 8 servings

TOOLS OF THE TRADE: APPLE SLICERS—GETTING TO THE CORE OF THE MATTER

If you have children and want to engage them in the fun of making apple pie, by all means buy one of those apple slicers or dividers. You've probably seen them: they have 2 handles and an arrangement of radiating blades with a circle in the center. You place the slicer on top of a peeled apple, push down hard, and voilà—you have a sliced, cored apple. Especially if kids are using it, you might want to cut a small slice off the bottom of the apple first, so that it doesn't wobble. Angle this cut so that when the apple sits there, the core runs straight up and down. The main drawback of these slicers is that it's difficult to cut evenly through the center of the apple; some of the core inevitably remains. The OXO company makes a well-designed apple slicer with slip-resistant rubberized handles.

Personally, I'm a creature of habit, and I like to slice my apples with a knife. I've used many kinds of paring knives for the job, settling on one I consider the best. It's the size of a small paring knife, but the blade is very narrow and has just a little flex. I don't know what it's called, but it looks like a mini fillet knife. The beauty of this knife is the control you have with the blade. You can scoop the core right out and you don't take half of the apple with it, which sometimes happens with full-size paring knives. And since the blade is so narrow and very sharp, it slices through the apple like a hot knife through butter. Mine has a wooden handle. It's made by Chicago Cutlery, and I believe I bought it for under $15.

Dense Apple Crumble Pie

This pie is based on one of my favorite recipes for apple bars. It's essentially the same recipe baked in a pie pan. This is the apple pie for anyone with a fear of rolling pastry. Instead of a traditional bottom crust, you have an oat crumb crust that's pressed into the pan. Sautéed apple chunks and dates are spooned into the crust, then the top—the same oat topping—is scattered over the apples. You end up with a compact, bar-like apple pie that's not only delicious, but sturdy enough to pack into brown-bag lunches and eat out of hand without making a mess. With the simple crumb crust and fewer-than-usual apples, this is a good recipe to make with kids.

CRUMB CRUST AND TOPPING:

1 CUP ALL-PURPOSE FLOUR

1 CUP OLD-FASHIONED ROLLED OATS (NOT INSTANT)

¾ CUP FIRMLY PACKED LIGHT BROWN SUGAR

⅓ CUP SWEETENED FLAKED COCONUT

½ TEASPOON GROUND CINNAMON

¼ TEASPOON SALT

10 TABLESPOONS (1¼ STICKS) COLD UNSALTED BUTTER, CUT INTO ¼-INCH PIECES

FILLING:

3 LARGE APPLES, PEELED, QUARTERED, AND CORED

2 TABLESPOONS UNSALTED BUTTER

¼ CUP FIRMLY PACKED LIGHT BROWN SUGAR

½ CUP CHOPPED PITTED DATES

1 TABLESPOON FRESH LEMON JUICE

1. To make the crust and topping, put the flour, oats, brown sugar, coconut, cinnamon, and salt in a food processor and pulse several times to mix. Remove the lid and scatter the butter pieces over the surface. Pulse again until the mixture forms coarse crumbs that hold together when you press them between your fingers. Stop the machine after several pulses to fluff the crumbs with a fork, pulling them up from the bottom of the processor.

2. Evenly spread a little more than half of the crumbs in the bottom and halfway up the sides of a lightly buttered 9-inch pie pan, pressing them into the pan. Refrigerate the crust and set the remaining crumbs aside as you make the filling. Preheat the oven to 400 degrees.

3. Cut each quarter section of apple in half lengthwise, then cut crosswise into chunks. Melt the butter in a medium-size nonreactive skillet over medium heat. Add the apples and cook, stirring, to soften somewhat, about 3

minutes. Stir in the brown sugar, dates, and lemon juice and cook for 1 minute more. Remove from heat and let cool for 5 minutes.

4. Scrape the filling and all the juice into the pie shell and spread it out evenly. Scatter the remaining crumbs evenly over the top of the pie, pressing them gently into the apples.

5. Put the pie directly on the center oven rack and bake for 20 minutes. Reduce the oven temperature to 375 degrees and bake until the top of the pie is golden brown and the apples are tender, another 20 to 25 minutes.

6. Transfer the pie to a cooling rack and let cool to room temperature before slicing.

Makes 8 to 10 servings

WASSAILING THE APPLE TREE

Our tradition of caroling at the holidays—"Here we go a-wassailing"—actually grew out of a much older pagan tradition of wassailing to crops and animals to wish them good health and prosperity. In time, the tradition became most commonly associated with apples. Written accounts from the 16th century speak of groups of young men who went from apple orchard to apple orchard, performing the wassailing ritual for pay or reward. This ritual came to be known as a howling or yowling—because of the banging, shooting, and yelling that accompanied it, to drive off evil spirits—and existed in various forms in England and America.

Traditionally, an apple community would visit the orchard at night, provisioned with guns, food, horns, and cider. They would gather round the oldest or most prolific tree—the one that best represented the bounty they hoped for. Cider was poured over the tree's roots, and pieces of toast or cake—offerings of gratitude to the spirits—would be hung or impaled on its branches. This was followed by a song or chant, such as this one, to pay their respects:

Here's to thee, old apple tree,
Whence thou mayst bud
And whence thou mayst blow
And whence thou mayst bear apples enow!
Hats full! Caps full!
Bushel-bushel-bags full!
And my pockets full too! Huzza!

This was repeated three times, followed by clamorous noisemaking to keep the evil spirits at bay.

I've taken part in such a ceremony at a friend's orchard in New Hampshire, but the tradition has essentially disappeared—though I understand it is still celebrated at a handful of orchards in England.

Apple Upside-Down Pan Pie

There are those who might argue that this pie, with its exposed apple slices, is really more of a tart than a pie. Perhaps. Still, I think of this as a pie. For one thing, it's not baked in a tart pan of any sort, but rather a skillet, which gives it the informality of a pie. Nor is the fruit arranged fussily, as fruit tarts generally are. What we do here is melt some butter and brown sugar in the skillet, add a layer of thickly sliced apples and another of diced apples, then cover with pastry and bake. You can serve the pie hot from the pan, but it's more fun to invert the whole thing onto a plate, exposing the caramelized apple slices. The final pie isn't very thick—only about an inch—because the direct heat between the pan and the apples causes the apples to compact quite a bit. But it is buttery rich and sweet—enough so that you can get 10 tidy servings from it.

You'll need some sort of oven-going skillet or sauté pan to make this in—meaning one without a wooden handle or other extremity that would be damaged by the heat. Cast iron is good, but I also have used a double-handled aluminum sauté pan, which works beautifully. Note that I recommend Golden Delicious apples, which will hold their shape better than most apples against the direct heat in the skillet.

1 recipe Best Butter Pie Pastry
   (PAGE 8), REFRIGERATED

FILLING:

¼ CUP (½ STICK) UNSALTED BUTTER

⅓ CUP FIRMLY PACKED LIGHT BROWN SUGAR

4 Golden Delicious apples, peeled,
   quartered, and cored

1 tablespoon fresh lemon juice

1. If you haven't already, prepare the pastry and refrigerate it until firm enough to roll, about 1 hour.

2. Select an ovenproof skillet or shallow sauté pan that measures roughly 9 inches across the bottom and 11 to 12 inches across the top. Over medium heat, melt the butter in the pan, then stir in the brown sugar. Heat until it bubbles, stirring until the mixture spreads across the pan more or less evenly. Remove from the heat. Preheat the oven to 400 degrees.

3. Cut 2 of the apples into thick slices and place them in the pan, flat side down. Don't bother to arrange them in even rows; you just want them down flat. Dice the remaining 2 apples and scatter the pieces evenly over the sliced apples. Sprinkle the lemon juice over all the apples.

4. On a sheet of lightly floured waxed paper, roll the pastry into a 12-inch circle with a floured rolling pin. Invert the pastry over the pan, center it, and peel off the paper. Tuck the edge of the pastry down the side of the pan; the residual warmth will allow the pastry to relax, so you can just push it down gently with a fork. Use the fork to poke several steam vents in the top of the pastry.

5. Put the pie directly on the center oven rack and bake for 20 minutes. Reduce the oven temperature to 375 degrees and bake until the top pastry is golden brown, an additional 20 to 25 minutes.

6. Transfer the pie to a cooling rack. Gently place a plate, as large as the pastry, over the pie. Wearing oven mitts and long sleeves to protect your arms from the caramel, immediately invert the pie onto the plate; it should drop right out. Remove the pan. Let cool for at least 10 minutes, then slice and serve.

Makes 8 to 10 servings

ROLLING PINS: ONE IS NEVER ENOUGH

If you have trouble rolling out pie dough, your rolling pin might be part of the problem. I've collected a number of rolling pins over the years—in part because I think they're beautiful and I love owning them, but also because I like different pins for different types of work. I might even use 2 pins for rolling 1 crust. For example, if I'm rolling out a butter pastry that's been in the fridge for several hours and has become quite firm, I like to loosen it up with my thin, tapered French-style pin; it lets me exert direct pressure on the dough and hastens the process. Then I'll switch to one of my larger ball-bearing pins for the final rolling.

When buying a rolling pin, avoid any whose handles are just sort of stuck into the ends of the pin; they won't last. I've broken off such handles rolling out a firm dough. On better pins, the handles are attached to a continuous steel rod that runs through the center of the roller. You can tell whether it's a good ball-bearing pin if you can hold it by the handle with one hand and spin the roller with the other: the roller should spin easily and for quite a few seconds. You may pay up to $40 for a good rolling pin, but believe me, it's worth it.

Apple Raisin Gingerbread Pie

Part apple pie, part spicy gingerbread, this is a little more involved than some of the recipes here—but then again, it's the best of both worlds. We begin by sautéing apple chunks in butter until they're barely tender, then mix them with applesauce. This filling is baked in the pastry for a while, then gingerbread batter is spread over the filling, and the pie is baked a little longer.

The finished pie is pretty much what you'd imagine—a moist apple raisin filling with a thin layer of gingerbread cake sitting right on top. It's scrumptious. Serve with lightly sweetened whipped cream.

1 RECIPE BEST BUTTER PIE PASTRY
(PAGE 8), REFRIGERATED

FILLING:

2 TABLESPOONS UNSALTED BUTTER

3 LARGE APPLES, PEELED, CORED, AND CUT
INTO BITE-SIZE CHUNKS

1 TABLESPOON FRESH LEMON JUICE

¼ CUP FIRMLY PACKED LIGHT BROWN SUGAR

1 CUP APPLESAUCE, HOMEMADE (PAGE 97)
OR STORE-BOUGHT

½ CUP RAISINS

GINGERBREAD TOPPING:

¼ CUP (½ STICK) UNSALTED BUTTER,
SOFTENED

¼ CUP FIRMLY PACKED LIGHT BROWN SUGAR

¼ CUP UNSULFURED MOLASSES

1 LARGE EGG, AT ROOM TEMPERATURE

½ TEASPOON PURE VANILLA EXTRACT

1 ¼ CUPS ALL-PURPOSE FLOUR

½ TEASPOON BAKING SODA

⅛ TEASPOON SALT

1 TEASPOON GROUND GINGER

¼ TEASPOON GROUND CINNAMON

¼ TEASPOON GROUND CLOVES

⅔ CUP BUTTERMILK

1. If you haven't already, prepare the pastry and refrigerate it until firm enough to roll, about 1 hour.

2. On a sheet of lightly floured waxed paper, roll the pastry into a 13½-inch circle with a floured rolling pin. Invert the pastry over a 9-inch deep-dish pie pan. Center it, then peel off the paper. Gently tuck the pastry into the pan, without stretching it, and sculpt the overhang into an upstanding ridge. Freeze the pie shell for at least 30 minutes.

3. To make the filling, melt the butter in a large skillet over medium heat. Add the apples and cook, stirring, until barely tender, 4 to 5 minutes. Immediately scrape them into a large mixing bowl and stir in the lemon juice, brown sugar, applesauce, and raisins. Preheat the oven to 400 degrees.

4. Turn the filling into the frozen pie shell, smoothing the top with your hands. Place directly on the center oven rack and bake for 30 minutes. After 30 minutes, reduce the oven temperature to 375 degrees. Put a sheet of aluminum foil over the pie, shiny side down; don't crimp it down over the pie, just lay it flat on top. Bake for 15 minutes more.

5. Meanwhile, prepare the gingerbread topping. Using an electric mixer, cream the softened butter, brown sugar, and molasses together in a medium-size mixing bowl. Beat in the egg and vanilla. Sift the flour, baking soda, salt, and spices together into a small mixing bowl. Blend half the dry mixture into the creamed ingredients. Add the buttermilk, blending until smooth, then blend in the rest of the dry ingredients.

6. Remove the pie from the oven. Scrape the gingerbread mixture over the filling and smooth it with a spoon. Put the pie back on the center rack and bake for another 25 minutes. When done, the cake will have likely developed fissures on the surface, and the gingerbread should feel springy to the touch in the center.

7. Transfer the pie to a cooling rack and let cool for at least 30 minutes before slicing. (I don't let this cool as long as other pies because there's very little loose juice in it; what there is seems to absorb up into the gingerbread.)

Makes 8 to 10 servings

Apple and Pear Open-Faced Pie

In Italian cooking, this sort of pie is often called a *crostata*, and it straddles the line between pie and tart. It is essentially what I refer to elsewhere as a peekaboo pie, only this is baked freeform on a baking sheet and not in a pie pan. Not only is it one of my favorite pies to make, but it's one that I've made time and again at cooking demonstrations to consistently enthusiastic crowds. The assembly here is simple: The dough is spread with a layer of ginger preserves, and the fruit is piled onto the crust. Then the uncovered border of pastry is folded over the filling, creating a sort of wide, frilly skirt to enclose the fruit.

So, pie or tart? Once you've tried it, I don't think it will matter.

1 RECIPE BEST BUTTER PIE PASTRY
(PAGE 8), REFRIGERATED

FILLING:

⅓ CUP SUGAR

1½ TABLESPOONS ALL-PURPOSE FLOUR

½ TEASPOON GROUND CINNAMON

2 LARGE GOLDEN DELICIOUS APPLES,
PEELED, QUARTERED, AND CORED

1 LARGE RIPE PEAR, QUARTERED AND CORED

GRATED ZEST OF 1 LEMON

⅓ CUP GINGER OR APRICOT PRESERVES

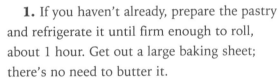

1. If you haven't already, prepare the pastry and refrigerate it until firm enough to roll, about 1 hour. Get out a large baking sheet; there's no need to butter it.

2. To make the filling, mix the sugar, flour, and cinnamon together in a small mixing bowl; set aside. Cut the apples and pears crosswise into bite-size chunks and put in a large mixing bowl. Add the sugar mixture and toss well to mix. Add the lemon zest and mix again. Set aside. Preheat the oven to 400 degrees.

3. On a sheet of lightly floured waxed paper, roll the pastry into a 13½-inch circle with a floured rolling pin. Invert the pastry onto the baking sheet, center it, and peel off the paper. Spread the preserves in an 8-inch circle in the center of the pastry, warming it if necessary to make it more spreadable. Carefully distribute the filling over the preserves, taking care to leave an uncovered pastry border of at least 2 inches all around.

4. Fold the edge of the pastry over the fruit, using a metal spatula, if necessary, to help you lift the dough. You'll need to do this in sections, working your way around the pie; as you do, the dough will self-pleat.

5. Put the baking sheet on the center oven rack and bake for 25 minutes, then reduce the oven temperature to 375 degrees and bake until the crust is golden brown and the filling bubbly, an additional 25 minutes or so.

6. Transfer the baking sheet to a cooling rack and let cool for at least 15 minutes before slicing. This is excellent served warm.

Makes 8 servings

AND IF THAT PERSONALS AD DOESN'T WORK, YOU CAN ALWAYS TRY THIS

There are any number of old traditions whereby a young lady would enlist the help of an apple peel for a glimpse into her future love life. A long-standing Scottish and Irish tradition maintains that if a girl so intended, she might learn the identity of her beloved by peeling the apple in one long continuous piece and tossing it over her left shoulder: the profile of the peel would reveal the profile of her future love. In another variation, the peel would reveal his initials. And if the peel broke, the young lady would, alas, remain unmarried.

Not surprisingly, the apple's ancient associations with love—the modern tradition of throwing rice at weddings was preceded by the custom of throwing apples—gave rise to other forms of romantic divination. If a girl wasn't sure which of several suitors she should choose, she might settle the issue by assigning the young men's names to each of several apple seeds and pushing the moistened seeds onto her forehead. One New England account of this tradition then has the girl chant the following:

Pippin! Pippin! Paradise!
Tell me where my true love lies!

The one that dropped off last was the fellow she should turn her attention to. If she then wanted to foretell her chances of marital bliss, it was said that counting the seeds in a given apple would give her a glimpse into their union: An even number meant a happy marriage. If a seed was cut in half, it would be an unhappy marriage. Two seeds meant widowhood.

Now, as then, should you have your sights set on that special someone—and tossing apple peels has proved less than fruitful—it might not be a bad idea to take the direct approach and simply bake a mouthwatering apple pie for the object of your affections. Call me old-fashioned, but I think a warm apple pie is rife with romantic possibilities.

Cox's Orange Pippin Pie with Cinnamon Streusel

The Cox's Orange Pippin is one of those apples that apple growers fawn over and fans clamor for when they can find them. The "orange" in the name refers to a faint red-orange, mottled skin. The flavor is softer than that of some Pippins—not so tart or sharp—and it's been described, variously, as spicy, nutty, honeyed, and pear-like, all suggestive of some of the ingredients that would work well in a pie made with them.

This pie, however, plays it fairly straight, which is often the way I like to play it when I find an apple of superior flavor. I don't use too much sweetener, but I do add a bit of sharpness with a little cider vinegar. An apple of this caliber needs a butter pastry, and for the topping I go with a simple cinnamon streusel. If you happen to live in New England, you can find Cox's Orange Pippins at Alyson's Apple Orchard in Walpole, New Hampshire (see page 179). Buy extra apples because you'll want to eat as many as you can out of hand. If you can't buy Cox's Orange Pippins, feel free to substitute another variety of apple.

1 RECIPE BEST BUTTER PIE PASTRY (PAGE 8), REFRIGERATED

FILLING:

8 CUPS PEELED, CORED, AND THINLY SLICED COX'S ORANGE PIPPIN APPLES

½ CUP SUGAR

1½ TABLESPOONS CIDER VINEGAR

2 TABLESPOONS ALL-PURPOSE FLOUR

2 TABLESPOONS APPLE BUTTER OR APPLESAUCE (OPTIONAL)

CINNAMON STREUSEL TOPPING:

1 CUP ALL-PURPOSE FLOUR

⅔ CUP SUGAR

1 TEASPOON GROUND CINNAMON

⅛ TEASPOON SALT

½ CUP (1 STICK) COLD UNSALTED BUTTER, CUT INTO ¼-INCH PIECES

1. If you haven't already, prepare the pastry and refrigerate it until firm enough to roll, about 1 hour.

2. On a sheet of lightly floured waxed paper, roll the pastry into a 13½-inch circle with a floured rolling pin. Invert the pastry over a 9-inch deep-dish pie pan. Center it, then peel off the paper. Gently tuck the pastry into the pan, without stretching it, and sculpt the overhang into an upstanding ridge. Put the pie shell in the freezer for at least 30 minutes.

3. To make the filling, combine the apples, sugar, and vinegar in a large mixing bowl; mix well. Set aside for 10 minutes. Preheat the oven to 400 degrees.

4. Sprinkle the flour over the fruit and mix. Stir in the apple butter, if using. Turn the filling into the frozen pie shell, smoothing the surface with your hands. Place the pie directly on the center oven rack and bake for 30 minutes.

5. While the pie bakes, make the topping. Combine the flour, sugar, cinnamon, and salt in a food processor. Remove the lid and scatter the butter pieces over the dry ingredients. Pulse the machine repeatedly, until the mixture resembles fine crumbs. Transfer the topping to a large mixing bowl and rub with your fingers to make large, buttery crumbs. Refrigerate.

6. After 30 minutes, remove the pie from the oven and place it on a large, dark baking sheet covered with aluminum foil. Reduce the oven temperature to 375 degrees. Carefully dump the streusel in the center of the pie, spreading it evenly over the surface with your hands. Press down gently to compact the streusel. Put the pie on the baking sheet back in the oven and bake until the juices bubble thickly around the edge, an additional 25 to 30 minutes.

7. Transfer the pie to a cooling rack and let cool for at least 1 hour before slicing.

Makes 8 to 10 servings

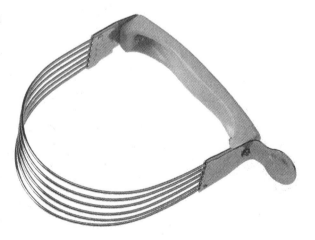

Andy's Cranberry Apple Pie with Walnut Crumb Topping

My friend Andy Johnson is a frugal New England fellow—a first-rate competition fiddler and latter-day Euell Gibbons who forages for at least some of his diet when the opportunity presents itself. Thus when Andy breezes into town once or twice each year in his ancient Honda—known affectionately as "The Pod," 300,000 miles and counting—he often has a bag of something he's gathered along the way: produce from a friend's garden, apples he's picked, fresh currants from a spot nobody else knows about. One year Andy arrived with a paper sack full of cranberries he had gathered from some bogs near his family's home along the New Hampshire seacoast. In turn, I baked them into a pie—this pie—which I make at least a couple of times a year in honor of Andy. In truth, I vary the formula a little from time to time. I sometimes use a pear in place of an apple. Occasionally I will add a top crust instead of a crumb topping. It would be very un-Andy to be too rigid about this. But I don't vary it much, and I doubt you will either, once you've tried it.

1 RECIPE BEST BUTTER PIE PASTRY
(PAGE 8), REFRIGERATED

FILLING:

6 CUPS PEELED, CORED, AND SLICED
APPLES

2 CUPS FRESH CRANBERRIES, PICKED OVER

½ CUP CHOPPED WALNUTS

⅓ CUP GRANULATED SUGAR

⅓ CUP PURE MAPLE SYRUP

1½ TABLESPOONS FRESH LEMON JUICE

GRATED ZEST OF 1 ORANGE

½ TEASPOON GROUND CINNAMON

½ TEASPOON GROUND CLOVES

3 TABLESPOONS ALL-PURPOSE FLOUR

WALNUT CRUMB TOPPING:

1 CUP WALNUTS

⅓ CUP GRANULATED SUGAR

⅓ CUP FIRMLY PACKED LIGHT BROWN SUGAR

¾ CUP ALL-PURPOSE FLOUR

¼ TEASPOON SALT

½ CUP (1 STICK) COLD UNSALTED BUTTER,
CUT INTO ¼-INCH PIECES

1. If you haven't already, prepare the pastry and refrigerate it until firm enough to roll, about 1 hour.

2. On a sheet of lightly floured waxed paper, roll the pastry into a 13½-inch circle with a floured rolling pin. Invert the pastry over a 9-inch deep-dish pie pan. Center it, then peel off the paper. Gently tuck the pastry into the pan, without stretching it, and sculpt the edge into an upstanding ridge. Place the pie shell in the freezer for at least 30 minutes.

3. To make the filling, mix the apples, cranberries, walnuts, and sugar together in a large mixing bowl. Set aside for 10 minutes. Preheat the oven to 400 degrees.

4. Add the remaining filling ingredients to the bowl, shaking the flour on at the end and mixing it in. Turn the filling into the frozen pie shell. Smooth the filling with your hands to even it out. Place the pie on a large, dark baking sheet covered with aluminum foil. Set the sheet on the center oven rack and bake for 35 minutes.

5. While the pie bakes, make the crumb topping. Put the walnuts and sugars in a food processor; pulse briefly to grind the nuts. Add the flour and salt and pulse again. Remove the lid and scatter the butter over the dry ingredients. Pulse the machine repeatedly, until the mixture resembles medium-fine crumbs. Transfer to a large mixing bowl, then rub the crumbs between your fingers to make large, buttery crumbs. Refrigerate.

6. After 35 minutes, remove the pie and baking sheet from the oven. Reduce the oven temperature to 375 degrees. Carefully dump the topping in the center of the pie, spreading the crumbs evenly over the surface with your hands. Tamp them down lightly. Return the pie on the baking sheet to the oven and bake until the juices bubble thickly around the edge, an additional 35 to 40 minutes. Loosely cover the pie with tented aluminum foil during the last 10 to 15 minutes of baking to keep the crumbs from browning too much.

7. Transfer the pie to a cooling rack and let cool for at least 1 hour before slicing.

Makes 8 to 10 servings

FREEZE THOSE CRANBERRIES

Every fall I wait until cranberries go on sale—usually right before the holidays—and buy a case to stash in the freezer. One bonus about frozen cranberries is how easy they are to chop: a sharp knife will glide right through them. By contrast, fresh cranberries offer a bit of resistance: your knife wants to roll off them rather than bite into them. Slicing matters aside, cranberries couldn't be simpler to freeze: just toss the bags in the freezer. If you're adding cold cranberries to a pie, you'll probably have to add 5 to 7 minutes to the total baking time.

As of this writing, the supply of cranberries has been up and the price has been down, making them a bargain. So act now and stash a case this year.

Apple Pecan Pumpkin-Butter Pie

This may well be my first choice for a Thanksgiving pie, since it features both apples and pumpkin. Unlike Pumpkin Applesauce Pie (page 92), this one uses pumpkin butter instead of canned pumpkin—pumpkin butter being more or less the equivalent of apple butter, a very thick reduction. It gives a very intense pumpkin flavor to the pie, so much so that people are often uncertain whether they're eating a pumpkin pie or an apple pie. I believe that you can find other brands of pumpkin butter, probably in health food stores, but the brand I love and have been using for years comes from a small company named Muirhead, out of Ringoes, New Jersey (see note). It isn't cheap, but the flavor and texture are so superior that I think it's worth the extra cost. The product I use is actually called Pecan Pumpkin Butter—the pecans are so finely ground you're aware only of the flavor, not the texture—and to sharpen the pecan emphasis, I add chopped pecans to the pie. I put this in a butter pastry and top it with a spiced streusel. Use a fresh, juicy, tart apple—I like Redcort, Jonagold, or Granny Smith. Even with juicy apples, the pie doesn't need any thickener; apparently there's enough fiber and body in the pumpkin butter to absorb the juice.

1 RECIPE BEST BUTTER PIE PASTRY (PAGE 8), REFRIGERATED

FILLING:

7 CUPS PEELED, CORED, AND SLICED APPLES

¼ CUP SUGAR

1 TABLESPOON FRESH LEMON JUICE

1 CUP SWEETENED PUMPKIN BUTTER (SEE HEADNOTE)

½ CUP CHOPPED PECANS

½ CUP RAISINS

SPICED STREUSEL TOPPING:

1 CUP ALL-PURPOSE FLOUR

⅔ CUP SUGAR

1 TEASPOON PUMPKIN PIE SPICE

¼ TEASPOON SALT

½ CUP (1 STICK) COLD UNSALTED BUTTER, CUT INTO ¼-INCH PIECES

1. If you haven't already, prepare the pastry and refrigerate it until firm enough to roll, about 1 hour.

2. On a sheet of lightly floured waxed paper, roll the pastry into a 13½-inch circle with a floured rolling pin. Invert the pastry over a 9-inch deep-dish pie pan. Center it, then peel off the paper. Gently tuck the pastry into the pan, without stretching it, and sculpt the overhang into an upstanding ridge. Freeze the pie shell for at least 30 minutes.

3. To make the filling, combine the apples, sugar, and lemon juice in a large mixing bowl. Mix well, then set aside for 10 minutes. Preheat the oven to 400 degrees.

4. Add the pumpkin butter, pecans, and raisins to the filling and mix. Scrape the filling into the frozen pie shell, smoothing the top of the fruit with your hands. While you're at it, try to bury the raisins under the top layer of apples so they don't scorch during the first 30 minutes of baking. Put the pie directly on the center oven rack and bake for 30 minutes. Check the pie after about 20 minutes. If the tops of the apples are getting too dark, loosely cover the filling with a piece of aluminum foil.

5. While the pie bakes, make the topping. Put the flour, sugar, pumpkin pie spice, and salt in a food processor and pulse several times to mix. Remove the lid and scatter the butter pieces over the dry ingredients. Pulse the machine repeatedly, until the mixture resembles fine crumbs. Dump the mixture into a large mixing bowl, then rub gently with your fingers to make large, buttery crumbs. Refrigerate.

6. After 30 minutes, remove the pie from the oven and place it on a large, dark baking sheet covered with aluminum foil. Reduce the oven temperature to 375 degrees. Carefully dump the streusel mixture in the center of the pie, spreading it evenly over the surface with your hands. Tamp it down gently. Put the pie on the baking sheet back in the oven and bake until you see juices bubbling thickly around the edge, an additional 30 to 35 minutes. If the topping starts to get too dark, cover the pie with loosely tented aluminum foil during the last 10 to 15 minutes of baking.

7. Transfer the pie to a cooling rack and let cool for at least 1 hour before slicing.

Makes 8 to 10 servings

Note: You can contact Muirhead at 43 Highway 202, Ringoes, NJ 08551, (800) 782-7803, www.muirheadfoods.com.

Apple Marmalade Pie

Many years ago, I was browsing through a cookbook when a recipe for Shaker lemon pie caught my eye. Rather than some ordinary lemon meringue pie, this one had thin—paper-thin—slices of lemon in it. And lots of sugar. The slices sat in the sugar overnight, at which point the rind—which you might think would be too bitter to use in a pie—had sweetened up nicely. It made a great pie, and eventually I adapted the idea of sugaring the rind and using it in this pie, whose runny, citrusy flavor I especially appreciate in the depths of winter.

What I do here is somewhat similar to the process I mentioned, only much simpler. First, I chop one orange and half a lemon in the food processor with some sugar, then let the mixture stand overnight. The next day, I mix it with sliced apples, vanilla, and cinnamon, then bake it in a pie shell. For lack of a better way to describe the taste of the filling, it's what you might expect apple marmalade to taste like: quite citrusy, with a pronounced apple taste. I add a crumb topping, but a top crust would work fine, too. It's excellent with vanilla ice cream.

1 RECIPE BEST BUTTER PIE PASTRY (PAGE 8), REFRIGERATED

FILLING:

1 NAVEL ORANGE, WASHED AND CUT INTO CHUNKS

½ LEMON, WASHED, SEEDED, AND CUT INTO CHUNKS

¾ CUP SUGAR

6 CUPS PEELED, CORED, AND SLICED APPLES

½ TEASPOON PURE VANILLA EXTRACT

¼ TEASPOON GROUND CINNAMON

3 TABLESPOONS ALL-PURPOSE FLOUR

BLOND STREUSEL TOPPING:

1 CUP ALL-PURPOSE FLOUR

⅔ CUP SUGAR

¼ TEASPOON SALT

6 TABLESPOONS (¾ STICK) COLD UNSALTED BUTTER, CUT INTO ¼-INCH PIECES

1 TABLESPOON MILK OR LIGHT CREAM

1. The day before you plan to bake the pie, put the orange chunks, lemon chunks, and sugar in the bowl of a food processor. Pulse the machine a number of times, breaking the fruit into small pieces—though not too small; you want a little texture left in the fruit because it adds a nice bit of chewiness. Transfer the mixture to a small mixing bowl and cover with plastic wrap. Refrigerate for at least 4 hours, preferably overnight.

2. If you haven't already, prepare the pastry and refrigerate it until firm enough to roll, about 1 hour.

3. On a sheet of lightly floured waxed paper, roll the pastry into a 13½-inch circle with a floured rolling pin. Invert the pastry over a 9-inch deep-dish pie pan. Center it, then peel off the paper. Gently tuck the pastry into the pan, without stretching it, and sculpt the overhang into an upstanding ridge. Place the pie shell in the freezer for at least 30 minutes. Preheat the oven to 400 degrees.

4. To make the filling, prepare the apples and place them in a large mixing bowl. Add the citrus fruit mixture, vanilla, and cinnamon; mix well. Shake the flour over the fruit and mix again. Turn the filling into the frozen pie shell, smoothing the surface with your hands. Place

the pie directly on the center oven rack and bake for 30 minutes.

5. While the pie bakes, make the streusel. Combine the flour, sugar, and salt in a food processor. Pulse briefly to mix. Remove the lid and scatter the butter pieces over the dry ingredients. Pulse the machine repeatedly, until the mixture resembles fine crumbs. Add the milk and pulse again, until the mixture starts to form large, buttery crumbs. Refrigerate.

6. After 30 minutes, remove the pie from the oven and place it on a large, dark baking sheet covered with aluminum foil. Reduce the oven temperature to 375 degrees. Carefully dump the crumbs in the center of the pie and spread them evenly over the surface with your hands. Press down gently to compact the streusel. Put the pie on the baking sheet back in the oven and bake until the juices bubble thickly around the edge, 35 to 40 minutes longer. Loosely cover the pie with tented aluminum foil during the last 15 minutes, if necessary, to prevent the topping from getting too brown.

7. Transfer the pie to a cooling rack and let cool for at least 1 hour before serving.

Makes 8 to 10 servings

CHAPTER 3

Distinctly Summer Apple Pies

Although some summer pie makers shift their attention almost exclusively to the sexy, elusive fruits of summer—the plums, peaches, and berries—I think it's a mistake to turn our collective back on the possibilities for summer apple pies, for a couple of reasons. The first is that apples have a way of softening and enhancing the flavor of some summer fruits, which I believe taste even better in a pie when they're blended with other fruits. Raspberries are a perfect example. I think an all-raspberry pie is too much of a good thing. A raspberry apple pie, with a clear but not overwhelming raspberry presence, is more appealing to me.

Consider, too, that summer is really the only time to make these pies, for the simple reason that the quality of apples available in summer—especially New Zealand–grown Granny Smith, Braeburn, and Gala varieties, among others—is much better than the quality of berries, peaches, plums, and other summer fruits you'll find in the supermarket in the winter. So it stands to reason

that you'll want to make these mixed-fruit pies when you have access to local summer fruits. Cost is another consideration, since imported summer fruits are much more expensive than imported apples.

Here, then, is a collection of apple pies you'll want to consider for the summer months. They're not here to muscle out the all-peach pies or the mixed-berry pies you and I love to bake. They're simply a reminder that even if the new crop is still a few months away, apples can hold a prominent place in your summer pies, sharing the spotlight with the season's best.

Nancy's Apple and Elderberry Pie

Nancy Phillips is one of my dearest friends in New Hampshire. In the early 1980s, she and her husband, Michael, moved to a farm in northern New Hampshire. Over the years, they have raised herbs and vegetables—and a beautiful daughter, Gracie—and have generally done a stellar job of living the country life. Nancy is an accomplished cook; among her specialties is this apple pie made with the elderberries that grow near the stream outside their back door. It's a pie that has special meaning because Michael, who formerly ran the apple orchard and cider mill down the road, is an apple expert and the author of *The Apple Grower: A Guide for the Organic Orchardist* (Chelsea Green, 1998).

In addition to making a great pie, Nancy tells me that the elder tree and elderberry possess a treasure-trove of healthful properties. The berries are immunity enhancing and have antiviral agents. The flowers make a great tea for treating fevers. The tree itself is widely revered. Nancy says that it is customary, in some places, to ask permission of the tree before you pick anything from it. If you like this sort of thing, I suggest that you buy a copy of Nancy and Michael's new book, *The Village Herbalist* (Chelsea Green, 2001). And don't forget to try the pie.

1 RECIPE THREE-GRAIN BUTTER PASTRY (PAGE 10), REFRIGERATED

FILLING:

6 CUPS PEELED, CORED, AND SLICED APPLES (SUCH AS NORTHERN SPY, GRANNY SMITH, OR GOLDEN DELICIOUS)

2 CUPS RIPE ELDERBERRIES, PICKED OVER

½ CUP MILD-TASTING HONEY, WARMED UNTIL LIQUEFIED

1 TABLESPOON FRESH LEMON JUICE

2 TABLESPOONS GRANULATED SUGAR

1 TABLESPOON CORNSTARCH

PINCH EACH OF GROUND CLOVES AND GROUND GINGER

OATMEAL CRUMB TOPPING:

1 CUP ALL-PURPOSE FLOUR

½ CUP OLD-FASHIONED ROLLED OATS (NOT INSTANT)

⅔ CUP FIRMLY PACKED LIGHT BROWN SUGAR

¼ TEASPOON SALT

¼ TEASPOON GROUND CINNAMON

½ CUP (1 STICK) COLD UNSALTED BUTTER, CUT INTO ¼-INCH PIECES

1. If you haven't already, prepare the pastry and refrigerate it until firm enough to roll, about 1 hour.

2. On a sheet of lightly floured waxed paper, roll the pastry into a 13½-inch circle with a floured rolling pin. Invert the pastry over a 9-inch deep-dish pie pan. Center it, then peel off the paper. Gently tuck the pastry into the pan, without stretching it, and sculpt the edge into an upstanding ridge. Place the pie shell in the freezer for at least 30 minutes.

3. Meanwhile, make the filling. Combine the apples, elderberries, honey, and lemon juice in a large mixing bowl. Toss well to mix, then set aside for 10 minutes. Preheat the oven to 400 degrees.

4. Mix the granulated sugar, cornstarch, and spices together in a small bowl. Sprinkle over the fruit and stir to combine. Turn the filling into the frozen pie shell, smoothing the top with your hands. Put the pie directly on the center oven rack and bake for 30 minutes.

5. While the pie bakes, make the oatmeal topping. Put the flour, oats, brown sugar, salt, and cinnamon in a food processor and pulse several times to mix. Remove the lid and scatter the butter pieces over the dry mixture. Pulse the machine repeatedly, until the mixture resembles fine crumbs. Empty the crumbs into a large mixing bowl and rub them between your fingers to make large, buttery crumbs. Refrigerate.

6. After 30 minutes, remove the pie from the oven and place it on a large, dark baking sheet covered with aluminum foil. Reduce the oven temperature to 375 degrees. Carefully dump the crumbs in the center of the pie, spreading them evenly over the entire surface with your hands. Tamp them down gently. Return the pie on the baking sheet to the oven and bake until the juices bubble thickly around the edge, an additional 30 to 40 minutes. Loosely cover the pie with tented aluminum foil during the last 15 minutes, if necessary, to prevent the top from getting too dark.

7. Transfer the pie to a cooling rack and let cool for at least 1 hour before serving.

Makes 8 to 10 servings

Apple Strawberry Pie with Mint Jelly

Here's another good summer apple pie made with fresh strawberries. It's very juicy, because of the strawberries, so I use cornstarch to help keep the filling from getting too runny. One optional touch you might want to consider is a spoonful of rose water, which you can use in addition to the mint jelly or in place of it. This is the perfect apple pie for early to midsummer, when you can get your hands on fresh local berries.

1 RECIPE ALL-AMERICAN DOUBLE CRUST (PAGE 2), REFRIGERATED

FILLING:

6 CUP PEELED, CORED, AND SLICED GRANNY SMITH APPLES

1 PINT RIPE STRAWBERRIES, RINSED, HULLED, AND THICKLY SLICED

½ CUP SUGAR

3 TABLESPOONS CORNSTARCH

PINCH OF GROUND NUTMEG

1 TABLESPOON FRESH LEMON JUICE

GRATED ZEST OF ½ LEMON

½ TEASPOON FOOD-GRADE ROSE WATER (OPTIONAL)

1 TABLESPOON MINT JELLY

GLAZE:

MILK

SUGAR

1. If you haven't already, prepare the pastry and refrigerate it until firm enough to roll, about 1 hour.

2. On a sheet of lightly floured waxed paper, roll the larger portion of the pastry into a 13½-inch circle with a floured rolling pin. Invert the pastry over a 9-inch deep-dish pie pan. Center it, then peel off the paper. Gently tuck the pastry down into the pan, without stretching it, and let the dough drape over the side of the pan. Refrigerate while you prepare the filling.

3. To make the filling, mix the apples and strawberries together in a large mixing bowl. Mix the sugar, cornstarch, and nutmeg together in a small mixing bowl, then add it to the fruit and toss well. Stir in the lemon juice, lemon zest, and rose water, if using. Set aside.

4. On another sheet of lightly floured waxed paper, roll the other piece of pastry into an 11½-inch circle. Turn the filling into the chilled pie shell, smoothing the surface with your hands.

Dot the filling with the mint jelly, dabbing it here and there.

5. Lightly moisten the edge of the pastry with a wet fingertip or pastry brush. Invert the top pastry over the filling, center it, and peel off the paper. Press the top and bottom pastries together at the dampened edge. Trim the pastry, leaving an even ½ inch all around, then sculpt the overhang into an upstanding ridge. Poke several steam vents in the top of the pie with a fork or paring knife; put a couple of the vents near the edge, so you can check the juices there later. Brush the top of the pie with milk and sprinkle with sugar.

6. Put the pie on a large, dark baking sheet covered with aluminum foil, place on the center oven rack, and bake for 30 minutes. Reduce the oven temperature to 375 degrees and bake until the juices—visible at the steam vents—bubble thickly, about another 30 minutes.

7. Transfer the pie to a cooling rack and let cool for at least 2 hours before serving.

Makes 8 to 10 servings

SKEWER THOSE APPLES

I keep a package of wooden skewers in my kitchen cabinet, and I use them as much for checking my apple pies as I do for making kabobs. They make excellent apple pie testers because they are long and pointy. Metal skewers, I've found, aren't pointy enough to be much help. And unlike the more common tester—an ordinary toothpick—you can insert a skewer way down into the center of the pie without burning your fingers.

I deliberately test my apple pie with a skewer before I think the apples are done. Different apples offer different kinds of resistance, and I like to test the waters and see just how much resistance my apples have to offer. This preliminary poking gives me some idea how much longer the pie needs to bake. If I have any doubt that the apples are sufficiently tender, I give the pie more time because I think undercooked apples are one of the worst sins an apple pie baker can commit: there you are, expecting a mouthful of soft, yielding apples, only to bite into a stack of half-cooked slices. I hate it when that happens.

Poke the skewer into one or two places, and if your pie has a top pastry, try to insert it through one of the steam vents. You want to be discreet about all of this, not leave your pastry looking like Swiss cheese. Remove the probe, rinse and dry it, and use it again and again.

Farm Stand Apple and Peach Pie

I have publicly lamented the fact that I've often had a difficult time finding good fresh peaches in New England. That situation has changed quite dramatically since I've started living part-time in Annapolis, Maryland. Good peaches are as easy to find in Maryland—I buy mine at a farm stand not two miles from my home—as good apples are in New England. This pie is a showcase for both. One of the things I love about a peach pie is the softness of it all—a tender top crust that almost melts into soft-cooked peaches. To keep that softness, I'm inclined to blend the peaches with an apple that cooks up nice and soft. Paula Red is my first choice—it's soft and arrives early to market, when peaches are still prime. McIntosh is also good, though perhaps not the earliest ones, since they're a bit on the firm side. As for the peaches, I like to match the whiteness of the apple's flesh with white peaches, which are very sweet, although—in my opinion, at least—they don't have as much of a peachy flavor as the traditional yellow-fleshed peaches do. For the crust, my first choice is an all-shortening crust, but the All-American Double Crust is great, too.

1 RECIPE SHORTENING DOUBLE CRUST (PAGE 4) OR ALL-AMERICAN DOUBLE CRUST (PAGE 2), REFRIGERATED

FILLING:

5 CUPS PEELED, CORED, AND THINLY SLICED APPLES

4 CUPS PEELED, PITTED, AND SLICED RIPE PEACHES

½ CUP SUGAR

2 TABLESPOONS CORNSTARCH

⅛ TEASPOON SALT

BIG PINCH OF GROUND NUTMEG

1 TABLESPOON FRESH LEMON JUICE

½ TEASPOON PURE VANILLA EXTRACT

2 TABLESPOONS COLD UNSALTED BUTTER, CUT INTO SMALL PIECES

GLAZE:

MILK

SUGAR

1. If you haven't already, prepare the pastry and refrigerate it until firm enough to roll, about 1 hour.

2. On a sheet of lightly floured waxed paper, roll the larger portion of the pastry into a 13½-inch circle with a floured rolling pin. Invert the pastry over a 9-inch deep-dish pie pan. Center it, then peel off the paper. Gently tuck the pastry into the pan, without stretching it, and let the overhang drape over the edge of the pan. Refrigerate.

3. While the pie shell chills, make the filling. Combine the apples and peaches in a large mixing bowl. In a small mixing bowl, mix the sugar, cornstarch, salt, and nutmeg. Add this mixture to the fruit and toss well. Add the lemon juice and vanilla and mix again. Set aside. Preheat the oven to 400 degrees.

4. On another sheet of lightly floured waxed paper, roll the other half of the pastry into an 11½-inch circle. Turn the filling into the chilled pie shell and smooth the fruit with your hands. Dot the top of the fruit with the butter.

5. Lightly moisten the edge of the pie shell with a wet fingertip or pastry brush. Invert the top pastry over the filling, center it, and peel off the paper. Press the top and bottom pastries together along the dampened edge. Trim the pastry with scissors or a paring knife, leaving an even ½-inch overhang all around, then sculpt the overhang into an upstanding ridge. Poke several steam vents in the top of the pie with a fork or paring knife; put a couple of the vents near the edge of the crust, so you can check the juices there later. Brush the top of the pie with a little milk and sprinkle lightly with sugar.

6. Put the pie directly on the center oven rack and bake for 30 minutes. Remove the pie from the oven and place it on a large, dark baking sheet covered with aluminum foil. Reduce the oven temperature to 375 degrees. Put the pie on the baking sheet back in the oven and bake until the juices bubble thickly at the edge, an additional 30 to 35 minutes.

7. Transfer the pie to a cooling rack and let cool for at least 2 hours—preferably longer, since this is a juicy pie—before slicing.

Makes 8 to 10 servings

Fresh Tomato and Apple Pie

I'll admit that, of all the pies in this book, perhaps this one sounds the weirdest. All the more reason to be thoroughly delighted when you discover for yourself how good it tastes. And that's not just me talking. I've actually served this pie at gatherings, intentionally not divulging the secret ingredient, to see how people respond. If someone asks what "the red pieces" are, I simply say "Take a guess." And guess they do, including fresh currants, raspberries, and strawberries. It never seems to occur to anyone that you can put fresh ripe tomatoes in an apple pie—in spite of the fact that green tomato and apple pie isn't all that unusual. Anyway, this is absolutely worth trying, but only with the best summer tomatoes and certainly not with canned tomatoes because the effect won't be the same. The flavor of the pie is wonderfully sweet, with a slight acidic edge thanks to the tomatoes. It's a harmonious blend of flavors. See what sort of reaction it gets from your own crew, but think twice about telling anyone beforehand what's in the pie. I use a crumb topping here, but I like this pie just as much with a top crust. Northern Spy or Granny Smith apples work well.

1 RECIPE BEST BUTTER PIE PASTRY
  (PAGE 8), REFRIGERATED

FILLING:

2 LARGE RIPE TOMATOES, SEEDED AND
  DICED

½ CUP PLUS 2 TABLESPOONS SUGAR

JUICE AND GRATED ZEST OF 1 LEMON

7 CUPS PEELED, CORED, AND SLICED
  APPLES (SEE HEADNOTE)

½ TEASPOON CHOPPED FRESH LEMON
  THYME LEAVES OR ¼ TEASPOON CHOPPED
  FRESH THYME LEAVES

1½ TABLESPOONS CORNSTARCH

TOPPING:

1 CUP ALL-PURPOSE FLOUR

⅔ CUP SUGAR

¼ TEASPOON SALT

PINCH OF GROUND NUTMEG

½ CUP (1 STICK) COLD UNSALTED BUTTER,
  CUT INTO ¼-INCH PIECES

1. If you haven't already, prepare the pastry and refrigerate it until firm enough to roll, about 1 hour.

2. On a large sheet of lightly floured waxed paper, roll the pastry into a 13½-inch circle with a floured rolling pin. Invert the pastry over a 9-inch deep-dish pie pan. Center it, then peel off the paper. Tuck the pastry into the pan, without stretching it, and sculpt the edge into an upstanding ridge. Place the pie shell in the freezer for at least 30 minutes.

3. In a large mixing bowl, combine the tomatoes, ½ cup of the sugar, and the lemon juice and zest. Set aside. Preheat the oven to 400 degrees.

4. Add the apples and thyme to the tomato mixture and toss well. Combine the remaining 2 tablespoons sugar and the cornstarch in a small mixing bowl. Add to the fruit and toss well. Turn the filling into the frozen pie shell, smoothing the top of the fruit with your hands. Place the pie directly on the center oven rack and bake for 30 minutes.

5. While the pie bakes, make the topping. Put the flour, sugar, salt, and nutmeg in a food processor and pulse several times to mix. Remove the lid and scatter the butter pieces over the dry mixture. Pulse the machine repeatedly, until the mixture resembles fine crumbs. Dump the crumbs into a large mixing bowl and rub them together with your fingertips to make large, buttery crumbs. Refrigerate.

6. Remove the pie from the oven and place it on a large, dark baking sheet covered with aluminum foil. Reduce the oven temperature to 375 degrees. Carefully dump the topping in the center of the pie and spread it evenly with your hands over the surface, tamping it down lightly. Put the pie on the baking sheet back on the center rack and bake until any juices—visible near the edge of the pie—bubble thickly, another 30 to 35 minutes.

7. Transfer the pie to a cooling rack and let cool for at least 1 hour before slicing.

Makes 8 to 10 servings

AND YOU THOUGHT MAKING ONE PIE WAS WORK?

"The brick ovens of colonial times were rated in terms of pies; there were 10-pie and even 20-pie ovens. Pies were eaten at every meal including breakfast, a pleasant custom that still persists. In the old days, especially on farms and especially in winter, pies were turned out by mass production. Enough for a week were routinely baked and put aside in a cold closet or unheated back room. Some housewives baked 100 pies at a time, froze them out in the snow (which did them no harm) and then thawed and warmed them for each meal in front of the fire blazing on the hearth. Pies went into the woods with logging crews and put out to sea on sailing ships as last, loving offerings of relatives ashore."
—Jonathan Norton Leonard, *American Cooking: New England* (Time-Life, 1970)

Logging Road Blackberry Apple Pie

When my kids were much younger, the high point of the summer was picking blackberries along the abandoned logging roads around our house. I knew of no better way to fritter away a sunny afternoon. We'd don long sleeves and hiking boots, strap leftover yogurt containers to our belts, and tromp off into the brush. When the picking was great, we'd end up with enough for an all-blackberry pie. And when it was just pretty good, we'd mix the berries with apples to make a pie like this one. In some ways, I like this mixed version even more because there are fewer seeds and there's certainly no lack of berry flavor. With perfectly ripe berries, I suppose you could skip step 2, where I crush the berries with the sugar and lemon juice. That habit developed because, in spite of my coaching, the kids would toss unripe berries into their containers; in their eyes, size seemed to be the main consideration. Crushing the berries was my way of masquerading the unripe ones, and it gave the apples a coating of berry sauce to bake in from the start. You'll pay too much for imported berries, so wait until summer berry season—and local berries—before you make this.

1 RECIPE ALL-AMERICAN DOUBLE CRUST (PAGE 2), REFRIGERATED

FILLING:

3 CUPS FRESH BLACKBERRIES, PICKED OVER

½ CUP PLUS 2 TABLESPOONS SUGAR

2 TABLESPOONS FRESH LEMON JUICE

6 CUPS CORED, PEELED, AND SLICED APPLES

2½ TO 3 TABLESPOONS CORNSTARCH

¼ TEASPOON GROUND NUTMEG

GLAZE (OPTIONAL):

MILK

SUGAR

1. If you haven't already, prepare the pastry and refrigerate it until firm enough to roll, about 1 hour.

2. While you're waiting for the dough to chill, put the blackberries in a large mixing bowl. Add ½ cup of the sugar and the lemon juice. Using a potato masher, crush the berries until they're well mashed but still have a bit of texture. Set aside.

3. On a sheet of lightly floured waxed paper, roll the larger portion of the pastry into a 13½-inch circle with a floured rolling pin. Invert the pastry over a 9-inch deep-dish pie pan. Center it, then peel off the paper. Gently tuck the pastry into the pan, without stretching it, and let the overhang drape over the edge of the pan. Refrigerate.

4. While the pie shell chills, finish making the filling. Add the apples to the crushed berries and toss well. Mix the remaining 2 tablespoons sugar with the cornstarch, using the greater amount of cornstarch if you think you'll be eating the pie while it is still relatively warm. Add the cornstarch mixture and nutmeg to the fruit and mix well. Set aside. Preheat the oven to 400 degrees.

5. On another sheet of lightly floured waxed paper, roll the other half of the dough into an 11½-inch circle. Turn the filling into the refrigerated pie shell and smooth the top with your hands. Lightly moisten the rim of the pie shell. Invert the top pastry over the filling, center it, and peel off the paper. Press the top and bottom pastries together along the dampened edge. Trim the pastry with scissors or a paring knife, leaving an even ½-inch overhang all around, then sculpt the overhang into an upstanding ridge. Poke several steam vents in the top of the pie with a fork or a paring knife; put a couple of the vents near the edge of the crust, so you can check the juices there later. If you want to glaze the pie, brush it with a little milk and sprinkle with sugar.

6. Put the pie directly on the center oven rack and bake for 30 minutes. Remove from the oven and place on a large, dark baking sheet covered with aluminum foil. Reduce the oven temperature to 375 degrees. Put the pie on the baking sheet back in the oven and bake until the top is golden brown and any juices—visible at the steam vents—bubble thickly, another 35 to 40 minutes.

7. Transfer the pie to a cooling rack and let cool briefly before serving.

Makes 8 to 10 servings

Apple Cherry Pie with Coconut Almond Crumb Topping

Sweet summer cherries, coconut, and almonds make for an irresistible pie combination. I can't get sour cherries often, but when I can, I like to use them here, increasing the sugar just slightly. As for pitting the cherries, there are various gadgets for doing so, and I've seen a trick for using a paper clip. But I just put them in a large bowl—to keep the splatter contained—and press down on the end of each cherry (the end opposite the stem) with my thumb. If the cherries are the least bit ripe, the pit will come right out.

1 RECIPE FLAKY CREAM CHEESE PASTRY (PAGE 14), REFRIGERATED

FILLING:

5 CUPS PEELED, CORED, AND SLICED APPLES

3 CUPS PITTED AND HALVED FRESH CHERRIES

3 TABLESPOONS AMARETTO

1 TEASPOON PURE VANILLA EXTRACT

1 TABLESPOON FRESH LEMON JUICE

½ CUP PLUS 2 TABLESPOONS SUGAR

2 TABLESPOONS CORNSTARCH

COCONUT ALMOND CRUMB TOPPING:

1 CUP ALL-PURPOSE FLOUR

⅔ CUP SUGAR

¼ TEASPOON SALT

½ CUP SLICED ALMONDS

½ CUP SWEETENED FLAKED COCONUT

6 TABLESPOONS (¾ STICK) COLD UNSALTED BUTTER, CUT INTO ¼-INCH PIECES

1 TABLESPOON MILK OR LIGHT CREAM

1. If you haven't already, prepare the pastry and refrigerate it until firm enough to roll, 1½ to 2 hours.

2. On a sheet of lightly floured waxed paper, roll the pastry into a 13½-inch circle with a floured rolling pin. Invert the pastry over a 9-inch deep-dish pie pan. Center it, then peel off the paper. Gently tuck the pastry into the pan, without stretching it, and sculpt the overhang into an upstanding ridge. Put the pie shell in the freezer for at least 30 minutes.

3. To make the filling, combine the apples, cherries, amaretto, vanilla, and lemon juice in a large mixing bowl; toss well. Mix in ½ cup of the sugar. Set aside for 10 minutes. Preheat the oven to 400 degrees.

4. In a small bowl, mix the remaining 2 tablespoons sugar with the cornstarch. Sprinkle over the fruit and toss well. Turn the filling into the frozen pie shell. Smooth the filling with your hands to even it out. Place directly on the center oven rack and bake for 35 minutes.

5. While the pie bakes, make the topping. Put the flour, sugar, salt, almonds, and coconut in a food processor and pulse several times to mix. Remove the lid and scatter the butter pieces over the dry ingredients. Pulse the machine repeatedly, until the mixture resembles fine crumbs. Add the milk and pulse again until the crumbs are more gravelly in texture. Refrigerate.

6. After 35 minutes, remove the pie from the oven and place it on a large, dark baking sheet covered with aluminum foil. Reduce the oven temperature to 375 degrees. Carefully dump the crumbs in the center of the pie and spread them evenly over the surface with your hands. Press on the crumbs gently to compact them. Put the pie on the baking sheet back in the oven and bake until the juices bubble thickly around the edge, another 35 to 40 minutes.

7. Transfer the pie to a cooling rack and let cool for at least 1 hour before slicing.

Makes 8 to 10 servings

Apple Plum Pie with Coconut Streusel

Living in New Hampshire for much of the year, I've grown accustomed to the fact that some of the fruit I get in the market—even during peak season—is going to need a nudge in the direction of full flavor. Plums are a prime example. It's very difficult to get a ripe, juicy plum with a pleasing texture. Still, I'm fond of plums in pies, and if I simmer them in sugar and a little bit of port, then mix them with sliced apples, they make a wonderful addition. For one thing, the simmering bleeds the color from the skins into the poaching liquid, which in turn tints the filling a deep shade of plum—much deeper, I've noticed, than if you simply add sliced plums to the pie (it doesn't hurt that I use ruby port for the poaching liquid). Cooking also softens the plums, which can be disheartengly firm, and releases their flavor.

Of course, if you're lucky enough to live where ripe, juicy plums drop from branches in the backyard, you can disregard all of this and make a wonderful half-and-half apple plum pie without any of these provisions. Use a double crust if you like; I prefer this coconut streusel.

1 RECIPE BEST BUTTER PIE PASTRY (PAGE 8), REFRIGERATED

FILLING:

6 OR 7 DARK-SKINNED PLUMS, HALVED AND PITTED

½ CUP RUBY PORT

½ CUP SUGAR

6 CUPS PEELED, CORED, AND SLICED APPLES

1 TABLESPOON FRESH LEMON JUICE

2 TABLESPOONS CORNSTARCH

COCONUT STREUSEL TOPPING:

1 CUP ALL-PURPOSE FLOUR

⅔ CUP SUGAR

¼ TEASPOON SALT

½ CUP SWEETENED FLAKED COCONUT

6 TABLESPOONS (¾ STICK) COLD UNSALTED BUTTER, CUT INTO ¼-INCH PIECES

1 TABLESPOON MILK OR LIGHT CREAM

1. If you haven't already, prepare the pastry and refrigerate it until firm enough to roll, about 1 hour.

2. On a sheet of lightly floured waxed paper, roll the pastry into a 13½-inch circle with a floured rolling pin. Invert the pastry over a 9-inch deep-dish pie pan. Center it, then peel off the paper. Gently tuck the pastry into the pan, without stretching it, and sculpt the overhang into an upstanding ridge. Place the pie shell in the freezer for at least 30 minutes.

3. To make the filling, slice 3 or 4 of the plums. Place them in a medium-size nonreactive saucepan with the port and ¼ cup of the sugar. Bring to a boil, cover, reduce the heat slightly, and cook at a low boil for 5 minutes. Remove the lid and continue to boil until the remaining liquid is syrupy, though not as thick as a glaze, 3 to 5 minutes. Remove from the heat. Scrape the fruit into a shallow pan and let cool. Preheat the oven to 400 degrees.

4. In a large mixing bowl, toss the apples with the lemon juice and cooked plums. Slice the remaining plums and add them, too. Mix the remaining ¼ cup sugar with the cornstarch in a small mixing bowl and sprinkle it over the fruit; toss well. Turn the filling into the frozen pie shell. Smooth the filling with your hands to even it out. Place the pie directly on the center oven rack and bake for 35 minutes.

5. As the pie bakes, make the coconut streusel. Put the flour, sugar, salt, and coconut in a food processor. Pulse several times. Remove the lid and scatter the butter pieces over the dry mixture. Pulse the machine repeatedly, until the mixture resembles fine crumbs. Add the milk and pulse the machine 2 or 3 times to incorporate. Dump the crumbs into a large mixing bowl and rub gently between your fingers to make large, buttery crumbs. Refrigerate.

6. After 35 minutes, remove the pie from the oven and place it on a large, dark baking sheet covered with aluminum foil. Reduce the oven temperature to 375 degrees. Carefully dump the crumbs in the center of the pie and spread them evenly over the surface with your hands. Press down gently to compact them. Put the pie on the baking sheet back in the oven and bake until the juices bubble thickly at the edge, about 40 minutes more. Loosely cover with tented aluminum foil during the last 20 minutes, if necessary, to prevent it from browning too much.

7. Transfer the pie to a cooling rack and let cool for at least 1 hour before serving.

Makes 8 to 10 servings

Summer Apple Raspberry Pie

This is a wonderful summer pie—the soft flavor of the apples providing a nearly perfect foil to the sweet-tart taste of the berries. In truth, I actually prefer this pie to an all-raspberry pie, which is almost too much of a good thing. Here the 3 cups of berries provide ample flavor, which soaks into the apples as the pie cools down—flavor that can disguise nicely some of the shortcomings of summer apples. If I happen to have a couple of good ripe peaches on hand, I'm likely to substitute one or two of them for one of the apples, adding yet another layer of flavor; peaches, raspberries, and apples are quite wonderful together. Do let this cool down before you slice it because the filling can be pretty soupy if you don't. But if that's the way you like it, go right ahead and slice warm. Just don't forget the vanilla or peach ice cream.

1 RECIPE ALL-AMERICAN DOUBLE CRUST
(PAGE 2), REFRIGERATED

FILLING:

6 CUPS PEELED, CORED, AND SLICED
GRANNY SMITH OR OTHER TART, JUICY
APPLES

3 CUPS FRESH RASPBERRIES, PICKED OVER

1 TABLESPOON FRESH LEMON JUICE

¼ TEASPOON GROUND NUTMEG

½ CUP PLUS 2 TABLESPOONS SUGAR

1½ TABLESPOONS CORNSTARCH

GLAZE:

MILK OR LIGHT CREAM

SUGAR

1. If you haven't already, prepare the pastry and refrigerate it until firm enough to roll, about 1 hour.

2. On a sheet of lightly floured waxed paper, roll the larger portion of the pastry into a 13½-inch circle with a floured rolling pin. Invert the pastry over a 9-inch deep-dish pie pan. Center it, then peel off the paper. Gently tuck the pastry into the pan, without stretching it, and let the edge of the pastry drape over the side of the pan. Refrigerate. Preheat the oven to 400 degrees.

3. To make the filling, combine the apples, raspberries, lemon juice, nutmeg, and ½ cup of the sugar in a large mixing bowl; toss well. Set aside for 10 minutes. In a small bowl, mix the remaining 2 tablespoons sugar with the cornstarch. Sprinkle over the fruit and mix well.

4. On another sheet of lightly floured waxed paper, roll the top pastry into an 11½-inch circle. Turn the filling into the refrigerated pie shell and smooth the top with your hands. Dampen the edge of the pie shell with a wet fingertip or pastry brush, then invert the top pastry over the filling, center it, and peel off the paper. Press the top and bottom pastries together along the dampened edge. Trim the pastry, leaving an even ½-inch overhang all around, then sculpt the overhang into an upstanding ridge. Poke several steam vents in the top of the pie with a fork or paring knife; put a couple of the vents near the edge of the crust, so you can check the juices there later. Brush the top of the pie with a little milk and sprinkle lightly with sugar.

5. Put the pie directly on the center oven rack and bake for 30 minutes. Remove the pie from the oven and place it on a large, dark baking sheet covered with aluminum foil. Reduce the oven temperature to 375 degrees. Put the pie on the baking sheet back in the oven and bake until the juices—visible at the steam vents—bubble thickly, another 35 to 40 minutes.

6. Transfer the pie to a cooling rack and let cool for at least 1 hour before slicing.

Makes 8 to 10 servings

DECORATIVE PIE EDGES

You can add a flourish to any apple pie with little more than a snip, twist, or imprint. When you have the time, a decorative edge is a fetching way to touch up your pie, especially if you're bringing it along to a party or potluck. Here are some simple ideas you might want to try. Most are meant for single-crust pies where a crumb top is added; some can be used for single- or double-crust pies.

Classic fluted edge: Start with your upstanding ridge of pastry. Hold the thumb and index finger of one hand close together, fingers pointing straight out with just a little space between them. Rest them against one side of the ridge, pressing gently from the other side—with your other index finger—aiming for the space between the fingers. Repeat all around.

Checkered edge: Start with your upstanding ridge of pastry. Refrigerate until firm. Using kitchen scissors or a sharp paring knife, cut the dough down to the pan's rim, leaving ¼ inch between the cuts. Push every other little square of dough slightly downward, creating a checkered up-and-down look.

Cutout pastry edge: Line your pie pan as usual, letting the pastry drape over the edge of the pan. Trim the pastry flush with the side of the pan. Using rolled out and then refrigerated dough, make small cutouts—hearts, circles (use a melon baller), leaves, and the like. Place them on the rim in a slightly overlapping manner, brushing them lightly with water so they stick.

Crimped edge: Start with a beefed-up flat edge, then press in any design that you please. The tines of a fork are a traditional imprint, but you can also use the business end of a teaspoon, pressed in upside down, or a lemon zester.

Strawberry Pink Lady Apple Pie

When I first heard the words "Pink Lady apple," I envisioned, perhaps naively, an apple with pink flesh—a delicate blush befitting a proper lady. Alas, it isn't the flesh but rather the skin of the petite, sweet-tart Pink Lady apple that's pink and yellow—pretty, but not exactly useful for creating what I wanted: a pie with a pink filling that would deliver what the apple's name suggests. I happened to be mulling over this issue in the summer, when the markets were full of local strawberries, which, it occurred to me would provide not just the color but the soft, seasonal flavor I was looking for. Happy to say, the combination worked beautifully.

This, then, is a wonderful summer apple pie, the sort of dessert you might take to a potluck dinner or family reunion or on a picnic. I've upped the summer ante here with a little rose water, to give the pie a floral bouquet— but it's by no means necessary if it means a special trip to the health food store. Do use the best local strawberries you can get your hands on, and add the full amount of flour for thickening if they're really fresh and ripe. I like this cream crumb topping, but a lattice top is also an excellent choice because it shows off the lovely filling. A slice of this alongside a scoop of vanilla ice cream makes for a classy summer dessert.

1 RECIPE BEST BUTTER PIE PASTRY (PAGE 8), REFRIGERATED

FILLING:

6 CUPS PEELED, CORED, AND SLICED PINK LADY OR OTHER APPLES

½ CUP GRANULATED SUGAR

GRATED ZEST OF 1 LEMON

2 TABLESPOONS FRESH LEMON JUICE

1 TEASPOON FOOD-GRADE ROSE WATER (OPTIONAL)

1 QUART RIPE STRAWBERRIES, RINSED, HULLED, AND SLICED

3 TO 4 TABLESPOONS ALL-PURPOSE FLOUR

CREAM CRUMB TOPPING:

1½ CUPS ALL-PURPOSE FLOUR

⅓ CUP GRANULATED SUGAR

⅓ CUP FIRMLY PACKED LIGHT BROWN SUGAR

½ TEASPOON GROUND CINNAMON

¼ TEASPOON SALT

1 TEASPOON BAKING POWDER

½ CUP PLUS 2 TABLESPOONS COLD HEAVY CREAM

1. If you haven't already, prepare the pastry and refrigerate it until firm enough to roll, about 1 hour.

2. On a sheet of lightly floured waxed paper, roll the pastry into a 13½-inch circle with a floured rolling pin. Invert the pastry over a 9-inch deep-dish pie pan. Center it, then peel off the paper. Gently tuck the pastry into the pan, without stretching it, and sculpt the overhang into an upstanding ridge. Place the pie shell in the freezer for at least 30 minutes.

3. To make the filling, combine the apples, granulated sugar, and lemon zest in a large mixing bowl; toss well. Blend the lemon juice and rose water, if using, and pour over the apples; toss again. Mix in the strawberries. Shake the flour over the fruit—using the greater amount if the berries are very juicy—and set aside. Preheat the oven to 400 degrees.

4. Turn the filling into the frozen pie shell. Smooth the filling with your hands to even it out. Place the pie directly on the center oven rack and bake for 30 minutes.

5. While the pie bakes, make the cream crumb topping. Combine the flour, sugars, cinnamon, salt, and baking powder in a food processor; pulse several times to mix. Pulsing the machine, add the cream in a slow, steady stream through the feed tube. Stop the machine as soon as the topping starts to form clumps; for the most part, it should be loose and granular-looking. Refrigerate.

6. After 30 minutes, remove the pie from the oven and place it on a large, dark baking sheet covered with aluminum foil. Reduce the oven temperature to 375 degrees. Carefully dump the crumbs in the center of the pie, spreading them evenly over the surface with your hands. Pat the crumbs gently to compact them. Place the pie on the baking sheet back in the oven and bake until the juices bubble thickly around the edge, another 40 to 45 minutes. The juices may not bubble as thickly as they do with some pies because the strawberries make this pie juicier than most. If the topping starts to get too dark, cover the pie with loosely tented aluminum foil for the last 15 minutes.

7. Transfer the pie to a cooling rack and cool for at least 1 hour before slicing. It may be rather runny if you cut it much before that.

Makes 8 servings

Blueberry Apple Lattice Pie

I like to mix other fruits with apples in my lattice-top pies, in part because with plain apple, the crust and filling are essentially the same color, so the lattice effect is not too striking. Berries and other colorful fruits provide a darker background and accentuate the lattice look.

Even though there's a gap between fresh local blueberries and apple season in most growing areas, at the urging of my better half, Bev—a diehard blueberry lover if ever there was one—I mixed the two in this pie, using juicy Granny Smith apples and the first of the fresh blueberries coming out of New Jersey. The combination made for a delicious pie whose filling is tinged a gorgeous light blue. Be sure you take the time to do as instructed, arranging some of the blueberries on top of the apples. Otherwise, they may all get buried underneath, and you won't get the full effect of their pretty color.

1 RECIPE ALL-AMERICAN DOUBLE CRUST
(PAGE 2), REFRIGERATED

FILLING:

7 CUPS PEELED, CORED, AND SLICED
GRANNY SMITH OR OTHER APPLES

1 PINT FRESH BLUEBERRIES, PICKED OVER

½ CUP SUGAR

2½ TABLESPOONS ALL-PURPOSE FLOUR

½ TEASPOON GROUND CINNAMON

2 TABLESPOONS FRESH LEMON JUICE

GLAZE:

MILK

SUGAR

1. Prepare the pastry as directed, making half of the pastry just slightly larger than the other. Shape the larger half into a disk and the other half into a square; both should be about ¾ inch thick. Wrap the pastry as usual and refrigerate it until firm enough to roll, about 1 hour.

2. On a sheet of lightly floured waxed paper, roll the disk of pastry into a 13½-inch circle with a floured rolling pin. Invert the pastry over a 9-inch deep-dish pie pan. Center it, then peel off the paper. Gently tuck the pastry into the pan, without stretching it, and sculpt the overhang into an upstanding ridge. Refrigerate.

3. Prepare the filling by combining the apples, half the blueberries, the sugar, flour, cinnamon, and lemon juice in a large mixing bowl; toss well. Set aside. Preheat the oven to 400 degrees.

4. On a sheet of lightly floured waxed paper, roll the remaining pastry into a 12 x 10-inch rectangle. With a pizza cutter or sharp knife, cut the pastry into 8 lengthwise strips, each 1¼ inches wide. (In other words, you should have 8 strips measuring 12 inches long by 1¼ inches wide.) Set aside.

5. Turn the filling into the refrigerated pie shell, moistening the rim of the shell slightly. Smooth the top of the filling, then scatter the remaining blueberries on top.

6. Lay 5 pastry strips vertically across the pie, evenly spaced, as shown in figure 1. Fold back strips 2 and 4, and lay another strip directly across the center of the pie, as shown in figure 2.

7. Unfold the folded dough strips, then fold backs strips 1, 3, and 5. Lay another perpendicular strip across the pie as shown in figure 3.

8. Unfold strips 1, 3, and 5, then fold them up the other way as shown in figure 4. Place another perpendicular strip across the pie, as shown in figure 4, then unfold strips 1, 3, and 5. Trim the strips, then pinch the ends of the strips into the edge of the pastry. Lightly brush the pastry strips with milk and sprinkle the pie with sugar.

9. Place the pie directly on the center oven rack and bake for 25 minutes. Remove the pie from the oven and place it on a large, dark baking sheet covered with aluminum foil. Reduce the oven temperature to 375 degrees. Return the pie on the baking sheet to the oven and bake just until the top is golden brown and any visible juices bubble thickly, another 40 to 45 minutes.

10. Transfer the pie to a cooling rack and let cool for at least 1 hour before slicing.

Makes 8 servings

Figure 1

Figure 2

Figure 3

Figure 4

Apple Strawberry Rhubarb Pie

Rhubarb doesn't get nearly as much attention or respect as it might, in part because I think many cooks try to tame its rather forward, tart personality with an onslaught of sugar or cooking—or both—resulting in a mushy-sweet, far-less-than-flattering portrayal. I'm a fan, but I do like a mixed-fruit rhubarb pie, strawberry being the standard, of course. I take a slightly different approach here by combining rhubarb with apples, which give the pie a certain firmness that rhubarb lacks. And then I add some strawberry preserves to insinuate the flavor that most of us have come to expect with rhubarb. It makes a great springtime pie, with either a top crust, as here, or a crumb topping. You can play up the seasonal theme even more by serving it with strawberry ice cream and perhaps a garnish of sliced fresh strawberries.

1 RECIPE ALL-AMERICAN DOUBLE CRUST (PAGE 2) OR SHORTENING DOUBLE CRUST (PAGE 4), REFRIGERATED

FILLING:

3½ CUPS PEELED RHUBARB STALKS CUT INTO ¼-INCH CHUNKS

⅔ CUP SUGAR

1 TABLESPOON FRESH LEMON JUICE

GRATED ZEST OF 1 LEMON

5 TO 6 CUPS PEELED, CORED, AND SLICED APPLES

2½ TABLESPOONS ALL-PURPOSE FLOUR

½ CUP STRAWBERRY PRESERVES

GLAZE:

MILK

SUGAR

1. If you haven't already, prepare the pastry and refrigerate it until firm enough to roll, about 1 hour.

2. On a sheet of lightly floured waxed paper, roll the larger portion of the pastry into a 13½-inch circle with a floured rolling pin. Invert the pastry over a 9-inch deep-dish pie pan. Center it, then peel off the paper. Gently tuck the pastry down into the pan, without stretching it, and let the edge of the pastry drape over the side of the pan. Refrigerate for 15 minutes.

3. To make the filling, mix the rhubarb, sugar, lemon juice, and lemon zest together in a large mixing bowl. Set aside for 10 minutes. Preheat the oven to 400 degrees.

4. On another sheet of lightly floured waxed paper, roll the top pastry into an 11½-inch circle. Stir the apples and flour into the rhubarb mixture, then stir in the strawberry preserves. Turn the filling into the refrigerated pie shell and smooth the top with your hands. Lightly moisten the edge of the shell with a wet fingertip or pastry brush. Invert the top pastry over the filling, center it, and peel off the paper. Press the top and bottom pastries together along the dampened edge. Trim the pastry with scissors or a paring knife, leaving an even ½-inch overhang all around, then sculpt the overhang into an upstanding ridge. Poke several steam vents in the top of the pie with a fork or paring knife; put a couple of the vents near the edge of the crust, so you can check the juices there later. Brush the top of the pie with a little milk and sprinkle lightly with sugar.

5. Put the pie on a large, dark baking sheet covered with aluminum foil, place on the center oven rack, and bake for 30 minutes. Reduce the oven temperature to 375 degrees and bake until any juices—visible at the steam vents—bubble thickly, another 30 to 40 minutes.

6. Transfer the pie to a cooling rack and let cool for at least 1 hour before slicing.

Makes 8 to 10 servings

COOL THAT APPLE PIE, PLEASE!

Alas, many are chagrined when I candidly admit that I'm not partial to hot apple pie. In the eyes of some, my admission is nothing short of sacrilege, an affront to the very institution of apple pie.

But let me assure you that there's logic to my bias. And it goes like this: When you cut into a hot apple pie and remove a slice, you leave a void—a void that quickly fills with lovely apple juice from the surrounding territory. You essentially drain the pie of its main flavor-bearing component, leaving a network of fruit bereft of its own juice.

In atonement for your sin, you gamely start spooning the juice from the void over individual servings, like a sailor frantically bailing a leaky boat, but the juice is never quite the same: thin, when it should have luscious body, and too hot for you to appreciate the complex apple flavors hidden within.

Left to cool for an hour or two, an apple pie undergoes a wonderful transformation. The power of your thickening agent kicks in. Instead of a puddle of thin juice, you're left with fruit that's evenly coated with semi-thickened juice. The fruit softens further as it reabsorbs its own juice. And the flavor of the pie, now that it's warm and no longer hot, is sharper and more complex.

Of course, I've never been able to convince my kids that any of this makes sense. They want to cut into my apple pie as soon as it's done. And often I do. But for me, it's never quite the same as an apple pie that's been allowed a proper rest.

CHAPTER 4

Very Apple Apple Pies

No sooner had the apple started thriving on American soil than our forefathers and mothers were faced with the predicament of what to do with the excess crop. Much of it was pressed into cider, the majority of which was not drunk fresh but hard. Indeed, some accounts I've read of the early settlers would lead one to believe that the homesteading arts—tilling the soil, growing food, building homes and outbuildings, and animal care—frequently took a back seat to the imbibing of hard liquor.

Nonetheless, our ancestors learned that any apples that didn't find their way into the root cellar and cider could also be turned into applesauce, apple butter, apple jelly, and boiled cider. And one suspects that those apple products often found their way into the earliest of American apple pies.

This chapter celebrates some of those apple products and explores the delectable question of how they can be added to our own apple pies. From personal experience, I can tell you that nothing enhances the flavor of apple pie like one of these items—so much so that including them in my own pies has become second nature. Especially if I'm making an apple pie and not using a specific recipe, I'm likely to spoon in a healthy measure of applesauce or apple butter, or I may pour a little boiled cider right into the filling.

The more you work with these apple products in your pies, the better you'll appreciate the impact each has. Applesauce makes for a slightly slushy filling, which I adore. Apple butter adds an intense flavor and firmer texture, while boiled cider gives the most pronounced apple taste of all. I hope you'll try all the pies here and discover their charms for yourself.

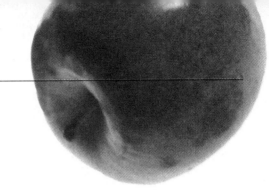

Shaker Boiled Apple Cider Pie

I have been making this pie for more than 20 years, since I first discovered boiled cider. If you're not familiar with boiled cider, it's not surprising. I know of only one source—Willis and Tina Wood (see Making Boiled Cider, page 91)—and, labor-intensive product that it is, competitors aren't exactly lining up. For the uninitiated, boiled cider is just that: cider that's been boiled down to roughly one-seventh of its original volume. Once the cider has been boiled, it becomes dark and syrupy with an intense apple flavor—thus it's a wonderful way to kick up the flavor of your pies.

This particular pie has a couple of apples in it, but the real attraction here is the cider maple custard that's poured over it and baked in the crust. So you end up with three filling layers: the apples on the bottom, the custard in the middle, and a sort of apple meringue on top. Even if you like warm apple pie, you have to serve this cold so the custard becomes as firm as possible; no cheating.

Incidentally, you can make your own boiled cider. It's easy to do, but if you don't want to bother, you can order it directly from the Woods. Because the pie is pretty sweet, I serve it with unsweetened whipped cream.

1 RECIPE BEST BUTTER PIE PASTRY
(PAGE 8) OR THREE-GRAIN BUTTER
PASTRY (PAGE 10), REFRIGERATED

FILLING:

3 TABLESPOONS UNSALTED BUTTER

2 LARGE GOLDEN DELICIOUS OR OTHER
FIRM-TEXTURED APPLES, PEELED, CORED,
AND SLICED

¾ CUP BOILED APPLE CIDER

¾ CUP PURE MAPLE SYRUP

PINCH OF SALT

⅛ TEASPOON GROUND NUTMEG

4 LARGE EGGS, SEPARATED

GARNISH:

UNSWEETENED WHIPPED CREAM

1. If you haven't already, prepare the pastry and refrigerate it until firm enough to roll, about 1 hour.

2. On a sheet of lightly floured waxed paper, roll the pastry into a 13½-inch circle with a floured rolling pin. Invert the pastry over a 9-inch deep-dish pie pan. Center it, then peel off the paper. Gently tuck the pastry down into the pan, without stretching it, and sculpt the edge so it comes up no higher than the rim of the pan. Place the pie shell in the freezer for at least 30 minutes.

3. To make the filling, melt 1 tablespoon of the butter in a medium-size skillet. Add the apples and cook over medium heat until the

BLUEBERRY APPLE
LATTICE PIE

Page 84

APPLE CHERRY PIE
WITH COCONUT
ALMOND CRUMB
TOPPING

Page 76

APPLE PIZZA PIE

Page 206

APPLE AND PEAR
HAND PIES WITH
RAISINS AND
WALNUTS

Page 200

FARM-STYLE
BUTTERMILK PIE
WITH FRIED
APPLE RINGS

Page 138

BAKED APPLE
DUMPLING PIE

Page 32

FROZEN APPLE
AND PEANUT BUTTER
CLOUD PIE

Page 214

HARVEST PIE
WITH AUTUMN
LEAVES

Page 34

slices are just tender, 5 to 6 minutes. Set aside, leaving the apples right in the pan. Preheat the oven to 350 degrees.

4. Heat the remaining 2 tablespoons butter, the boiled cider, and maple syrup together in a small saucepan just until the butter melts. Pour the liquid into a large mixing bowl; let cool somewhat, about 10 minutes. Blend in the salt and nutmeg.

5. Put the egg yolks in a small mixing bowl and stir in a ladleful of the cider mixture. Blend well, then blend this back into the warm cider mixture.

6. Put the egg whites in a large mixing bowl and beat with an electric mixer until they just hold soft peaks. Add the whites to the cider mixture. Whisk the mixture briefly, but don't try to totally incorporate the whites into the liquid. The liquid will settle to the bottom, for the most part, and the whites will remain on top.

7. Spread the apple slices evenly in the frozen pie shell. Pour the custard over the apples. Place the pie on the center oven rack and bake until set, about 45 minutes. To see if the pie is done, jiggle it gently; the filling should be firm and not move in waves. If you're uncertain, give it another 5 minutes.

8. Transfer the pie to a cooling rack and let cool to room temperature. Refrigerate for at least 2 hours before slicing. I like it best when it has chilled overnight. Slice and serve with the whipped cream.

Makes 8 to 10 servings

MAKING BOILED CIDER

Willis and Tina Wood make boiled cider in their maple syrup evaporator, boiling down fresh cider to one-seventh its original volume. If you'd like to try your hand at making your own boiled cider, here's what you do.

Start with good, fresh, preservative-free cider, preferably from a local producer. Pour 7 cups of it into a large saucepan—not a heavy-duty one, because toward the end you'll be pouring this back and forth into a measuring cup to check the volume, so you don't want a heavy pan. Bring the cider to a boil, then keep it at a boil until you think it has condensed down to about 1½ cups. At that point, check by pouring the cider into a heatproof measuring cup. Pour it back into the pan and continue to boil until the liquid is reduced to just over 1 cup. Err on the side of caution, because if you boil it too much, you'll end up with apple jelly—good stuff, but not what you're hoping for here. Either use the boiled cider right away or pour it into a jar, seal, and refrigerate. It will keep for months.

I've made this a number of times, and it's always great—though, frankly, never quite the same as Willis and Tina's. I think it's the special blend of apples they use in their cider, their years of experience making it, and their overall knowledge of the process that just can't be translated in a short recipe. You can contact Wood's Cider Mill at 1482 Weathersfield Center Road, Springfield, VT 05156, (802) 263-5547, www.woodscidermill.com.

Pumpkin Applesauce Pie

Pumpkin and apples might sound like an unlikely match in a pie, but the two have a long history as pie partners. In their book *Pumpkin Companion* (Brick Tower Press, 1996), Elizabeth Brabb and Bruce T. Paddock tell us that one of the first pies made by the colonists was a hollowed-out pumpkin stuffed with apples, spices, sugar, and milk, then baked. According to the authors, flour was often scarce in the New England colonies, and this method was probably a way to help conserve it. I haven't tried this old-fashioned technique, but I have made many pies by blending some chunky applesauce with the smooth pumpkin and most of the other ingredients you find in pumpkin pie. And it works beautifully. I prefer chunky applesauce to smooth because I like to show off the fact that the pie has apples; otherwise, the apple flavor is too subtle for some people to detect.

As you might guess, this is a great Thanksgiving and all-around holiday pie. I like it best cold—the apple flavor is more noticeable that way—but I realize that there are those for whom warm pumpkin pie has no equal.

1 RECIPE BEST BUTTER PIE PASTRY
   (PAGE 8), REFRIGERATED

FILLING:

3 LARGE EGGS, AT ROOM TEMPERATURE

¼ CUP PURE MAPLE SYRUP

1 TEASPOON PURE VANILLA EXTRACT

¾ CUP FIRMLY PACKED LIGHT BROWN SUGAR

1½ TABLESPOONS ALL-PURPOSE FLOUR

½ TEASPOON SALT

½ TEASPOON GROUND CINNAMON

½ TEASPOON GROUND GINGER

¼ TEASPOON GROUND CLOVES

¼ TEASPOON GROUND NUTMEG

1 CUP CHUNKY APPLESAUCE, HOMEMADE
   (PAGE 97) OR STORE-BOUGHT

1 CUP CANNED PUMPKIN PUREE

1. If you haven't already, prepare the pastry and refrigerate it until firm enough to roll, about 1 hour.

2. On a sheet of lightly floured waxed paper, roll the pastry into a 13½-inch circle with a floured rolling pin. Invert the pastry over a 9-inch deep-dish pie pan. Center it, then peel off the paper. Gently tuck the pastry into the pan, without stretching it, and sculpt the edge into an upstanding ridge. Place the pie shell in the freezer for at least 30 minutes, then partially prebake the pie shell according to the instructions on page 19. Let cool partially on a wire rack as you put together the filling. Preheat the oven to 350 degrees.

3. Whisk the eggs in a medium-size mixing bowl until foamy and blended. Whisk in the maple syrup and vanilla; set aside.

4. In a small mixing bowl, combine the brown sugar, flour, salt, and spices. Whisk this into the eggs. Blend in the applesauce and pumpkin, whisking until smooth. Ladle the filling into the partially baked crust.

5. Place the pie directly on the center oven rack and bake for 50 to 55 minutes. To check the pie for doneness, give the pan a quick little jab. The filling should not move in waves, but instead should appear set in the center. The sides may have puffed, but don't leave the pie in until the center puffs up because this is an indication that the pie is overbaked. One other thing: when the pie is done, the outer area of the pie will have a flat finish, but the center will be more glossy.

6. Eat the pie warm, if you like. Or let the pie cool thoroughly, then refrigerate, loosely covered with a sheet of waxed paper, and serve chilled.

Makes 8 to 10 servings

Apple Applesauce Cherry Pie

This pie has less in common with the bulging apple pies I typically make than it does with the French fruit tarts I'm also fond of baking. Which is to say that there's much less fruit—just a single layer of apples and another of applesauce blended with cherry preserves—and a very flaky, tart-like top and bottom pastry. The finished height of the pie is only about half as high as the pan, and it has a flat top, which makes for a nice neat slice. This is the pie to make when you want something a little more refined than a big, buff American-style pie—say for a small dinner party. The dusting of confectioners' sugar is really all the accompaniment it needs. Still, I can't resist serving small scoops of cherry vanilla ice cream on the side.

1 RECIPE FLAKY CREAM CHEESE PASTRY
(PAGE 14), REFRIGERATED

FILLING:

1 TABLESPOON GRANULATED SUGAR

1½ TEASPOONS ALL-PURPOSE FLOUR

¼ TEASPOON GROUND CINNAMON

1 LARGE APPLE, PEELED, HALVED
LENGTHWISE, AND CORED

¾ CUP APPLESAUCE, HOMEMADE (PAGE 97)
OR STORE-BOUGHT

⅓ CUP CHERRY PRESERVES

GLAZE AND DUSTING:

MILK

GRANULATED SUGAR

CONFECTIONERS' SUGAR

1. If you haven't already, prepare the pastry and refrigerate it until firm enough to roll, about 1 hour.

2. This pie can be baked in either a 9-inch deep-dish pie pan, as most of my pies are, or a regular 9-inch pie pan. In either case, on a sheet of lightly floured waxed paper, roll half of the pastry into an 11-inch circle with a floured rolling pin. Invert the pastry over the pan, center it, and peel off the paper. Gently tuck the pastry into the pan, without stretching it, and let the edge of the pastry run up the side of the pan. Refrigerate for 10 minutes.

3. Meanwhile, start making the filling. Mix the granulated sugar, flour, and cinnamon together in a small mixing bowl; set aside. Put the apple halves on a cutting board, flat sides down, and cut straight down into even slices slightly less than ¼ inch thick. Sprinkle the sugar mixture evenly over the chilled pie shell and arrange the apple slices in a single layer in the shell.

4. In another small mixing bowl, blend the applesauce and cherry preserves together. Spread the mixture evenly over the apples. Refrigerate while you roll the other half of the pastry into a 10-inch circle on a sheet of lightly floured waxed paper. With a wet fingertip, lightly moisten the rim of the pie shell. Invert the pastry over the filling, center it, and peel off the paper. Pinch the pastries together—you'll be working below the rim of the pan now—and sculpt them into a level rim. It's not easy working down in the pan like this, but don't worry; just pinch the edges together as best you can and make an even edge. Refrigerate the pie while you preheat the oven to 400 degrees.

5. Just before baking, lightly brush the top pastry with milk and sprinkle with granulated sugar. Using a paring knife or fork, poke several evenly spaced steam vents in the top of the pie. Place the pie directly on the center oven rack and bake for 15 minutes. Reduce the oven temperature to 375 degrees and bake for another 25 minutes. When the pie is done, it won't be bubbly like most fruit pies. Total baking time is your best indicator of doneness.

6. Transfer the pie to a cooling rack and let cool for 30 minutes. Put a couple of tablespoons of confectioners' sugar in a sieve and shake it over the pie. Continue to cool the pie, slicing and serving it when it is slightly warm or at room temperature.

Makes 8 to 10 servings

Blushing Apple Applesauce Pie

Have you ever started to make a favorite recipe, only to find—halfway into it—that you're missing some key ingredients? Me, too, which is how the whole applesauce pie thing started way back when. There I would be, seized by the urge to make an apple pie, blithely rolling the crust and preheating the oven, when I'd discover that I had only three or four apples. Now what? Three or four apples make for a pretty skimpy pie. Then I would spy half a jar of applesauce in the deep reaches of my fridge, and in no time flat I'd have the rest of that jar emptied right into the apple filling. At some point, when the jar of applesauce wasn't too full, I added some leftover cranberry sauce as well; thus was born the blushing applesauce pie. These days I don't make this by accident—I make it on purpose, and it's one of my favorite apple pies.

1 RECIPE ALL-AMERICAN DOUBLE CRUST (PAGE 2), REFRIGERATED

FILLING:

7 CUPS PEELED, CORED, AND SLICED APPLES

⅓ CUP SUGAR

1 TABLESPOON FRESH LEMON JUICE

½ TEASPOON GROUND CINNAMON

3 OR 4 TABLESPOONS ALL-PURPOSE FLOUR

1 CUP CANNED WHOLE-BERRY CRANBERRY SAUCE

1 CUP APPLESAUCE, HOMEMADE (PAGE 97) OR STORE-BOUGHT

GLAZE:

MILK

SUGAR

1. If you haven't already, prepare the pastry and refrigerate it until firm enough to roll, about 1 hour.

2. On a sheet of lightly floured waxed paper, roll the larger portion of the pastry into a 13½-inch circle with a floured rolling pin. Invert the pastry over a 9-inch deep-dish pie pan. Center it, then peel off the paper. Gently tuck the pastry down into the pan, without stretching it, and let the excess pastry drape over the side of the pan. Refrigerate.

3. To make the filling, mix the apples, sugar, lemon juice, and cinnamon together in a large mixing bowl. Set aside for 10 minutes. Preheat the oven to 400 degrees.

4. On another sheet of floured waxed paper, roll the top pastry into an 11½-inch circle.

Sprinkle 3 tablespoons of the flour over the apples and mix it in. If the apples are very juicy, use the remaining 1 tablespoon flour. Stir in the cranberry sauce and applesauce. Turn the filling into the refrigerated pie shell and smooth the top with your hands. Lightly moisten the edge of the shell with a wet fingertip or pastry brush. Invert the top pastry over the filling, center it, and peel off the paper. Press the top and bottom pastries together at the dampened edge. Trim the pastry with scissors or a paring knife, leaving an even ½ inch all around, then sculpt the overhang into an upstanding ridge. Poke several steam vents in the top of the pie with a fork or paring knife; put a couple of the vents near the edge of the pie, so you can check the juices there later. Brush the top of the pie with a little milk and sprinkle with sugar.

5. Place the pie on a large, dark baking sheet covered with aluminum foil, place on the center oven rack, and bake for 30 minutes. Reduce the oven temperature to 375 degrees and bake until any juices—visible at the steam vents—bubble thickly, about another 30 minutes.

6. Transfer the pie to a cooling rack and let cool at least somewhat before slicing.

Makes 8 to 10 servings

CINNAMON CIDER APPLESAUCE

Applesauce adds body, flavor, and moisture to pies. Store-bought works fine; I use it all the time. But in the fall, when apples are abundant and cheap, I like to make my own. I'll often buy a few bags of "drops" just for this purpose. Drops are apples that have fallen from the trees instead of being picked. They're less expensive since they might have a bruise or two, but otherwise they're fresh and juicy. McIntosh apples are great for sauce, by the way. Here's how I make it.

4 OR 5 LARGE APPLES, PEELED, CORED, AND CUT
   INTO LARGE CHUNKS

1 CUP FRESH APPLE CIDER

PINCH OF SALT

¼ TO ⅓ CUP SUGAR, TO YOUR TASTE

1½ TABLESPOONS FRESH LEMON JUICE

¼ TO ½ TEASPOON GROUND CINNAMON

1. Put the apples, cider, salt, and sugar in a medium-size nonreactive saucepan. Bring to a boil, cover, and reduce the heat to a low boil. Cook the apples, covered, until tender, about 15 minutes. Check after about 10 minutes to make sure there's enough liquid in the pan to keep the apples from sticking. When the apples are done, remove from heat and let cool for 15 minutes.

2. Transfer the apples to a food processor and process with the lemon juice and cinnamon, keeping the sauce on the smooth or chunky side, whichever you prefer.

3. Transfer to a bowl and let cool thoroughly. Transfer to a jar, cover tightly, and refrigerate. It will keep this way for a good week, but it's not likely to be around that long.

Makes about 2 cups

Oatmeal-Raisin Apple–Apple Butter Pie

Here's my tip for would-be blue-ribbon apple pie bakers: apple butter. Apple butter, as you probably already know, is a mixture of apples, sweetener, and spice that's been cooked down and processed to a smooth puree—something like applesauce, only more so. As such, it makes an unmistakable apple statement when used in an apple pie. It gives the pie the flavor it might otherwise lack if the apples are flavor challenged, and some of the moisture it may be missing if the apples are dry. In this particular pie, I use a lot of apple butter—to good effect, I believe, at least judging from those who've told me that they've never eaten an apple pie quite so good. There's less sugar in this pie than in most, since the apple butter is already sweetened. And there's no additional spice, as there tends to be quite a bit in most apple butters. You can seek out locally made or regional brands of apple butter, but if you come up short, Smucker's makes an excellent product that you can find in any supermarket. I like to play up the whole apple oatmeal fantasy thing here with not only an oatmeal crumb topping but an oatmeal pastry as well. It's a wonderful pie crust, and you'll probably end up using it for quite a few of your own pies.

1 RECIPE THREE-GRAIN BUTTER PASTRY (PAGE 10), REFRIGERATED

FILLING:

9 TO 10 CUPS PEELED, CORED, AND SLICED APPLES

¼ CUP GRANULATED SUGAR

JUICE AND GRATED ZEST OF 1 LEMON

1½ TABLESPOONS ALL-PURPOSE FLOUR

1 CUP SPICED APPLE BUTTER, HOMEMADE (PAGE 101) OR STORE-BOUGHT

¾ CUP RAISINS

OATMEAL CRUMB TOPPING:

1 CUP ALL-PURPOSE FLOUR

½ CUP OLD-FASHIONED ROLLED OATS (NOT INSTANT)

⅔ CUP FIRMLY PACKED LIGHT BROWN SUGAR

¼ TEASPOON SALT

½ CUP (1 STICK) COLD UNSALTED BUTTER, CUT INTO ¼-INCH PIECES

1. If you haven't already, prepare the pastry and refrigerate it until firm enough to roll, about 1 hour.

2. On a sheet of lightly floured waxed paper, roll the pastry into a 13½-inch circle with a floured rolling pin. Invert the pastry over a 9-inch deep-dish pie pan. Center it, then peel off the paper. Gently tuck the pastry into the pan, without stretching it, and sculpt the edge into an upstanding ridge. Place the pie shell in the freezer for at least 30 minutes.

3. To make the filling, combine the apples, granulated sugar, and lemon juice and zest in a large mixing bowl. Mix well, then set aside for 10 minutes. Preheat the oven to 400 degrees.

4. Sprinkle the flour over the apples and mix well. Stir in the apple butter and raisins. Turn the filling into the frozen pie shell. Smooth the filling with your hands to even it out. Place the pie directly on the center oven rack and bake for 35 minutes.

5. While the pie bakes, make the crumb topping. Put the flour, oats, brown sugar, and salt in a food processor and pulse several times to mix. Remove the lid and scatter the butter pieces over the dry mixture. Pulse the machine repeatedly, until the mixture resembles fine crumbs. Empty the crumbs into a large mixing bowl and rub them between your fingers until you have large, buttery crumbs. Refrigerate.

6. After 35 minutes, remove the pie from the oven and place it on a large, dark baking sheet covered with aluminum foil. Reduce the oven temperature to 375 degrees. Carefully dump the crumbs in the center of the pie, spreading them over the entire surface with your hands. Tamp them down lightly. Return the pie on the baking sheet to the oven and bake until the juices bubble thickly around the edge, an additional 35 to 40 minutes. Loosely cover the pie with tented aluminum foil during the last 15 minutes of baking to keep the top from browning too much.

7. Transfer the pie to a cooling rack and let cool for at least 1 hour before slicing.

Makes 8 to 10 servings

Chunky Apple–Apple Butter Pie

I've spoken about how well apple butter can work as a flavor enhancer for apple pies. In my other apple butter pie (page 98), the apple butter is essentially used to dress the apples, coating each one with apple flavor. Here I use it somewhat differently—not unlike the way the boiled cider is used in the pie on page 90—in a custard that's poured over the apples after they've been partially cooked (in that variation, we sauté the apples, whereas here we bake them right in the crust). The oven temperature is lowered, then the pie is baked further, just until the custard is set. Do eat this cold, not warm. When the pie is warm, there tends to be loose liquid at the bottom, but if you wait until it is cold, most of the liquid will be reabsorbed into the filling.

1 RECIPE BEST BUTTER PIE PASTRY
(PAGE 8), REFRIGERATED

FILLING:

5 CUPS PEELED AND CORED APPLES CUT
INTO LARGE CHUNKS

1 TABLESPOON SUGAR

2½ TABLESPOONS ALL-PURPOSE FLOUR

¾ CUP PURE MAPLE SYRUP

3 TABLESPOONS UNSALTED BUTTER

1 CUP SPICED APPLE BUTTER, HOMEMADE
(PAGE 101) OR STORE-BOUGHT

4 LARGE EGGS, LIGHTLY BEATEN

½ TEASPOON PURE VANILLA EXTRACT

⅛ TEASPOON SALT

1. If you haven't already, prepare the pastry and refrigerate it until firm enough to roll, about 1 hour.

2. On a sheet of lightly floured waxed paper, roll the pastry into a 13½-inch circle with a floured rolling pin. Invert the pastry over a 9-inch deep-dish pie pan. Center it, then peel off the paper. Gently tuck the pastry into the pan, without stretching it, and sculpt the overhang into an upstanding ridge. Place the pie shell in the freezer for at least 30 minutes. Preheat the oven to 400 degrees during the last 10 minutes.

3. To make the filling, mix the apples, sugar, and flour together in a large mixing bowl. Turn the filling into the frozen pie shell, arranging the apples so they're more or less level on top.

Place the pie directly on the center oven rack and bake for 30 minutes.

4. While the pie bakes, warm the maple syrup and butter together in a small saucepan over medium heat just until the butter melts. Pour into a medium-size mixing bowl. Whisk in the apple butter, then blend in the remaining filling ingredients. Set aside.

5. Remove the pie from the oven and place it on a large, dark baking sheet covered with aluminum foil. Reduce the oven temperature to 350 degrees. Stir the apple butter filling, then slowly ladle it over the apples, covering all of them. The filling will probably come very close to the top of the pastry. Place the pie on the baking sheet back on the center rack and bake for an additional 30 minutes. When done, the edges will be somewhat puffy and have a flat finish; the center is likely to be more glossy and not puffed, or only very slightly so. In any event, none of the filling should be soupy-loose if you jiggle the pie.

6. Transfer the pie to a cooling rack and let cool to room temperature. Refrigerate for at least several hours, preferably overnight, before slicing.

Makes 8 to 10 servings

SPICED APPLE BUTTER

If you've ever made applesauce, you've come close to making apple butter, which is essentially applesauce cooked down to a thicker consistency.

3 TO 4 POUNDS APPLES, PEELED, CORED, AND
  CUT INTO LARGE CHUNKS
1 ½ CUPS FRESH APPLE CIDER
2 TABLESPOONS PEELED AND MINCED CANDIED
  GINGER
⅓ CUP SUGAR
1 ½ TABLESPOONS FRESH LEMON JUICE

1. Preheat the oven to 375 degrees. Combine the apples, cider, and ginger in a large nonreactive pot. Bring to a boil. Cover, reduce the heat to medium, and cook at a low boil, stirring occasionally, until the apples turn to mush, 20 to 25 minutes.

2. Remove from the heat and stir in the sugar and lemon juice. Transfer about half of the apple mixture to a food processor and process to a fine puree. Pour into a shallow ovenproof casserole. Repeat for the remaining apple mixture, pouring the puree into the same casserole.

3. Put the casserole in the oven and bake for 30 minutes, stirring once or twice. Reduce the oven temperature to 350 degrees and cook, stirring occasionally, until the apple butter has darkened and thickened and is reduced by nearly half, 45 to 55 minutes.

4. Remove from the oven and let cool. Transfer to jars, screw on the lids, and refrigerate. This will keep for at least 2 weeks.

Makes 2½ to 3 cups

CHAPTER 5

Special Occasion Apple Pies

An apple pie is reason enough to celebrate, but sometimes we want a pie that suits the occasion in a particular fashion: a birthday pie, perhaps; one you can assemble and freeze today but bake next week when your company is due; or a sweet little pie you can make for your valentine.

Here's a selection of recipes for those occasions and others. Some are tied to a particular event, but others are just plain special—the cause for celebration is up to you. Use your imagination. Do you have an upcoming trip to California wine country? Or would you like to note the anniversary of such a trip with your traveling companion? You'll find a wine country pie here that fits the bill. Are you organizing a tailgate party for a group of friends? Almost any of the pies in this collection will work beautifully, but there's one in this chapter I've baked for a Mexican theme tailgate party. Is a pie-loving friend about to celebrate a birthday? I have a special birthday pie here that I like to make for my sweetheart.

Treating someone to an apple pie isn't flashy. It doesn't cost much, and it requires only a little of your time. But the love, happiness, and goodwill you can generate with a simple gift of a special occasion apple pie are way out of proportion to the modest investment you'll make.

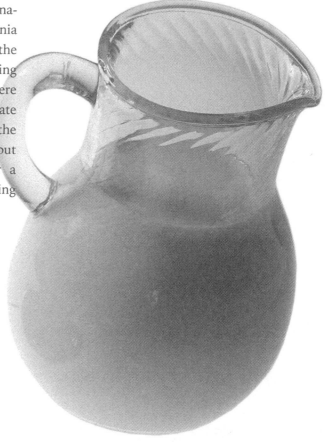

Bev's Apple Crumb Birthday Pie

My better half, Bev, is such an apple pie lover that she prefers it to birthday cake, and I'm happy to oblige on her special day.

The pie she likes is essentially my favorite crumb-topped pie—favorite for its extravagant amount of crumb topping, the sheer volume of fruit, and the addition of raisins: no fancy, schmancy flourishes necessary. Don't try to cram this amount of filling into a smaller pie pan than the one specified: you'll only end up with a mess on the oven floor. Of course, it wouldn't be a birthday pie without ice cream. Bev likes hers piled high with vanilla.

1 RECIPE BEST BUTTER PIE PASTRY (PAGE 8) OR THREE-GRAIN BUTTER PASTRY (PAGE 10), REFRIGERATED

FILLING:

10 CUPS PEELED, CORED, AND SLICED APPLES (A MIXTURE OF FIRM-TEXTURED AND SOFT APPLES IS BEST)

⅓ CUP GRANULATED SUGAR

¼ CUP FIRMLY PACKED LIGHT BROWN SUGAR

¾ CUP RAISINS

JUICE AND GRATED ZEST OF 1 LEMON

¼ TEASPOON GROUND NUTMEG

¼ CUP ALL-PURPOSE FLOUR

OATMEAL CRUMB TOPPING:

1 CUP ALL-PURPOSE FLOUR

½ CUP OLD-FASHIONED ROLLED OATS (NOT INSTANT)

⅔ CUP FIRMLY PACKED LIGHT BROWN SUGAR

½ TEASPOON GROUND CINNAMON

¼ TEASPOON SALT

½ CUP (1 STICK) COLD UNSALTED BUTTER, CUT INTO ¼-INCH PIECES

1. If you haven't already, make the pastry and refrigerate it until firm enough to roll, about 1 hour.

2. On a sheet of lightly floured waxed paper, roll the pastry into a 13½-inch circle with a floured rolling pin. Invert the pastry over a 9-inch deep-dish pie pan. Center it, then peel off the paper. Gently tuck the pastry down into the pan, without stretching it, and sculpt the edge into an upstanding ridge. Place the pie shell in the freezer for at least 30 minutes.

3. To make the filling, mix the apples, sugars, raisins, lemon juice and zest, and nutmeg together in a large mixing bowl. Set aside for 10 minutes. Preheat the oven to 400 degrees.

4. Sprinkle the flour over the apples and mix well. Turn the filling into the frozen pie shell, smoothing it with your hands to even it out. Place the pie on a large, dark baking sheet covered with aluminum foil and bake on the center oven rack for 35 minutes.

5. While the pie bakes, make the crumb topping. Put the flour, oats, brown sugar, cinna-mon, and salt in a food processor, pulsing several times to mix. Remove the lid and scatter the butter pieces over the dry mixture. Pulse the machine repeatedly, until the mixture resembles fine crumbs. Empty the crumbs into a large mixing bowl and rub them between your fingers to make large, buttery crumbs. Refrigerate.

6. After 35 minutes, remove the pie from the oven. Reduce the oven temperature to 375 degrees. Carefully dump the crumbs in the center of the pie, spreading them over the entire surface with your hands. Tamp them down lightly. Put the pie on the baking sheet back in the oven and bake until the juices bubble thickly around the edge, an additional 35 to 40 minutes. Loosely cover the pie with aluminum foil during the last 15 minutes of baking to keep the top from browning too much.

7. Transfer the pie to a cooling rack and let cool for at least 1 hour before slicing.

Makes 8 to 10 servings

Valentine's Apple Pie for Two

Everyone needs a little apple pie recipe for two—for you and that someone special. This is just such a creation—a petite apple cherry pie with a decorative arrangement of hearts on top. If you have a 7-inch pie pan, that would be perfect here. Since I don't have one that size, I use a 7-inch cake pan, which I butter well before putting in the pastry, so I can easily turn the cooled pie out of the pan and present this on a pretty serving platter. I flavor the apples with cherry preserves to tint them a blushing valentine red. This is optional, but I also like to heighten the cherry flavor with 2 tablespoons of cherry juice concentrate, which you can order from King Orchards (see page 107) or find in many health food stores. Mass-market brands are also available in most supermarkets. I think you'll enjoy making this for your sweetheart. I do.

1 RECIPE ALL-AMERICAN DOUBLE CRUST (PAGE 2), REFRIGERATED

FILLING:

3 APPLES, PEELED, CORED, AND SLICED

¼ CUP SUGAR

1 TABLESPOON FRESH LEMON JUICE

3 TO 4 TABLESPOONS CHERRY PRESERVES

2 TABLESPOONS CHERRY JUICE CONCENTRATE (OPTIONAL)

1 TABLESPOON CORNSTARCH

GLAZE:

MILK

SUGAR

1. If you haven't already, prepare the pastry, dividing it into roughly equal thirds, making one piece slightly larger than the other two. Wrap and refrigerate until firm enough to roll, about 1 hour. Butter a 7-inch cake pan or equivalent size gratin dish and set aside.

2. On a sheet of lightly floured waxed paper, roll the larger piece of dough into an 11½-inch circle with a floured rolling pin. Invert the pastry over the pan, center it, and peel off the paper. Tuck the pastry into the pan, without stretching it, and let the edge of the pastry drape over the side of the pan. Refrigerate.

3. While the dough chills, roll out another piece of dough on a sheet of lightly floured waxed paper a little less than ⅛ inch thick. Place it in the freezer until you're ready to cut out the heart decorations.

4. Combine the apples, sugar, and lemon juice in a large bowl. Set aside for 10 minutes.

5. Stir in the cherry preserves and concentrate, if using. Shake the cornstarch over the fruit and mix very well to combine. Set aside. Preheat the oven to 400 degrees.

6. On another sheet of lightly floured waxed paper, roll the third piece of pastry into an 8-inch circle. Dampen the edge of the pie shell with a finger or pastry brush. Turn the filling into the shell, smoothing the fruit with your hands. Invert the top pastry over the filling, center it, and peel off the paper. Press the pastries together along the dampened edge. Trim the pastry with scissors or a paring knife to an even ½ inch all around, then sculpt the overhang into a rolled edge or upstanding ridge. Brush the top of the pie lightly with milk.

7. Get the rolled pastry from the freezer and let it sit at room temperature for a minute or so before you cut it. Using a heart-shaped cookie cutter or working freehand, cut hearts to go on top of the pastry. If they're small, you can make a border of them all around the perimeter. If they're a little larger, you can put one on each half of the pie. Or put one big heart in the middle—with an arrow going through it. Brush the decorations with a little milk and sprinkle the top with sugar. Poke 2 or 3 steam vents near the edge, so you can check the juices there later.

8. Place the pie directly on the center oven rack and bake for 30 minutes. Remove from the oven and place on a large, dark baking sheet covered with aluminum foil. Reduce the oven temperature to 375 degrees. Return the pie on the baking sheet to the oven and bake for

another 30 minutes. You won't necessarily see any juices bubbling up, but the pie should be done after 1 hour of baking.

9. Transfer the pie to a cooling rack and let cool. You can eat this anytime if you've made it in a pie pan. If you've made it in a cake pan, cool the pie for at least 5 hours, then invert it onto a plate, loosening the sides with a knife. Then invert the pie again onto a serving platter.

Makes 2 servings

KING ORCHARDS CHERRIES

I've had the pleasure of baking some great pies made with Michigan McIntosh apples from King Orchards, near Central Lake, Michigan. The company is owned and run by Betsy King and family, who offer not just their exemplary apples but wonderful cherries. Their dried tart cherries are the best I've eaten: plump, chewy, and delicious.

One of their most sought after products is Tart Cherry Juice Concentrate, which I knew was a great flavoring for apple pie but didn't realize has numerous health benefits as well. One study has found that cherry growers and their families, who ate above-average amounts of tart cherries, had fewer signs of heart disease and a lower risk of cancer compared to the general population.

If you want to find out more, and learn how you might order King Orchards' products, you can contact them at 4620 North M-88, Central Lake, MI 49622, (877) YES-KING, www.kingorchards.com.

Apple and Champagne Grape Pie

The first time I tasted tiny champagne grapes, I could not believe how sweet they were—literally, as sweet as candy. So it made perfect sense when I eventually learned that these are the grapes dried currants are made from. They're so sweet, in fact, that you scarcely need any added sugar when making this pie. I mix a couple of tablespoons of sugar with the cornstarch, just so I'm satisfied that the cornstarch won't lump, but you could leave the sugar out altogether if you like.

If you've ever picked tart red currants right off the bush, you have some idea how champagne grapes cling to the branches. Picking them off one by one is pretty tricky because they're rather soft and fragile, so I just sort of rake them off with my fingertips; it's much easier that way. I don't often see champagne grapes in the market, but I enjoy this pie so much that I make a point of buying them a few times a year just to make this pie.

1 RECIPE ALL-AMERICAN DOUBLE CRUST
(PAGE 2), REFRIGERATED

FILLING:

6 CUPS PEELED, CORED, AND SLICED
APPLES

2 CUPS CHAMPAGNE GRAPES

2 TABLESPOONS SUGAR

1½ TABLESPOONS CORNSTARCH

2 TABLESPOONS RED WINE

1 TABLESPOON FRESH LEMON JUICE

GLAZE:

MILK

SUGAR

1. If you haven't already, prepare the pastry and refrigerate it until firm enough to roll, about 1 hour.

2. On a sheet of lightly floured waxed paper, roll the larger portion of the pastry into a 13½-inch circle with a floured rolling pin. Invert the pastry over a 9-inch deep-dish pie pan. Center it, then peel off the paper. Gently tuck the pastry into the pan, without stretching it, and let the excess pastry drape over the side of the pan. Refrigerate for at least 15 minutes, loosely covered with plastic wrap. Preheat the oven to 400 degrees.

3. To make the filling, combine the apples and grapes in a large mixing bowl. Mix the sugar and cornstarch together in a small mixing bowl; shake it over the fruit and mix well. Add the wine and lemon juice and mix again. Turn the filling into the refrigerated pie shell and smooth the top with your hands.

4. On another sheet of lightly floured waxed paper, roll the top pastry into an 11½-inch circle. Dampen the edge of the pie shell with a wet fingertip or pastry brush. Invert the top pastry over the filling, center it, and peel off the paper. Press the top and bottom pastries together along the dampened edge. Trim the pastry with scissors or a paring knife, leaving an even ½ inch all around, then sculpt the overhang into an upstanding ridge. Poke several steam vents in the top of the pie with a fork or paring knife; put a couple of the vents near the edge of the crust, so you can check the juices there later. Brush the top of the pie with a little milk and sprinkle lightly with sugar.

5. Put the pie directly on the center oven rack and bake for 30 minutes. Remove the pie from the oven and place on a large, dark baking sheet covered with aluminum foil. Reduce the oven temperature to 375 degrees. Put the pie on the baking sheet back in the oven and bake until any juices—visible at the steam vents— bubble thickly, another 35 to 40 minutes.

6. Transfer the pie to a cooling rack and let cool for at least 1 hour before slicing.

Makes 8 to 10 servings

CHECK THAT JUICE

For most of the recipes in this collection, I've recommended using anywhere from about 1 to 4 tablespoons of flour to thicken the apple pie filling, or an equivalent amount of cornstarch. These recommendations are based on the relative juiciness of the apples I used in testing the recipes and the presence of other ingredients that would necessitate more or less thickening power.

Keep in mind, though, that these recommendations are fairly flexible and should be taken with a grain of salt, for the simple reason that my apples might be juicier than yours, or vice versa, depending on a lot of things, including the age of the apples and how long they've been in storage. This is one of the reasons I nearly always recommend sugaring your fruit and letting it stand for 10 minutes before adding the flour. After those 10 minutes, you'll have a good indication of just how juicy your apples are by looking at the liquid that's accumulated in the bowl. If there's lots of juice, you'll need a fair amount of thickener. Not too much juice means you'll probably need less. So keep an eye on that juice and adjust the amount of thickener you're using if the situation seems to warrant it.

Apple Apricot Peekaboo Pie

This is one of the only pies in this collection where the filling is arranged rather than just mixed and turned into the crust. In that regard, I will admit that it's more of a tart and less of a pie. But for the moment at least, I'm going to overlook that fact because it's such an attractive open-faced dessert, and there are times—such as when you're entertaining—when a sophisticated pie like this is appropriate. You can use any pastry you like here, but it should be large enough to roll into a 14-inch circle without making it too thin.

That's equivalent to about two-thirds of the All-American Double Crust (page 2) or the Shortening Double Crust (page 4). I like the Whole Wheat Double Crust for its earthy contrast to an otherwise uptown pie. The dough is rolled, apricot preserves are smeared in the center, and thin apple slices are arranged over that, with bits of dried apricots placed in the voids between the apples. The sides are folded over the fruit, making a frilled edge, then the pie is baked. Serve this warm for best eating, within 30 minutes of baking.

1 RECIPE WHOLE WHEAT DOUBLE CRUST
(PAGE 6), REFRIGERATED

FILLING:

2 LARGE GOLDEN DELICIOUS APPLES,
PEELED AND CORED

½ CUP APRICOT PRESERVES

½ CUP FINELY DICED DRIED APRICOTS

1. If you haven't already, prepare the pastry and refrigerate it until firm enough to roll, about 1 hour.

2. Halve the apples lengthwise. To slice them, put the flat side down on a cutting board and cut them into lengthwise slices ⅛ inch thick, cutting straight down through the apple, not on an angle. Take all of the smaller end slices and chop them finely. Set aside both the chopped and sliced apples. Preheat the oven to 400 degrees.

3. On a sheet of lightly floured waxed paper, roll the pastry into a 14-inch circle with a floured rolling pin. Invert the pastry onto a

large, ungreased baking sheet. Center it, then peel off the paper.

4. Smear ¼ cup of the apricot preserves in the center of the pastry in a circle about 8 inches in diameter. Cover with the chopped apples. Arrange the apple slices over the chopped apples in an overlapping fashion. Make them neat, but you don't have to get too carried away with precision; they're going to soften and relax in the oven anyway. Place pieces of dried apricot here and there between the apple slices. Try to put them below the upper plane of the apples so they won't scorch.

5. Fold the edge of the pastry up over the outer area of the fruit; the dough will self-pleat, creating a frilled edge with exposed apples in the center. Warm the remaining ¼ cup preserves in a small saucepan and brush it over the exposed apples. Put the baking sheet on the center oven rack and bake for 30 minutes, then reduce the temperature to 375 degrees and bake until the pie is juicy and bubbly, about 15 minutes more.

6. Transfer the baking sheet to a cooling rack and let the pie cool briefly before slicing.

Makes 8 servings

HOW TO STORE APPLES

In the short term, a bag of fresh apples will keep in the refrigerator for several weeks. But say you've found some prize Northern Spy or other apples, and you'd like to keep them around for pie making into the winter. How should you store them?

First, know that some apples keep better than others. Generally speaking, those include apples picked at their prime. Apples that are too green will have storage problems, as will those that have been picked beyond their maturity. Among the best storage apples are Northern Spy, Winesap, and Rome Beauty. Ask your local apple grower which apples he or she recommends for storage.

For long-term storage, choose a cool location with relatively high humidity. The ideal storage temperature is 32 to 34 degrees. Below that, apples will freeze, causing the cell structure to break down and consequently ruin the apples.

Storage apples must be in perfect, unblemished condition. Choose them carefully; any with bruises or soft spots should be used as soon as possible. Wrap apples individually in black-and-white newsprint bunched up around the apples. Don't use paper with color photos, as the colored ink may contaminate the apples. Place the apples in a box and store it in a dark place. Check the apples once a week to see how they're faring. Damp spots on the newsprint are an indication that an apple is rotting. Finally, don't store apples next to potatoes. They put off a gas that will hasten the demise of stored apples. Apples stored under ideal conditions can keep for 4 to 5 months.

A Freeze-and-Bake Apple Pie

This is a handy item—a pie you can assemble ahead, freeze, and then pop in the oven when you need it. A freezer pie has a number of requirements that run counter to fresh pie wisdom. For one, there can't be too much filling, or the pie won't bake properly: the top and bottom will get overcooked before the apples are fully cooked. For another, although I try to get my fresh apple pies good and juicy before they go into the crust—by sugaring the apples and letting them sit for a few minutes—I go out of my way here to keep them "dry," so their juice doesn't dampen the bottom pastry. (You'll notice that I don't even use lemon juice, just the zest.) Much as I hate to tie up a glass pie pan in the freezer for a few days or weeks, I strongly suggest that you don't prepare this pie in a disposable aluminum pan because the combination of the cold pie and reflective aluminum is likely to result in a soggy bottom crust. This is an altogether excellent pie.

1 RECIPE ALL-AMERICAN DOUBLE CRUST
   (PAGE 2) OR SHORTENING DOUBLE CRUST
   (PAGE 4), REFRIGERATED

FILLING:

2 TEASPOONS PLUS 2 TABLESPOONS ALL-
   PURPOSE FLOUR

2 TEASPOONS PLUS ½ CUP SUGAR

6 CUPS PEELED, CORED, AND THINLY SLICED
   APPLES

GRATED ZEST OF 1 LEMON

1. If you haven't already, prepare the pastry and refrigerate it until firm enough to roll, about 1 hour.

2. On a sheet of lightly floured waxed paper, roll the larger portion of the pastry into a 13½-inch circle with a floured rolling pin. Invert the pastry over a 9-inch deep-dish pie pan. Center it, then peel off the paper. Gently tuck the pastry down into the pan, without stretching it, and let the edge of the pastry drape over the side of the pan. Place the pie shell in the freezer while you continue working on the pie.

3. Mix the 2 teaspoons flour and 2 teaspoons sugar together in a small mixing bowl. Remove the pie shell from the freezer and sprinkle this dry mixture over the bottom of the shell; it should help absorb any juice the apples might throw off before the pie freezes solid. Put the pie shell back in the freezer.

4. Combine the apples, the remaining 2 tablespoons flour, the remaining ½ cup sugar, and the lemon zest in a large mixing bowl; toss well to mix. Scrape the filling into the pie shell, taking a little time to arrange the apples so that they form a fairly tight-fitting, compact layer. Smooth the top with your hands. Put the pie back in the freezer.

5. On another sheet of lightly floured waxed paper, roll the top pastry into an 11½-inch circle. Remove the pie from the freezer and let it sit at room temperature just long enough for the overhanging dough to become supple; it should take only 2 to 3 minutes. Lightly moisten the edge of the pie shell with a pastry brush or your fingertips. Invert the top pastry over the filling, center it, and peel off the paper. Press

the pastries together along the dampened edge. Trim the pastry, leaving an even ½ inch all around, then sculpt the overhang into an upstanding ridge. Poke several steam vents in the top of the pie with a fork or paring knife; put a couple of them near the edge, so you can check the juices there when you bake the pie.

6. Put the pie back in the freezer until the top pastry is good and firm, then cover it completely with aluminum foil and slip the pie into a large plastic bag. Freeze for up to 2 weeks.

7. To bake the pie, remove it from the freezer 15 to 20 minutes before you plan to bake it. Preheat the oven to 375 degrees. Bake the pie directly on the center oven rack until the juices bubble thickly at the edge, about 1¼ hours.

8. Transfer the pie to a cooling rack and let cool for at least 1 hour before slicing.

Makes 8 to 10 servings

Teresa's Apple and Jalapeño Tailgate Pie

I was at a Navy home football tailgate party—I live in Annapolis, Maryland, part-time—and the conversation wound its way to the subject of apple pie, as it often did during the stretch that I was working on this book. The focus of the conversation was this: what sort of apple pie would be appropriate for the very party we were attending? Simple enough, except for the fact that this tailgate party—for the past 10 consecutive years—had had a Mexican theme. Naturally, the concept of a tequila pie was offered up numerous times (which should give you some indication of the sort of crowd this was), as was a chili powder pie,

salsa pie, and several other versions that made even those sound appetizing by comparison. Finally, my friend Teresa Baird hit upon the idea of using jalapeño jelly to sweeten the pie—an idea I immediately liked. So I got to work on that pie the very next week, and it turned out beautifully. Will a spicy hot jalapeño apple pie be to everyone's liking? Probably not. But if you think there's a chance this will appeal, don't hesitate to try it. The gourmet section of my supermarket stocks a good red-colored jalapeño jelly made by Knott's Berry Farm. If your market doesn't stock this brand, the manager might be able to order it.

1 RECIPE BEST BUTTER PIE PASTRY (PAGE 8), REFRIGERATED

FILLING:

8 CUPS PEELED, CORED, AND SLICED GRANNY SMITH OR OTHER TART, JUICY APPLES

2 TABLESPOONS SUGAR

2 TEASPOONS FRESH LEMON JUICE

¾ CUP JALAPEÑO JELLY, STIRRED TO LOOSEN

¼ TEASPOON GROUND CINNAMON

2 TEASPOONS ALL-PURPOSE FLOUR

2 TO 3 TABLESPOONS CHOPPED PICKLED JALAPEÑO PEPPERS, TO YOUR TASTE (OPTIONAL)

CORNMEAL STREUSEL TOPPING:

¾ CUP ALL-PURPOSE FLOUR

¼ CUP FINE YELLOW CORNMEAL

⅔ CUP SUGAR

¼ TEASPOON SALT

½ CUP (1 STICK) COLD UNSALTED BUTTER, CUT INTO ¼-INCH PIECES

1. If you haven't already, prepare the pastry and refrigerate it until firm enough to roll, about 1 hour.

2. On a sheet of lightly floured waxed paper, roll the pastry into a 13½-inch circle with a floured rolling pin. Invert the pastry over a 9-inch deep-dish pie pan. Center it, then peel off the paper. Gently tuck the pastry down into the pan, without stretching it, and sculpt the edge into an upstanding ridge. Place the pie shell in the freezer for at least 30 minutes.

3. To make the filling, mix the apples, sugar, and lemon juice together in a large mixing bowl. Add the jalapeño jelly and mix again. Stir in the cinnamon and flour. Mix in the jalapeño peppers, if using. Set the filling aside for 10 minutes. Preheat the oven to 400 degrees.

4. Turn the filling into the frozen pie shell. Smooth the filling with your hands to even it out. Place the pie on a large, dark baking sheet covered with aluminum foil and bake on the center oven rack for 30 minutes.

5. While the pie bakes, make the topping. Put the flour, cornmeal, sugar, and salt in a food processor and pulse several times to mix. Remove the lid and scatter the butter pieces over the dry ingredients. Pulse the machine repeatedly, until the mixture resembles fine crumbs. Empty the crumbs into a large mixing bowl and rub them between your fingers to make large, buttery crumbs. Refrigerate.

6. After 30 minutes, remove the pie from the oven. Reduce the oven temperature to 375 degrees. Carefully dump the crumbs in the center of the pie, spreading them evenly over the surface with your hands. Tamp them down lightly. Put the pie on the baking sheet back in the oven and bake until the juices bubble thickly around the edge, an additional 30 minutes. Loosely cover the pie with tented aluminum foil during the last 15 minutes of baking if the top starts to get too brown.

7. Transfer the pie to a cooling rack and let cool for at least 1 hour before slicing.

Makes 8 to 10 servings

Sausage, Apple, and Prune Potpies

Not quite a sweet pie, not a savory one, this is essentially a dinner pie and dessert pie rolled into one. For these individual potpies, I like to use the standard 10-ounce Pyrex custard cups you can find in almost any supermarket or housewares store. I line them with pastry—the buttery All-American Double Crust is best for a dinner pie—then layer in a lightly sugared apple prune mixture and smoked sausage. A pinch of thyme gives the pies a savory bent, and a bit of mint jelly ties the flavors together beautifully. These are already on the rich side, so consider this next suggestion optional: sometimes I like to layer a couple of slabs of cheddar cheese on top of each pie when the pies come out of the oven. The cheese softens up and tastes great with the apples and sausage.

I'd suggest serving these for a ski lodge party or after some other cold weather event, when appetites are sharp and adventurous.

1 RECIPE ALL-AMERICAN DOUBLE CRUST
(PAGE 2), DIVIDED AS INSTRUCTED IN STEP
1 AND REFRIGERATED

FILLING:

3 LARGE JUICY APPLES, PEELED, CORED,
AND SLICED CROSSWISE

2 TABLESPOONS SUGAR

¼ CUP CHOPPED PITTED PRUNES

¼ TEASPOON DRIED THYME

⅓ POUND KIELBASA OR OTHER SMOKED
(FULLY COOKED) SAUSAGE, DICED

1 TABLESPOON MINT JELLY

TOPPING:

CHEDDAR CHEESE (OPTIONAL)

1. Prepare the pastry as directed, dividing it as follows: Lift the pastry out of the bowl onto a sheet of lightly floured waxed paper. Press it into a large, thick rectangle and divide the rectangle in half, making one half slightly larger than the other. Divide the larger half into 4 equal pieces; these will be the bottom crusts. Divide the other half of the dough into 4 equal pieces; these will be the top crusts. Shape each piece into a thick disk and place the disks on a small baking sheet lined with plastic wrap. Cover with plastic wrap and refrigerate for at least 1 hour.

2. When you're almost ready to start the assembly, prepare the filling. Combine the apples, sugar, prunes, and thyme in a large mixing bowl and mix well. Set aside. Preheat the oven to 400 degrees and get out four 10-ounce custard cups.

3. Working with one of the larger pieces of dough at a time, roll the dough into a 7½- to 8-inch circle on a sheet of lightly floured waxed paper with a floured rolling pin. Before you lift the dough into the custard cup, make four 1½-inch slits at the 12, 3, 6, and 9 o'clock positions. The slits will allow the dough to neatly self-pleat when you tuck it into the cup. Invert the dough onto your hand and carefully lower the pastry into the cup. Tuck it into the bottom and sides of the cup, without stretching it, and let the dough hang over the edge of the cup. Refrigerate while you repeat this procedure for the remaining cups.

4. Spoon an equal amount of the apple filling into each of the 4 cups, then add some of the diced sausage. Dot the top of each filled cup with one quarter of the mint jelly.

5. On fresh sheets of lightly floured waxed paper, roll each of the remaining pieces of dough into a 5½-inch circle. Moisten the edge of each pie shell and lift the top pastry into place, pressing the top and bottom pastries together at the dampened edge. As you do so, push the pastry down into the cup slightly, then trim the overhanging dough with a paring knife. Poke several steam vents in the top pastry.

6. Put the cups on a large, dark baking sheet covered with aluminum foil and place on the center oven rack. Bake the pies for 25 minutes, then reduce the oven temperature to 375 degrees and bake for an additional 20 minutes. When the pies are done, you may or may not see the juices bubbling up onto the crusts.

7. Transfer the pies to a cooling rack. If you're using the cheddar cheese (see headnote), lay a couple of slices on top of each pie as soon as the pies come out of the oven. Let the pies cool for at least 10 minutes before eating. Be careful, because these little pies will trap very hot steam for quite some time.

Makes 4 main-dish servings

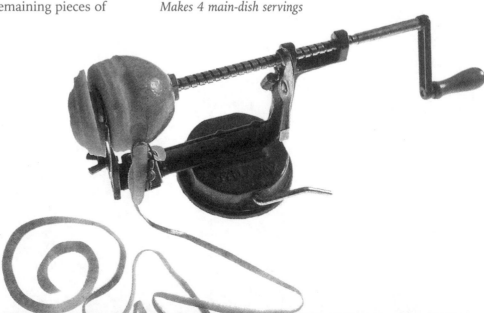

Individual Apple and Plum Pies with Streusel Topping

This is not only a fine recipe; it's a model for practically any sort of individual mixed-fruit apple pie that you'd like to make. I use small Italian prune plums here because I like their flavor and color and, for whatever reason, they seem to be superior to other plums I'm able to find at the height of plum season. You could just as easily use blackberries, blueberries, sliced peaches or nectarines, or a handful of fresh cranberries.

A note about individual pies made in 10-ounce custard cups: these make for a pretty substantial dessert. Thus the rest of the meal should be on the light side—perhaps just a brothy soup and a bit of salad. You'll want plenty of room for dessert. A big scoop of ice cream is overkill with these pies, but do consider making Vanilla Custard Sauce (page 33) and serving it chilled, in a small pitcher on the side.

1 RECIPE ALL-AMERICAN DOUBLE CRUST (PAGE 2) OR SHORTENING DOUBLE CRUST (PAGE 4), DIVIDED AS INSTRUCTED IN STEP 1 AND REFRIGERATED

FILLING:

3 LARGE APPLES, PEELED, QUARTERED, AND CORED

6 TO 8 SMALL ITALIAN PRUNE PLUMS, QUARTERED LENGTHWISE AND PITTED

⅓ CUP SUGAR

1 TABLESPOON FRESH LEMON JUICE

GRATED ZEST OF 1 LEMON

½ TABLESPOON ALL-PURPOSE FLOUR

STREUSEL TOPPING:

½ CUP ALL-PURPOSE FLOUR

⅓ CUP SUGAR

¼ TEASPOON SALT

⅛ TEASPOON GROUND CINNAMON

¼ CUP (½ STICK) COLD UNSALTED BUTTER, CUT INTO ¼-INCH PIECES

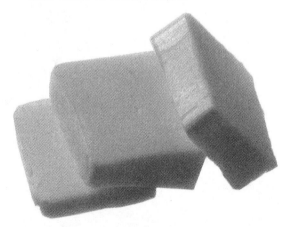

1. Prepare the pastry as directed, dividing it as follows: Lift the pastry out of the bowl and onto a sheet of lightly floured waxed paper. Press it into a large, thick rectangle and divide the rectangle in half, making one half slightly larger than the other. Divide the large half into 4 equal pieces; these will be the bottom crusts. Shape each piece into a thick disk and place the disks on a plate lined with plastic wrap. Cover with plastic wrap and refrigerate until firm enough to roll, at least 1 hour. Flatten the other half of the dough into a thick disk. Wrap that half in plastic wrap and refrigerate or freeze for later, using it to make a pie shell.

2. When you're almost ready to start the assembly, prepare the filling. Slice the apples crosswise into thin slices. Combine the apples, plums, sugar, lemon juice, lemon zest, and flour in a large mixing bowl and mix well. Set aside. Preheat the oven to 400 degrees and get out four 10-ounce Pyrex custard cups.

3. Working with one piece of dough at a time, roll the dough into a 7½- to 8-inch circle on a sheet of lightly floured waxed paper with a floured rolling pin. Before you lift the dough into the custard cup, make four 1½-inch-long slits at the 12, 3, 6, and 9 o'clock positions. The slits will allow the dough to neatly self-pleat when you tuck it into the cup. Invert the dough onto your hand and carefully lower the pastry into the cup. Tuck it into the bottom and sides of the cup, without stretching it, and let the dough hang over the edge of the cup. Turn the overhang back and under, shaping it into a thick edge level with the top of the cup. Refrigerate while you repeat this procedure for the remaining cups.

4. Spoon an equal amount of the filling into each of the 4 cups. Place the cups on a large, dark baking sheet covered with aluminum foil, put on the center oven rack, and bake for 25 minutes.

5. While the pies bake, make the streusel topping. Put the flour, sugar, salt, and cinnamon in a food processor and pulse several times to mix. Remove the lid and scatter the butter pieces over the dry ingredients. Pulse the machine repeatedly, until the mixture resembles fine crumbs. Dump the crumbs into a large mixing bowl and rub them gently between your fingers to make large, buttery crumbs. Refrigerate.

6. After 25 minutes, remove the pies and the baking sheet from the oven. Reduce the oven temperature to 375 degrees. Divide the topping evenly among the pies, spreading it evenly over the surface and tamping it down lightly with your hand. Put the pies on the baking sheet back in the oven and bake for about 20 minutes longer. When the pies are done, you will probably see juices bubbling in each cup.

7. Transfer the pies to a cooling rack and let cool for at least 30 minutes before serving.

Makes 4 servings

Apple Bread-Pudding Pie

Here's a cross between two great American comfort desserts—apple pie and bread pudding—the latter spooned over the former midway through the baking. It emerges from the oven looking almost like any other bread pudding, crusty and golden brown—until you remove a slice and reveal distinct layers of pastry crust, apples, and bread pudding. As you might imagine, this is not a dessert for the faint of appetite. Plan to serve it in the dead of winter when a seriously hearty dessert will be most appreciated.

1 RECIPE BEST BUTTER PIE PASTRY (PAGE 8), REFRIGERATED

APPLE FILLING:

3 GALA OR OTHER FIRM-TEXTURED, JUICY, SWEET APPLES, PEELED AND CORED

⅓ CUP SUGAR

1 TABLESPOON FRESH LEMON JUICE

¼ TEASPOON GROUND CINNAMON

1 TABLESPOON ALL-PURPOSE FLOUR

BREAD PUDDING:

ABOUT 6 SLICES SLIGHTLY DRY, FIRM-TEXTURED, WHITE BREAD

1½ CUPS LIGHT CREAM, HALF-AND-HALF, OR MILK

⅓ CUP SUGAR

1 TEASPOON PURE VANILLA EXTRACT

GRATED ZEST OF 1 ORANGE

PINCH OF SALT

3 LARGE EGGS

TOPPING:

UNSALTED BUTTER, CUT INTO SMALL PIECES

SUGAR

1. If you haven't already, prepare the pastry and refrigerate it until firm enough to roll, about 1 hour.

2. On a sheet of lightly floured waxed paper, roll the larger portion of the pastry into a 13½-inch circle with a floured rolling pin. Invert the pastry over a 9-inch deep-dish pie pan. Center it, then peel off the paper. Gently tuck the pastry into the pan, without stretching it, and sculpt the edge into an upstanding ridge. Place the pie shell in the freezer for at least 30 minutes.

3. To make the filling, quarter the apples lengthwise, then cut each section into thin, crosswise slices. Combine the apples with the rest of the filling ingredients in a large mixing bowl. Set aside for 10 minutes. Preheat the oven to 400 degrees.

4. Turn the filling into the pie shell. Place directly on the center rack of the oven and bake for 30 minutes.

5. As soon as the pie starts to bake, make the pudding. Cut the bread into ¾-inch cubes and put them in a large mixing bowl; you will need 4 cups of cubes. Heat the cream in a small saucepan until hot to the touch and pour into a medium-size mixing bowl. Stir in the sugar, vanilla, orange zest, and salt. Break the eggs into another bowl and whisk until frothy. Blend them into the cream mixture, then pour the liquid over the bread, stirring gently so all of the bread is dampened. Set aside, stirring gently once or twice in the next 20 minutes.

6. After 30 minutes, remove the pie from the oven and place on a large, dark baking sheet covered with aluminum foil. Reduce the oven temperature to 375 degrees. Carefully spoon the pudding mixture over the apples, distributing it evenly. Pour on as much custard as you can without letting it spill over. Dot the top of the pie with several small pieces of butter and sprinkle generously with sugar. Put the pie on the baking sheet back in the oven and bake until the bread pudding is golden and cooked through, another 30 to 35 minutes.

7. Transfer the pie to a cooling rack and let cool for at least 30 minutes before slicing. This pie is excellent warm.

Makes 8 to 10 servings

Vanilla Bean Apple Cherry Pie

Every foodie I know has his or her own little thing— something he or she is uncommonly passionate or fanatical about. One of my things is vanilla beans. I know they're expensive and extract is easier to use. But there's just something about the flavor of vanilla beans. For the record, the vanilla bean has more than 250 flavor notes associated with it, and I think you can taste all of them in this wonderful pie. First I scrape the seeds from the bean into the sugar and rub them together; the seeds tend to clump when you scrape them, and this step disperses them, ensuring that the vanilla flavor permeates the pie. Then, when the pie filling goes into the shell, I place the whole bean right in the center of the filling because baking the bean brings out even more vanilla flavor. (Don't forget to remove it when you cut the pie. It can be rinsed, air-dried, and used again to flavor custards, mulled drinks, and other dishes.)

One of vanilla's flavor notes is cherry—it can actually enhance the taste of cherries, so I add cherry preserves since they go well with both the apples and the vanilla. I like this crumb topping, but a top crust is great here, too.

1 RECIPE BEST BUTTER PIE PASTRY
   (PAGE 8), REFRIGERATED

FILLING:

½ CUP SUGAR

1 VANILLA BEAN

8 CUPS PEELED, CORED, AND SLICED
   APPLES

1 TABLESPOON FRESH LEMON JUICE

⅓ CUP CHERRY PRESERVES

2 TABLESPOONS ALL-PURPOSE FLOUR

CRUMB TOPPING:

1 CUP ALL-PURPOSE FLOUR

⅔ CUP SUGAR

¼ TEASPOON SALT

⅛ TEASPOON GROUND NUTMEG

½ CUP (1 STICK) COLD UNSALTED BUTTER,
   CUT INTO ¼-INCH PIECES

1. If you haven't already, prepare the pastry and refrigerate it until firm enough to roll, about 1 hour.

2. On a sheet of lightly floured waxed paper, roll the pastry into a 13½-inch circle with a floured rolling pin. Invert the pastry over a

9-inch deep-dish pie pan. Center it, then peel off the paper. Gently tuck the pastry into the pan, without stretching it, and sculpt the overhang into an upstanding ridge. Place the pie shell in the freezer for at least 30 minutes.

3. To make the filling, measure the sugar into a large mixing bowl. Halve the vanilla bean lengthwise, then use a paring knife to scrape out the seeds and add them to the sugar. Rub the sugar and seeds together, then add the apples, lemon juice, and cherry preserves and mix well. Set aside for 10 minutes. Preheat the oven to 400 degrees.

4. Shake the flour over the apples and mix well. Turn the filling into the frozen pie shell. Take the whole vanilla bean and bury it in the center of the pie, just under the top layer of apples. Smooth the top of the filling with your hands, then place the pie directly on the center oven rack. To help guard against the vanilla bean drying out, cover the pie with loosely tented aluminum foil. Bake for 30 minutes.

5. While the pie bakes, make the topping. Combine the flour, sugar, salt, and nutmeg in a food processor; pulse to mix. Remove the lid and scatter the butter pieces over the dry ingredients. Pulse the machine repeatedly, until the mixture resembles fine crumbs. Transfer the mixture to a large mixing bowl and rub it between your fingers to make large, buttery crumbs. Refrigerate.

6. After 30 minutes, remove the pie from the oven and place it on a large, dark baking sheet covered with aluminum foil. Reduce the oven temperature to 375 degrees. Carefully dump the crumbs in the center of the pie, spreading them evenly over the surface with your hands. Press down gently to compact them. Put the pie on the baking sheet back in the oven and bake until the juices bubble thickly around the edge, about 35 minutes. Cover the pie with loosely tented aluminum foil during the last 15 minutes, if necessary, to prevent the streusel from getting too brown.

7. Transfer the pie to a cooling rack and let cool for at least 1 hour before serving.

Makes 8 to 10 servings

MORE ABOUT THOSE VANILLA BEANS

Thomas Jefferson—our most epicurean of presidents—was very fond of vanilla, which he had encountered in France while serving as ambassador. But upon his return to native soil, he wasn't able to find it. So he wrote a letter to the chargé d'affaires in Paris, with instructions to send him "a packet of 50 pods which may come very well in the middle of a packet of newspapers." In other words, send me some vanilla beans, even if you have to smuggle them in.

Look for shiny, supple beans with a leathery texture. The pods should never be dry or brittle. Buy whole pods 5 to 7 inches long, an indication that they've grown to full maturity. Stay away from partial or cut beans, a sign that they might have had mold cut away.

Tropical Apple Pie with Coconut Crumb Topping

The tropics are a long way from the apple orchards of North America, but the distance is bridged quite nicely in this delicious pie. In the tropics, I'd no doubt make this with fresh pineapple, guava, passion fruit, and papaya. Living here in New Hampshire, it's a whole lot simpler to buy a couple of cans of tropical fruit salad.

I save some of the juice and stir in coconut extract before adding it to the filling. And then I top the pie with a coconut crumb crust. If you can't afford to get away this winter on a tropical vacation, throw a tropics getaway party—complete with Hawaiian shirts, leis, and margaritas—and serve this pie for dessert.

1 RECIPE BEST BUTTER PIE PASTRY
(PAGE 8) OR FLAKY CREAM CHEESE
PASTRY (PAGE 14), REFRIGERATED

FILLING:

5 CUPS PEELED, CORED, AND SLICED
APPLES

TWO 15-OUNCE CANS TROPICAL FRUIT
SALAD (ABOUT 3 CUPS)

⅓ CUP SUGAR

2½ TABLESPOONS CORNSTARCH

½ TEASPOON PURE COCONUT EXTRACT

1 TABLESPOON FRESH LIME JUICE

COCONUT CRUMB TOPPING:

1 CUP ALL-PURPOSE FLOUR

⅔ CUP SUGAR

¼ TEASPOON SALT

½ CUP SWEETENED FLAKED COCONUT

6 TABLESPOONS (¾ STICK) COLD UNSALTED
BUTTER, CUT INTO ¼-INCH PIECES

1 TABLESPOON MILK OR LIGHT CREAM

1. If you haven't already, prepare the pastry and refrigerate it until firm enough to roll, about 1 hour.

2. On a sheet of lightly floured waxed paper, roll the pastry into a 13½-inch circle with a floured rolling pin. Invert the pastry over a 9-inch deep-dish pie pan. Center it, then peel off the paper. Gently tuck the pastry into the pan, without stretching it, and sculpt the overhang into an upstanding ridge. Place the pie shell in the freezer for at least 30 minutes.

3. To make the filling, put the apples in a large mixing bowl. Drain the fruit salad, reserving ⅓ cup of the juice in a small mixing bowl. Add the fruit to the apples. In another small mixing bowl, mix together the sugar and cornstarch. Add this mixture to the fruit and toss well. Stir the coconut extract and lime juice into the reserved tropical fruit juice. Pour this over the fruit and mix well. Preheat the oven to 400 degrees.

4. When the oven is heated, turn the filling into the frozen pie shell. Smooth the top of the filling with your hands to even it. Put the pie directly on the center oven rack and bake for 35 minutes.

5. While the pie bakes, make the coconut crumb topping. Put the flour, sugar, salt, and coconut in a food processor and pulse several times to mix. Remove the lid and scatter the butter pieces over the dry ingredients. Pulse the machine repeatedly, until the mixture resembles fine crumbs. Add the milk and pulse again. Transfer the mixture to a large mixing bowl and rub it between your fingers to make large, buttery crumbs. Refrigerate.

6. After 35 minutes, remove the pie from the oven and place it on a large, dark baking sheet covered with aluminum foil. Reduce the oven temperature to 375 degrees. Carefully dump the crumbs in the center of the pie, spreading them evenly over the entire surface with your hands. Press the crumbs down gently. Put the pie on the baking sheet back in the oven and bake until the juices bubble thickly around the edge, 35 to 40 minutes longer. Loosely cover the pie with tented aluminum foil during the last 15 minutes of baking if the topping is getting too dark.

7. Transfer the pie to a cooling rack and let cool for at least 1 hour before slicing.

Makes 8 to 10 servings

Apple Pie Frangipane

If you like to bake, or at least peruse baking books, you've no doubt run across recipes for something called pear tart frangipane—a tart of poached pear halves with a cake-like almond topping baked around them. I've made various versions of this tart over the years, and if the recipes tend to be a bit involved, the result is always spectacularly good. In fact, the idea is no less wonderful when applied to apple pie. Unlike the pear tart, I don't poach the apples in this version, which saves a good deal of time. I simply cut them into

chunks—chunks, as opposed to slices, to get a properly dense layer of fruit—and bake the fruit for 45 minutes. Then I cover the fruit with the almond topping, which is made right in the food processor, and bake for 20 minutes more.

I play up the almond theme here with a couple of tablespoons of amaretto mixed into the apples and another tablespoon blended into the topping. My preferred way to eat this is slightly warm, with vanilla ice cream.

1 RECIPE BEST BUTTER PIE PASTRY
(PAGE 8), REFRIGERATED

FILLING:

4 GOLDEN DELICIOUS APPLES, PEELED,
QUARTERED, AND CORED

⅓ CUP SUGAR

2 TABLESPOONS AMARETTO

1 TABLESPOON FRESH LEMON JUICE

1½ TABLESPOONS ALL-PURPOSE FLOUR

ALMOND CAKE TOPPING:

1 CUP RAW WHOLE ALMONDS WITH SKINS
ON

½ CUP SUGAR

3 TABLESPOONS ALL-PURPOSE FLOUR

2 TABLESPOONS SWEETENED OR
UNSWEETENED FLAKED COCONUT

1 TEASPOON BAKING POWDER

¼ TEASPOON SALT

¼ CUP (½ STICK) UNSALTED BUTTER,
SOFTENED

2 LARGE EGGS

1 TABLESPOON AMARETTO

1 TEASPOON PURE VANILLA EXTRACT

1. If you haven't already, prepare the pastry and refrigerate it until firm enough to roll, about 1 hour.

2. On a sheet of lightly floured waxed paper, roll the pastry into a 13½-inch circle with a floured rolling pin. Invert the pastry over a 9-inch deep-dish pie pan. Center it, then peel off the paper. Gently tuck the pastry into the pan, without stretching it, and sculpt the overhang into an upstanding ridge. Put the pie shell in the freezer for at least 30 minutes.

3. To make the filling, cut the apple quarters crosswise into thin slices. Combine in a large mixing bowl with the sugar, amaretto, and lemon juice. Set aside for 10 minutes. Preheat the oven to 400 degrees.

4. Shake the flour over the fruit and mix well. Turn the filling into the frozen pie shell, smoothing the top of the fruit with your hands. Place the pie directly on the center oven rack and bake for 30 minutes. Reduce the oven temperature to 375 degrees, cover the pie loosely with tented aluminum foil, and bake for another 15 minutes.

5. After you cover the pie, make the topping. Put the almonds, sugar, flour, coconut, baking powder, and salt in a food processor. Pulse the machine repeatedly, until the nuts are very finely ground, almost powdery. Add the remaining topping ingredients and pulse again, several times, until the mixture is evenly blended, scraping down the side of the bowl with a rubber spatula.

6. When the 15 minutes have elapsed, remove the pie from the oven. Spoon the topping evenly over the fruit, spreading it with the back of the spoon to smooth it. Put the pie back in the oven and bake until the topping is cooked through and dark golden brown, about 20 minutes more.

7. Remove the pie from the oven and place on a cooling rack. Slice and serve while the pie is still warm, if possible.

Makes 8 servings

Not-Quite-a-Mile-High Apple Ginger Pie

My first encounter with a mile-high pie was when I worked at a small bakery in New Jersey, before moving to New Hampshire. The fellow I worked for made more apple pies in a single evening than I ever imagined possible. He would have four or five high school girls come after school and do nothing but peel, core, and slice apples on a couple of those hand-cranked machines. They would fill several plastic garbage cans with the slices, then the baker would add massive quantities of brown sugar, cinnamon, and other essentials. Finally, he'd all but shovel the filling into the pie shells—great mountains of slices teetering from impossible heights and cascading down onto the extra-large baking sheets he baked them on. It was quite a spectacle.

Those pies, like this one, while starting out a mile high, inevitably ended up only about half a mile high—because, of course, apples will cook down and compact quite a bit. Just know that if you really want to impress someone with this baby, you might want to have him there as you're assembling it. Not that the finished pie is a letdown. On the contrary, it's quite tall and mounded, as apple pies go, and incredibly delicious and crowd-pleasing. You'll notice that it has a crumb topping—I don't recommend a pastry top, for reasons I've already mentioned and because of the extended baking time, which would overcook the crust. I like Granny Smith apples here, for their juiciness, but any kind will do.

1 RECIPE BEST BUTTER PIE PASTRY
(PAGE 8), REFRIGERATED

FILLING:

16 CUPS PEELED, CORED, AND SLICED
APPLES (10 TO 12 APPLES)

¾ CUP GRANULATED SUGAR

¼ CUP FRESH LEMON JUICE

⅓ CUP ALL-PURPOSE FLOUR

½ CUP GINGER PRESERVES

CRUMB TOPPING:

1 CUP ALL-PURPOSE FLOUR

¾ CUP OLD-FASHIONED ROLLED OATS (NOT
INSTANT)

¾ CUP FIRMLY PACKED LIGHT BROWN SUGAR

½ CUP WALNUT HALVES OR PIECES

¼ TEASPOON SALT

10 TABLESPOONS (1¼ STICKS) COLD
UNSALTED BUTTER, CUT INTO ¼-INCH
PIECES

1. If you haven't already, prepare the pastry and refrigerate it until firm enough to roll, about 1 hour.

2. On a sheet of lightly floured waxed paper, roll the pastry into a 13½-inch circle with a floured rolling pin. Invert the pastry over a 9-inch deep-dish pie pan. Center it, then peel off the paper. Gently tuck the pastry into the pan, without stretching it, and sculpt the overhang into an upstanding ridge. Place the pie shell in the freezer for at least 30 minutes.

3. To make the filling, combine the apples—you'll need an extra-large mixing bowl for this, or you can use a stockpot if you don't have a large enough bowl—granulated sugar, and lemon juice. Set aside for 10 minutes. Preheat the oven to 400 degrees.

4. Shake the flour over the apples and toss well to mix. Stir in the ginger preserves. Put the frozen pie shell on a large, dark baking sheet covered with aluminum foil. Transfer the apple filling and all the juices to the shell. I find it easiest just to lift them in with my hands, smooth the top, and pour on the juices. Put the pie on the baking sheet on one of the lower oven racks—you'll need the headspace—and bake for 45 minutes. Reduce the oven temperature to 375 degrees and bake for another 15 minutes.

5. During those last 15 minutes, make the topping. Put the flour, oats, brown sugar, walnuts, and salt in a food processor and pulse 6 or 7 times to chop the nuts well. Remove the lid and scatter the butter pieces over the dry mixture. Pulse the machine repeatedly, until the mixture resembles coarse crumbs. Dump the mixture into a large mixing bowl and gently rub it between your fingers to make large, buttery crumbs. Refrigerate.

6. When the 15 minutes have elapsed, remove the pie from the oven. Carefully dump the crumbs in the center of the pie, spreading them evenly over the surface with your hands. Tamp them down gently. Put the pie on the baking sheet back in the oven and bake for an additional 45 minutes. Loosely cover the pie with tented aluminum foil during the last 15 to 20 minutes if the topping starts to get too brown. Near the end of the baking, check the apples with a skewer (see page 69), if you have one, to see if the apples are tender.

7. Transfer the pie to a cooling rack and let cool for at least 2 hours before slicing.

Makes 8 to 10 servings

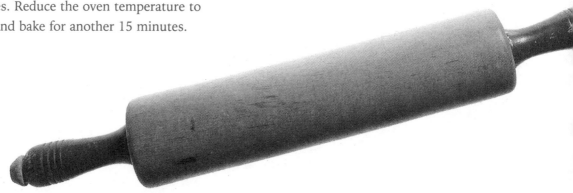

Wine Country Green Grape and Apple Pie

There I was one bleak New Hampshire winter afternoon, wondering what sort of apple pie I might make if I lived in California wine country—that being the place I would have gladly teleported myself to had it not been for an otherwise full schedule of shoveling snow, nursing the flu, and writing ridiculously large checks for heating oil. As fortune would have it, the refrigerator was stocked with a couple of useful items for creating just such a theme pie: green grapes and an open bottle of white wine, which I promptly combined with some sliced apples and sugar, tucked into a crust, and slid into the oven. Since the color scheme was very light, I decided to top the pie with what I call a blond streusel—blond because, unlike many of my crumb toppings, it has no brown sugar, cinnamon, or nuts: nothing that would darken what I saw as my sunny California pie. Since then, I've made this on other gloomy winter days, and it never fails to lift my spirits. The winy flavor of the pie is perfect with a soft-flavored ice cream, such as peach or strawberry.

1 RECIPE BEST BUTTER PIE PASTRY
(PAGE 8), REFRIGERATED

FILLING:

6 CUPS PEELED, CORED, AND SLICED
APPLES

2 CUPS SEEDLESS GREEN GRAPES CUT INTO
HALVES

¼ CUP CHARDONNAY, PINOT GRIGIO, OR
OTHER WHITE WINE

½ CUP PLUS 2 TABLESPOONS SUGAR

2 TABLESPOONS CORNSTARCH

BLOND STREUSEL TOPPING:

1 CUP ALL-PURPOSE FLOUR

⅔ CUP SUGAR

¼ TEASPOON SALT

6 TABLESPOONS (¾ STICK) COLD UNSALTED
BUTTER, CUT INTO ¼-INCH PIECES

1 TABLESPOON MILK OR LIGHT CREAM

1. If you haven't already, prepare the pastry and refrigerate it until firm enough to roll, about 1 hour.

2. On a sheet of lightly floured waxed paper, roll the pastry into a 13½-inch circle with a floured rolling pin. Invert the pastry over a 9-inch deep-dish pie pan. Center it, then peel off the paper. Gently tuck the pastry into the pan, without stretching it, and sculpt the overhang into an upstanding ridge. Place the pie shell in the freezer for at least 30 minutes. Preheat the oven to 400 degrees.

3. To make the filling, combine the apples, grapes, wine, and ½ cup of the sugar in a large mixing bowl; toss well to mix. Set aside for 10 minutes.

4. In a small mixing bowl, mix the remaining 2 tablespoons sugar with the cornstarch. Sprinkle over the filling and toss well to mix. Turn the filling into the frozen pie shell, smoothing the surface with your hands. Place the pie directly on the center oven rack and bake for 35 minutes.

5. While the pie bakes, make the streusel topping. Combine the flour, sugar, and salt in a food processor. Remove the lid and scatter the butter pieces over the dry ingredients. Pulse the machine repeatedly, until the mixture resembles fine crumbs. Add the milk and pulse again. Dump the mixture into a large mixing bowl and gently rub it between your fingers to make large, buttery crumbs. Refrigerate.

6. After 35 minutes, remove the pie from the oven and place it on a large, dark baking sheet covered with aluminum foil. Reduce the oven temperature to 375 degrees. Carefully dump the crumbs in the center of the pie, spreading them evenly over the surface with your hands. Press down gently to compact them. Put the pie on the baking sheet back in the oven and bake until the juices bubble thickly around the edge, 35 to 40 minutes. Loosely cover the pie with tented aluminum foil during the last 15 minutes, if necessary, to prevent the streusel from getting too brown.

7. Transfer the pie to a cooling rack and let cool for at least 1 hour before serving.

Makes 8 to 10 servings

Tipsy Apple and Dried Cranberry Pie with Grand Marnier

Perhaps you don't think of apple pie when you think of holiday desserts, but I do, and I'll bet I'm not the only New Englander who does. How does one give apple pie a festive profile? Dried cranberries, for one thing—they're just right for the season. You can use dried cranberries from the health food store, but Craisins—sweetened dried cranberries you can find in any super-market—are generally less expensive and perfect for the job. Before adding them to the filling, I like to soak them in Grand Marnier, which goes into the filling, too; that's where the "tipsy" part of the recipe title comes in. That said, this isn't really a kid's apple pie. But adults will love it, and it's guaranteed to be a hit at any holiday party.

1 RECIPE ALL-AMERICAN DOUBLE CRUST (PAGE 2), REFRIGERATED

FILLING:

½ CUP DRIED CRANBERRIES

⅓ CUP GRAND MARNIER OR OTHER ORANGE LIQUEUR

8 TO 9 CUPS PEELED, CORED, AND SLICED APPLES

½ CUP SUGAR

GRATED ZEST OF 1 ORANGE

JUICE OF 1 LEMON

¼ CUP ALL-PURPOSE FLOUR

⅛ TEASPOON GROUND CLOVES

GLAZE:

MILK

SUGAR

1. If you haven't already, prepare the pastry and refrigerate it until firm enough to roll, about 1 hour. Put the dried cranberries in a small mixing bowl and add the Grand Marnier. Set aside to soak.

2. On a sheet of lightly floured waxed paper, roll the larger piece of pastry into a 13½-inch circle with a floured rolling pin. Invert the pastry over a 9-inch deep-dish pie pan. Center it, then peel off the paper. Gently tuck the pastry into the pan, without stretching it, and let the edge of the pastry drape over the side of the pan. Refrigerate for at least 15 minutes. Preheat the oven to 400 degrees.

3. To make the filling, mix the apples, sugar, orange zest, and lemon juice in a large mixing bowl. Mix in the cranberries and Grand Marnier. Sprinkle the flour and cloves over the filling and mix well. Turn the filling into the refrigerated pie shell and smooth the top with your hands to even it out.

4. On another sheet of lightly floured waxed paper, roll the top pastry into an 11½-inch circle. Lightly moisten the edge of the pie shell with a wet fingertip or pastry brush. Invert the top pastry over the filling, center it, and peel off the paper. Press the top and bottom pastries together along the dampened edge. Trim the pastry with scissors or a paring knife, leaving an even ½-inch overhang all around, then sculpt the overhang into an upstanding ridge. Poke several steam vents in the top of the pie with a fork or paring knife; put a couple of the vents near the edge of the crust, so you can check the juices there later. Brush the top of the pie with a little milk and sprinkle lightly with sugar.

5. Put the pie directly on the center oven rack and bake for 30 minutes. Remove the pie from the oven and place on a large, dark baking sheet covered with aluminum foil. Reduce the oven temperature to 375 degrees. Put the pie on the baking sheet back in the oven and bake until any juices—visible at the steam vents— bubble thickly, another 30 to 40 minutes.

6. Transfer the pie to a cooling rack and let cool for at least 1 hour before slicing.

Makes 8 to 10 servings

CHAPTER 6

The Cream of the Crop

Even when you take the time to bake an apple pie from scratch—using the crispest apples, the best butter, and fragrant brown sugar and cinnamon—some people just aren't satisfied unless you serve that pie with ice cream or whipped cream. I know because I'm one of those people. Of course, there are exceptions to this state of affairs, the most notable being when an apple pie has something creamy baked right into it.

Here's a chapter devoted to just such a group of pies. It's a diverse lineup, including a couple of apple pies that taste like cheesecake; another pie, inspired by the Shakers, has a rose water custard that's poured over the apples and baked just until set; and still another is an old-fashioned farm-style buttermilk pie in which the custard is baked around pan-fried apple rings. There are similarities among these pies, but the most notable thing they have in common is how well each of the various custards and creams complements the apples in question.

Although these pies are no more difficult to bake than others, one cautionary note is worth mentioning: anytime you're cooking a custard, either on the stovetop or in the oven, it pays to be watchful. You never want to cook a custard too long or at too high a temperature because overcooked custard gets tough, often separates,

and loses most of its luxuriously silky charm. So pay careful attention to baking times and procedures with all of these pies. And if you err in the baking, err on the side of undercooking rather than overcooking.

These are decidedly rich pies, and most hark back to a time when dairy products were used more liberally than they are today. In short, they're not your everyday apple pies. But they are a real treat when you want your cream *in* your apple pie instead of on the side.

Marlborough Pie

According to Judith Jones, the esteemed cookbook editor at Knopf and co-author—with her late husband, Evan—of *The L.L. Bean Book of* New *New England Cookery* (Random House, 1987), Marlborough pie is an old British recipe that's also sometimes known in New England as Deerfield pie. I've come across a number of such recipes in cookbooks, and, with allowance for variations, this is always an apple custard pie and was traditionally served for Thanksgiving. The apples are sometimes sliced very thinly, but more often than not they're grated—as they are here—then cooked on the stovetop before going into the pie filling. This last step, the cooking, is an important one, because you essentially end up with very fine applesauce, which yields a pie with a fine custard filling with just a bit of apple texture. (I've also tried this with uncooked apples and the result wasn't quite the same.) A favorite apple here is the McIntosh or Paula Red, both of which will cook up good and soft. You'll note that I use Grand Marnier or Triple Sec to cook the apples. This isn't traditional; brandy, applejack, or another spirit is more common. I simply like the orange flavoring the other two impart. You can eat this warm, but I much prefer it chilled. Also, this is not one of those pies with an excess of filling, so it will fit nicely into a store-bought frozen 9-inch deep-dish pie shell.

1 RECIPE BEST BUTTER PIE PASTRY
(PAGE 8), REFRIGERATED

FILLING:

4 LARGE APPLES (SEE HEADNOTE), PEELED

2 TABLESPOONS UNSALTED BUTTER

⅓ CUP GRAND MARNIER, TRIPLE SEC, OR
BRANDY

¼ CUP PLUS ⅓ CUP SUGAR

1 CUP HEAVY CREAM

3 LARGE EGGS

½ TEASPOON PURE VANILLA EXTRACT

PINCH OF GROUND NUTMEG

1. If you haven't already, prepare the pastry and refrigerate it until firm enough to roll, about 1 hour.

2. On a sheet of lightly floured waxed paper, roll the pastry into a 13½-inch circle with a floured rolling pin. Invert the pastry over a 9-inch deep-dish pie pan. Center it, then peel off the paper. Gently tuck the pastry into the pan, without stretching it, and sculpt the edge into an upstanding ridge. Place the pie shell in the freezer for at least 30 minutes, then fully prebake it according to the instructions on page 19. Let cool partially on a wire rack as you put together the filling. Preheat the oven to 350 degrees.

3. To make the filling, grate the apples down to the core on the large holes of a box-style grater. Melt the butter in a large, nonreactive sauté pan—nonstick is handy here—and add the apples, Grand Marnier, and ¼ cup of the sugar. Bring the apple mixture to a boil, stirring often, then reduce the heat slightly and continue to simmer rapidly until the apples are very soft and most of the liquid has evaporated, about 10 minutes. Remove from the heat.

4. Combine the heavy cream and remaining ⅓ cup sugar in a small saucepan, stirring over medium heat just until the sugar melts. Remove from the heat and let cool briefly. Meanwhile, whisk the eggs in a large mixing bowl until foamy. Blend in the warm cream, about one-third at a time, then blend in the vanilla, nutmeg, and cooked apples, stirring until smooth.

5. Slowly pour the filling into the baked pie shell. Smooth the filling with a fork, then place the pie directly on the center oven rack and bake for about 35 minutes. When the pie is done, the center will be set—not runny—and the pie will probably puff slightly. The custard isn't likely to brown, so don't wait for that, or you may overcook the filling.

6. Transfer the pie to a rack and let cool. Eat warm or wait until thoroughly cooled, then cover loosely with waxed paper and refrigerate overnight before slicing. Take out of the refrigerator 15 to 20 minutes before serving it to soften the crust, which is quite firm when cold.

Makes 8 to 10 servings

MY PASTRY BRUSH

You can make pie without one, but a pastry brush fills a niche that's almost impossible to accommodate with any other tool: brushing flour off your pie pastry. Seems like a minor thing, getting rid of excess flour, but it really isn't. If you fail to brush the excess flour from the edge of your pastry, where it generally builds up, you'll have a difficult time getting your top and bottom pastries to stick together. Which, in turn, will leave a void where juices may bubble out.

One thing to watch: a damp pastry brush doesn't do the best job of removing flour because, as you brush, the flour clumps up in the hairs. That's why I generally dampen the edge of the pie shell with my finger and keep my pastry brush dry. The other alternative is to have 2 brushes, one for wet work and one for dry. My pastry brush, which I have had for years, is about 1½ inches wide—a good size for a variety of baking jobs.

Farm-Style Buttermilk Pie with Fried Apple Rings

I've never actually seen a recipe like this in an old cookbook, but it's the sort of pie one imagines might have been served on farms of an earlier day, when buttermilk was the everyday byproduct of churning butter and fried apples were served with great country breakfasts or for dinner with ham. First, we fry up thick apple rings—and you really must cook them until they're tender because they won't get any softer once they're surrounded by the buttermilk custard. The rings go into a prebaked pie shell, but you'll find that once you pour on the custard, they will rise to the top of the pie, where they will stay and form an attractive circle pattern. In fact, if they don't rise, just nudge them a little with a fork so that they float to the surface. The pie is baked until the custard is set, then cooled and refrigerated before serving. I suppose you could serve it warm, but I think the custard tastes so much better when it's cold.

1 RECIPE BEST BUTTER PIE PASTRY
(PAGE 8), REFRIGERATED

FILLING:

2 GOLDEN DELICIOUS APPLES

1½ TABLESPOONS UNSALTED BUTTER

2 TABLESPOONS GRANULATED SUGAR

1 CUP FIRMLY PACKED LIGHT BROWN SUGAR

3 TABLESPOONS ALL-PURPOSE FLOUR

3 LARGE EGGS PLUS 1 LARGE EGG YOLK

1 TEASPOON PURE VANILLA EXTRACT

1½ CUPS BUTTERMILK

3 TABLESPOONS UNSALTED BUTTER,
MELTED AND COOLED

1. If you haven't already, prepare the pastry and refrigerate it until firm enough to roll, about 1 hour.

2. On a sheet of lightly floured waxed paper, roll the pastry into a 13½-inch circle with a floured rolling pin. Invert the pastry over a 9-inch deep-dish pie pan. Center it, then peel off the paper. Gently tuck the pastry into the pan, without stretching it, and sculpt the edge into an upstanding ridge. Place the pie shell in the freezer for at least 30 minutes, then fully prebake it according to the instructions on page 19. Let cool on a wire rack as you put together the filling. Preheat the oven to 350 degrees.

3. As the pie shell cools, prepare the filling. Leaving the skins on, cut the apples into crosswise slices about ¾ inch thick. Core each slice and select the 6 best-looking slices. Melt the 1½ tablespoons butter in a large skillet and add the apple slices, sprinkling 1 tablespoon of the granulated sugar over them. Fry over medium heat for about 4 minutes, then flip the slices and fry them on the other side for another few minutes, until nearly tender. Sprinkle the remaining 1 tablespoon granulated sugar over the apples and flip once more. Cook for another minute or two, until the slices are tender. Transfer the slices to a plate.

4. Meanwhile, combine the brown sugar and flour in the bowl of a food processor. Pulse to mix. Add the eggs and yolk and the vanilla. Process until smooth. Add the buttermilk and melted butter and process just until blended.

5. Put one apple ring in the center of the prebaked pie shell and arrange the others around it. Very slowly pour the buttermilk custard over the apples. If the slices don't rise, lift them up with a fork. Put the pie directly on the center oven rack and bake for about 45 minutes. To check for doneness, give the pie pan a poke. The custard shouldn't move in waves, but instead should seem set in the center; don't overbake.

6. Transfer the pie to a cooling rack and let cool thoroughly. Cover with plastic wrap and refrigerate for at least several hours before serving.

Makes 8 to 10 servings

MARION CUNNINGHAM, THE FANNIE FARMER BAKER, ON APPLE PIE

Marion Cunningham, well-known food authority and author of, among other books, *The Fannie Farmer Baking Book* (Random House, 1996), had this to say in a conversation about apple pie.

"If we're talking about supermarket apples—and let's face it, that's where most of us buy them—I like the flavor and juiciness of both the Fuji apple and Gravenstein. I think they hold up better than some when they're baked in a pie. In general, though, I don't think apples are as juicy as they used to be because so many of them spend too much time in cold storage. They aren't as bad as the stone fruits we get today, however. I feel sorry for the newest generations of cooks. Most of them have never tasted a good fresh peach or plum or nectarine. As for the top, I prefer a crumb crust to a top crust."

Cottage Cheese–Cheesecake Apple Pie

Yet another custard apple pie, this one in the manner of some Italian-style cheesecakes I've made and tasted over the years. Those tend to use ricotta cheese; this one uses cottage cheese, which I think yields a smoother and more pleasantly tangy result. This pie has a buttery pastry, a layer of sautéed apples, and a top layer of citrus-flavored cottage cheese custard, shot throughout with dried currants. It needs no accompaniment other than good strong coffee and makes a great dessert with any lighter Italian meal. If you want to make this using a frozen pastry shell, use two sliced apples instead of three.

1 RECIPE BEST BUTTER PIE PASTRY
   (PAGE 8), REFRIGERATED

FILLING:

½ CUP DRIED CURRANTS

1½ TABLESPOONS GRAND MARNIER OR
   OTHER ORANGE LIQUEUR

2 TABLESPOONS UNSALTED BUTTER

3 GOLDEN DELICIOUS OR OTHER FIRM-
   TEXTURED COOKING APPLES, PEELED,
   CORED, AND SLICED

¼ CUP PLUS ⅓ CUP SUGAR

1½ CUPS SMALL OR REGULAR CURD
   COTTAGE CHEESE

2 LARGE EGGS

½ TEASPOON PURE VANILLA EXTRACT

GRATED ZEST OF 1 LEMON

1½ TABLESPOONS ALL-PURPOSE FLOUR

1. If you haven't already, prepare the pastry and refrigerate it until firm enough to roll, about 1 hour.

2. On a sheet of lightly floured waxed paper, roll the pastry into a 13½-inch circle with a floured rolling pin. Invert the pastry over a 9-inch deep-dish pie pan. Center it, then peel off the paper. Gently tuck the pastry into the pan, without stretching it, and sculpt the edge into an upstanding ridge. Place the pie shell in the freezer for at least 30 minutes, then fully prebake it according to the instructions on page 19. Let cool partially on a wire rack as you put together the filling. Preheat the oven to 350 degrees.

3. Combine the currants and Grand Marnier in a small mixing bowl; mix well. Set aside.

4. Melt the butter in a large, preferably non-stick sauté pan. Stir in the apples and ¼ cup of the sugar and cook over medium heat, stirring often, until the apples are tender but not mushy, 8 to 10 minutes. Remove from the heat and let the apples cool somewhat.

5. While the apples are cooling, put the remaining ⅓ cup sugar, the cottage cheese, eggs, vanilla, lemon zest, and flour in a food processor and process until very smooth, as much as 30 to 45 seconds. Add the currants and liqueur and pulse once or twice just to blend them in.

6. Scrape the apples into the crust and smooth them with a fork. Remove the processor blade from the bowl, then slowly pour the custard over the apples, jiggling the pie so the custard settles.

7. Put the pie directly on the center oven rack and bake until the custard is set in the center, 35 to 40 minutes. It should puff only a little, and the top should not develop fissures or turn brown.

8. Transfer the pie to a cooling rack and let cool thoroughly. Cover the top with a sheet of waxed paper and refrigerate for at least several hours before serving. Remove the pie from the refrigerator about 15 minutes before you plan to slice it.

Makes 10 servings

PICKS AND PIE PANS

Over the years, I've used and collected quite an array of pie pans—metal, glass, ceramic, and, naturally, the disposable aluminum kind. Some I've bought for their beauty, a few because they are collectible, and others because I found them at yard sales and couldn't resist a bargain.

Each of my pans has its charms, but if I had to choose a single pan for the rest of my pie-making days, it would without question be my standard 9-inch deep-dish Pyrex pie pan. Or perhaps I should say pans; I have five or six of them, and they're the ones I reach for time and again when I'm making apple and most other fruit pies. Indeed, it's the pan I used almost exclusively—for the sake of standardization—for testing the recipes in this book.

How can I account for this loyalty? Cost, for one. If you shop around, you can probably find these deep-dish pans for under $5 at a discount store or outlet. If I drop off a pie at a friend's house and forget to pick up the pan, I'm not out $35. Pyrex pans also are durable, almost indestructible; I can't remember ever breaking one. And they're reasonably attractive, too, with a fluted upper rim. Besides basic clear glass, they're also available in light blue and a pretty pink shade. They won't rust, either. I used to collect those old-fashioned stamped metal pans, but inevitably—usually when they were left in the dish drainer—a few drops of water would sit in them, and they'd get rust spots. And life is just too short to deal with rust.

Almond Custard Pie

Here's another custard pie I love, this one based on a type of tart one often sees in French cookbooks. We begin by cooking the apples—something I do with almost all of my custard pies since otherwise the apples will float to the surface and will not bake properly surrounded by all the custard. (Use an apple that will hold its shape when you sauté it—Golden Delicious or one of the other firm ones listed in A Pie Maker's Guide to Apple Varieties, page xv.) While the apples cool, I make an almond custard flavored with both almond extract and ground almonds. The apples go into the prebaked pastry first, the custard is poured over the top, and the pie is baked until the custard is firm.

This is not the pie to make if you're looking for something to turn out in a snap, but it's a great special occasion pie, especially for nut lovers and around the holidays.

1 RECIPE BEST BUTTER PIE PASTRY
   (PAGE 8), REFRIGERATED

FILLING:

2 TABLESPOONS UNSALTED BUTTER

4 LARGE FIRM-TEXTURED APPLES (SEE
   HEADNOTE), PEELED, CORED, AND CUT
   INTO 1-INCH CHUNKS

2 TABLESPOONS RUM OR BRANDY

¾ CUP SUGAR

1 CUP HEAVY CREAM

¼ CUP MILK

3 LARGE EGGS

½ TEASPOON PURE ALMOND EXTRACT

¾ CUP RAW WHOLE ALMONDS, FINELY
   GROUND IN THE FOOD PROCESSOR

1. If you haven't already, prepare the pastry and refrigerate it until firm enough to roll, about 1 hour.

2. On a sheet of lightly floured waxed paper, roll the pastry into a 13½-inch circle with a floured rolling pin. Invert the pastry over a 9-inch deep-dish pie pan. Center it, then peel off the paper. Gently tuck the pastry into the pan, without stretching it, and sculpt the edge into an upstanding ridge. Place the pie shell in the freezer for at least 30 minutes, then partially prebake it according to the instructions on page 19. Let cool partially on a wire rack as you put together the filling. Preheat the oven to 350 degrees.

3. Melt the butter in a large, preferably nonstick sauté pan. Stir in the apples, rum, and ¼ cup of the sugar. Bring to a boil, then reduce the heat slightly and simmer, stirring often, until the apples are tender but not mushy, 8 to 10 minutes. Remove the pan from the heat and let the apples cool slightly while you prepare the custard.

4. Blend the heavy cream, milk, and remaining ½ cup sugar in a small saucepan. Heat gently, stirring, just until the sugar melts. Remove from the heat. In a medium-size mixing bowl, whisk the eggs until foamy, then blend in the hot cream mixture about one third at a time. Blend in the almond extract and ground almonds.

5. Spoon the apples into the prebaked pie shell, then slowly pour the almond custard over them, jiggling the pie to settle the custard. Place the pie directly on the center oven rack and bake until the top of the pie is a light golden brown and the custard is set, 40 to 45 minutes.

6. Transfer the pie to a cooling rack and let cool thoroughly before slicing. Or cover the cooled pie with a sheet of waxed paper or plastic wrap and refrigerate overnight before slicing.

Makes 8 to 10 servings

HOLY PIE COUNCIL!

Bet you didn't know there was something called the American Pie Council. Well, there is, and—naturally—the organization even has its own Web site, www.piecouncil.org. Based in Lake Forest, Illinois, this nonprofit outfit is "devoted to pie-making, pie-eating, pie-selling, and the preservation of our fading pie heritage." The council publishes its own newsletter, *Pie Times,* "the sole pie-focused publication available," and sponsors National Pie Day (January 23) and the Great American Pie Festival, the first of which was held in Celebration, Florida, in February 2002.

Linda Hoskins, the American Pie Council's director, told me that—not surprisingly—apple pie is America's favorite pie, adding that one survey from a couple of years back found that 31 percent of Americans, when asked what their favorite comfort dessert was, said apple pie à la mode. And just in case you're wondering, we use 23 million pounds of apples a year in this country to make our apple pies.

Hoskins, who doesn't bake pies herself, is partial to tangy Key lime pie. But, she says, if she had to eat one kind of pie every day, it would indeed be crumb-topped apple pie.

Apple Cheesecake Pie

I used to have a little sideline selling cheesecakes to local restaurants, and I learned an awful lot about cheesecake. One thing I learned is that cheesecake must be one of America's favorite desserts, and I believe surveys support me on this. I sold mocha cheesecakes with bits of brownie; amaretto cheesecakes with almond crusts; cherry, blueberry, and cranberry cheesecakes. And they all sold like nobody's business. Which led me to believe that if I teamed up a cheesecake with an apple pie, I might be onto something good—and I believe I am. First I partially cook the apples in the crust, then I pour a vanilla cheesecake layer on and bake a little longer at a much lower heat—heat being the bane of a good cheesecake. Finally, I top it with sweetened sour cream once the pie has cooled somewhat. If you know someone who loves cheesecake and apple pie—and surely you must—this may end up being his or her idea of heaven.

1 RECIPE BEST BUTTER PIE PASTRY
(PAGE 8), REFRIGERATED

APPLE FILLING:

4 LARGE APPLES, PEELED, CORED, AND
THINLY SLICED

⅓ CUP SUGAR

2½ TABLESPOONS ALL-PURPOSE FLOUR

1 TABLESPOON FRESH LEMON JUICE

CHEESECAKE FILLING:

10 OUNCES CREAM CHEESE, SOFTENED
(DON'T USE LOWFAT OR NONFAT)

½ CUP SUGAR

2 LARGE EGGS, AT ROOM TEMPERATURE

⅓ CUP SOUR CREAM (DON'T USE LOWFAT OR
NONFAT)

½ TEASPOON PURE VANILLA EXTRACT

1 TEASPOON GRATED LEMON ZEST

SOUR CREAM TOPPING:

1 CUP SOUR CREAM (DON'T USE LOWFAT OR
NONFAT)

2 TABLESPOONS SUGAR

1. If you haven't already, prepare the pastry and refrigerate it until firm enough to roll, about 1 hour.

2. On a sheet of lightly floured waxed paper, roll the pastry into a 13½-inch circle with a floured rolling pin. Invert the pastry over a 9-inch deep-dish pie pan. Center it, then peel off the paper. Gently tuck the pastry down into the pan, without stretching it, and sculpt it into an upstanding ridge. Place the pie shell in the freezer for at least 30 minutes. Preheat the oven to 400 degrees.

3. To make the apple filling, mix the apples, sugar, flour, and lemon juice in a large mixing bowl. Scrape the filling into the pie shell and smooth it with your hands. Place the pie pan on a large, dark baking sheet covered with aluminum foil. Set the pie on the baking sheet on the center oven rack and bake for 30 minutes.

4. While the pie bakes, make the cheesecake filling. Using an electric mixer, in a large mixing bowl cream the cream cheese, gradually adding the sugar. Add the eggs one at a time, blending well but not overbeating; you don't want to beat too much air into the mixture. Scrape down the sides of the bowl as needed. Blend in the sour cream, vanilla, and lemon zest; set aside.

5. After 30 minutes, reduce the oven temperature to 325 degrees. Remove the baking sheet and pie from the oven. Slowly pour the cheesecake filling over the apples, spreading the mixture evenly with the back of a spoon. Put the pie on the baking sheet back in the oven and bake for about 25 minutes more. When the pie is done, the cheesecake layer will have puffed slightly but not too much.

6. Transfer the pie to a cooling rack and let cool for about 30 minutes, long enough for the top to settle down.

7. To make the sour cream topping, combine the sour cream and sugar in a small saucepan. Stirring over low heat, warm the mixture to only slightly more than body temperature, then immediately pour over the center of the pie, jiggling the pie so the sour cream creeps right up to the pastry. Put the pie back on the cooling rack and let cool to room temperature.

8. Loosely cover the cooled pie with tented aluminum foil, then refrigerate for at least 4 hours, preferably longer, before slicing.

Makes 8 to 10 servings

Sour Cream Apple Crumb Pie

It's not unusual to see this kind of apple pie in recipe collections from states where dairy farming is serious business. What you have here is a more or less traditional foundation of an apple pie—apples, sugar, spices—baked to a turn, then covered with a generous helping of lightly sweetened sour cream and a graham cracker topping. Once those have been added, the pie goes back in the oven for a few minutes, just long enough for the sour cream to settle into the upper crevices of the pie and the crumbs to brown. The result is really quite attractive and delicious. Because of the sour cream, it's one of those pies I much prefer cold. A couple of my kids put this pie on their short list of favorites in this book.

1 RECIPE BEST BUTTER PIE PASTRY (PAGE 8), REFRIGERATED

FILLING:

8 CUPS PEELED, CORED, AND SLICED APPLES

½ CUP SUGAR

GRATED ZEST OF 1 LEMON

¼ TEASPOON GROUND CINNAMON

¼ TEASPOON GROUND CARDAMOM

3 TABLESPOONS ALL-PURPOSE FLOUR

SOUR CREAM TOPPING:

1¼ CUPS SOUR CREAM (DON'T USE LOWFAT OR NONFAT)

¼ CUP SUGAR

½ TEASPOON PURE VANILLA EXTRACT

GRAHAM CRACKER TOPPING:

7 WHOLE GRAHAM CRACKERS

2 TABLESPOONS SUGAR

¼ TEASPOON GROUND CINNAMON

3 TABLESPOONS UNSALTED BUTTER, MELTED

1. If you haven't already, prepare the pastry and refrigerate it until firm enough to roll, about 1 hour.

2. On a sheet of lightly floured waxed paper, roll the pastry into a 13½-inch circle with a floured rolling pin. Invert the pastry over a 9-inch deep-dish pie pan. Center it, then peel off the paper. Gently tuck the pastry down into the pan, without stretching it, and sculpt it into an upstanding ridge. Put the pie shell in the freezer for at least 30 minutes.

3. To make the filling, mix the apples, sugar, lemon zest, cinnamon, and cardamom in a large mixing bowl and set aside for 10 minutes. Preheat the oven to 400 degrees.

4. Sprinkle the flour over the apples and mix well. Turn the filling into the frozen pie shell. Put the pie on a large, dark baking sheet covered with aluminum foil and bake on the center oven rack for 30 minutes.

5. After 30 minutes, reduce the oven temperature to 375 degrees. Form a large sheet of foil into a shallow bowl shape and slide it over the pie. Bake for an additional 20 minutes.

6. Meanwhile, prepare both toppings. Whisk the sour cream topping ingredients together in a medium-size mixing bowl. Set aside. Put the graham crackers and sugar in a food processor and process into fine crumbs. Transfer to a small mixing bowl and stir in the cinnamon and melted butter. Stir the mixture with a fork, then rub it between your fingers to make a uniform mixture. Refrigerate.

7. After the pie has baked for the additional 20 minutes, reduce the oven temperature to 350 degrees. Take the pie out and evenly pour or spoon the sour cream topping over the pie, spreading it with the back of a spoon. Carefully dump the crumbs in the center of the pie, spreading them evenly over the surface with your hands. Put the pie on the baking sheet back in the oven and bake for 7 to 8 minutes but no longer. The crumb topping might take on a toasted hue, but don't let it darken.

8. Transfer the pie to a cooling rack. Let cool thoroughly, then loosely cover the pie with foil and refrigerate for at least several hours before slicing.

Makes 8 to 10 servings

Apple Rose Water–Custard Pie

This is yet another of my Shaker-inspired recipes. Here apples are baked in a crust and surrounded with a lovely rose water custard. There are a couple of ways to make an apple custard pie, though this is the most reliable in my opinion. In this version, the custard is poured over the apples, covered with foil—to protect the delicate custard from overbaking—and baked as an open-faced pie. I've also made essentially the same pie with a top crust, pouring the custard through a hole in the crust about midway through the baking. The problem is, you run the risk of adding too much custard, which then leaks out through a breach in the crust.

And, worst of all, you can't really tell when the custard has set—not a good thing since an underbaked custard will be runny and an overbaked one will be grainy. With the method described here, you can size up the situation easily because the custard is exposed and doneness is easy to gauge. Do make sure to sculpt the crust up a little higher than the rim of the pan, so the pie will hold as much custard as possible. (Any leftover custard can be baked in a cup.) The rose water, available at any health food store, gives the custard a wonderful floral tone, but you can omit it and add another teaspoon of vanilla.

1 RECIPE BEST BUTTER PIE PASTRY (PAGE 8), REFRIGERATED

APPLE FILLING:

4 LARGE APPLES, PEELED, CORED, AND CUT INTO LARGE CHUNKS

¼ CUP SUGAR

¼ TEASPOON GROUND NUTMEG

GRATED ZEST OF 1 ORANGE

2 TABLESPOONS ALL-PURPOSE FLOUR

ROSE WATER CUSTARD:

5 LARGE EGG YOLKS

¼ CUP SUGAR

1 ½ CUPS HEAVY CREAM

¼ CUP MILK

1 TEASPOON FOOD-GRADE ROSE WATER

½ TEASPOON PURE VANILLA EXTRACT

1. If you haven't already, prepare the pastry and refrigerate it until firm enough to roll, about 1 hour.

2. On a sheet of lightly floured waxed paper, roll the pastry into a 13½-inch circle with a floured rolling pin. Invert the pastry over a 9-inch deep-dish pie pan. Center it, then peel off the paper. Gently tuck the pastry down into the pan, without stretching it, and sculpt it into an upstanding ridge that rises about ¼ inch above the rim of the pan. Place the pie shell in the freezer for at least 30 minutes.

3. To make the apple filling, combine the apples, sugar, nutmeg, and orange zest in a large mixing bowl. Set aside for 10 minutes. Preheat the oven to 400 degrees.

4. Stir the flour into the apple mixture, then scrape the filling into the frozen pie shell, smoothing it with your hands. Place the pie directly on the center oven rack and bake for 30 minutes. After 25 minutes, reduce the oven temperature to 350 degrees.

5. Meanwhile, make the custard. Stir the egg yolks and sugar together in a medium-size mixing bowl. Heat the heavy cream and milk together nearly to a boil in a medium-size saucepan over medium heat. Remove from the heat, ladle a little of the hot cream into the yolks, and blend well. Add a little more hot cream and stir again. Add the tempered egg yolks back to the hot cream and mix well. Stir in the rose water and vanilla.

6. After 30 minutes, remove the pie from the oven. Carefully ladle the custard over the apples, adding enough so that it nearly reaches the top of the crust. Place the pie back in the oven and cover with a large sheet of tented aluminum foil. Bake the pie until the custard is set—jiggle the pie and poke it with a knife to check it—another 30 to 35 minutes. The custard should not turn brown or crack.

7. Transfer the pie to a cooling rack. Let cool thoroughly, then cover with a sheet of waxed paper or plastic wrap and refrigerate for at least several hours before serving.

Makes 8 to 10 servings

CHAPTER 7

Apple Pie Pure and Wholesome

I don't even try anymore to keep up with what's healthy for me and what isn't. The concept of healthy eating seems to be a moving target, and no sooner do you get a bead on the bull's-eye than the rules change. One day butter is bad for you, the next day butter is fine—it's margarine you have to watch out for. Then everyone stops talking about butter altogether; it's the antioxidants that really matter. So eat lots of kale. And fish. Next thing you know, we'll all be putting pulverized fish scales in our smoothies because of the fiber.

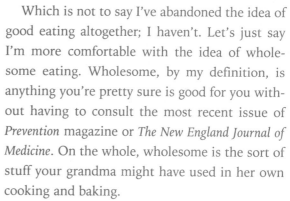

Which is not to say I've abandoned the idea of good eating altogether; I haven't. Let's just say I'm more comfortable with the idea of wholesome eating. Wholesome, by my definition, is anything you're pretty sure is good for you without having to consult the most recent issue of *Prevention* magazine or *The New England Journal of Medicine*. On the whole, wholesome is the sort of stuff your grandma might have used in her own cooking and baking.

That, by way of introducing this section on wholesome apple pies. Here you will find pies that aren't necessarily designed to pass muster at a Pritikin clinic. Rather, they're simply pies with wholesome touches: a bit of honey and a whole wheat crust here; some molasses and a whole wheat streusel there; skins left on the apples in another version. There's even, believe it or not, an apple pie made without sugar or honey or any sweetener at all—a great discovery for those whose diets don't allow added sugar.

Frankly, I believe any apple pie made from scratch is a wholesome dish. These are just a little more so, and that makes them extra special for some.

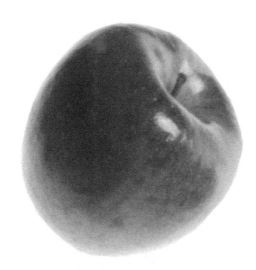

Apple Oatmeal Pie with Checkerboard Lattice

Most of the recipes in this book use either cornstarch or flour for thickening; this one uses oatmeal. The result is somewhat different from what you normally get: the filling and juices aren't uniformly thickened. Instead, what juices you see are on the thin side, with plump pieces of apple juice–engorged oats mixed in among the apples. It's a little like eating your morning oats, only in a pie. For the top crust, I make what I call a checkerboard lattice—a solid top pastry that I've cut squares in, checkerboard style. It's not supposed to be a fast version of a lattice top, just a different sort of decorative crust. It's simple to make, as long as you roll and refrigerate the top pastry so that it's firm enough to cut evenly. Use any juicy apple here.

1 RECIPE ALL-AMERICAN DOUBLE CRUST (PAGE 2), REFRIGERATED

FILLING:

8 CUPS PEELED, CORED, AND SLICED JUICY APPLES

½ CUP FIRMLY PACKED LIGHT BROWN SUGAR

JUICE AND GRATED ZEST OF 1 LEMON

½ CUP RAISINS

⅓ CUP OLD-FASHIONED ROLLED OATS (NOT INSTANT)

½ TEASPOON GROUND CINNAMON

GLAZE:

MILK

GRANULATED SUGAR

1. If you haven't already, prepare the pastry and refrigerate it until firm enough to roll, about 1 hour.

2. On a large sheet of lightly floured waxed paper, roll the larger portion of the pastry into a 13½-inch circle with a floured rolling pin. Invert the pastry over a 9-inch deep-dish pie pan. Center it, then peel off the paper. Tuck the pastry down into the pan, without stretching it, and let the edge of the pastry drape over the side of the pan. Refrigerate.

3. Meanwhile, roll the other half of the pastry into an 11½-inch circle on another large sheet of lightly floured waxed paper. Line a large baking sheet with yet another sheet of waxed paper and invert the pastry onto this sheet. Place the pastry and baking sheet in the refrigerator for at least 30 minutes.

4. To make the filling, combine the apples, brown sugar, and lemon juice and zest in a large mixing bowl; toss well. Set aside for 10 to 15 minutes. Preheat the oven to 400 degrees.

5. Remove the top pastry from the refrigerator. Using a ruler or other very thin straight edge, gently press the edge into the dough to barely score it, making the score marks about 1 inch apart. Score the pastry one way, then the other, checkerboard fashion. You won't be cutting precisely on these marks; they're only a guide. Using a sharp paring knife, cut out squares of dough—a little smaller than the squares you see—in an alternating checkerboard arrangement. (In other words, if this were a real checkerboard, you'd be cutting out only the black squares, or the red ones.) Leave a continuous border of pastry at the edge. The reason you're making the cutouts a little smaller than the squares you see is to make sure the pastry holds together. Remove the pastry squares and save these scraps for another use.

6. Add the raisins, oats, and cinnamon to the apples and mix. Turn the filling into the chilled pie shell, smoothing the top of the filling with your hands. Moisten the edge of the pie shell with a wet fingertip or pastry brush, then invert the checkerboard pastry over the filling. Press the pastries together along the dampened edge, then trim the overhang with scissors or a paring knife to an even ½ inch all around. Sculpt the edge of the pastry into an upstanding ridge. Brush the top pastry lightly with milk and sprinkle with granulated sugar.

7. Place the pie directly on the center oven rack and bake for 30 minutes. Remove from the oven and place on a large, dark baking sheet covered with aluminum foil. Reduce the oven temperature to 375 degrees. Put the pie on the baking sheet back in the oven and bake until the juices bubble vigorously inside the pie—you'll be able to look right in along the edge and see—another 35 to 40 minutes.

8. Transfer the pie to a cooling rack and let cool for at least 1 hour before serving.

Makes 8 to 10 servings

Skins-On Apple Pie in a Whole Wheat Crust

The good news is that apples are very healthy: there's all that fiber in the skin, and antioxidants galore. So a strong case could be made for leaving the skins on your apples when you make a pie. The bad news? Too much skin just doesn't cut it in an apple pie. The chewy texture is intrusive. But here's one good way to minimize the problem and make a delicious skins-on apple pie: just cut the apples into small dice, no more than ½ inch or so. What you get in the baked pie is a little bit of the chewy skin texture, but in manageable pieces. It's very pleasant, nothing obtrusive about it. There's something else here for the healthy-eating crowd—the whole wheat pastry, which makes an attractive, grainy container for the filling.

As for which apples to choose, I've had good luck with locally grown Gala apples and other small varieties whose skins aren't so thick. Golden Delicious are also good, but then you miss out on the red skins. Incidentally, the skins in the pie don't stay bright red. They bleed their color down into the apple bits, leaving you with a light pink streak. It's very pretty. If you're so inclined, the top piece of this whole wheat pastry can be woven into a lattice, as for the lattice-top pie on page 84.

1 RECIPE WHOLE WHEAT DOUBLE CRUST
(PAGE 6), REFRIGERATED

FILLING:

7 CUPS QUARTERED, CORED, AND DICED
APPLES (SEE HEADNOTE)

½ CUP SUGAR

1½ TABLESPOONS FRESH LEMON JUICE

GRATED ZEST OF 1 LEMON

2½ TABLESPOONS ALL-PURPOSE FLOUR

GLAZE:

MILK

SUGAR

1. If you haven't already, prepare the pastry and refrigerate it until firm enough to roll, 30 to 45 minutes.

2. On a sheet of lightly floured waxed paper, roll the larger portion of the pastry into a 13½-inch circle with a floured rolling pin. Invert the pastry over a 9-inch deep-dish pie pan. Center it, then peel off the paper. Tuck the pastry into the pan, without stretching it, and let the excess pastry drape over the side of the pan. Refrigerate.

3. To make the filling, combine the apples, sugar, lemon juice, and lemon zest in a large mixing bowl and mix well. Set aside for 10 minutes. Preheat the oven to 400 degrees.

4. On another sheet of lightly floured waxed paper, roll the other half of the pastry into an 11½-inch circle. Shake the flour over the filling and mix. Turn the filling into the refrigerated pie shell, smoothing the top of the filling with your hands. Moisten the edge of the pie shell with a pastry brush or wet fingertip. Invert the top pastry over the filling, center it, and peel off the paper. Press the pastries together along the dampened edge. Using scissors or a paring knife, trim the overhang to an even ½ inch all around. Sculpt the edge into an upstanding ridge. Make a number of steam vents in the top pastry with a fork or paring knife; put a few of them along the edge, so you can check the juices there later. Lightly brush the top of the pie with milk and sprinkle with sugar.

5. Bake the pie directly on the center oven rack for 30 minutes. Remove the pie from the oven and place it on a large, dark baking sheet covered with aluminum foil. Reduce the oven temperature to 375 degrees. Return the pie on the baking sheet to the oven and bake until any visible juices bubble thickly through the steam vents, another 30 to 40 minutes.

6. Transfer the pie to a cooling rack and let cool for at least 1 hour before slicing.

Makes 8 to 10 servings

FOIL THOSE DARK EDGES

Experienced pie makers have seen it happen time and again, especially with double-crust pies: the rest of the pie is baked to a nice golden brown, but the perimeter—the very edge of the pie—is much darker. There are lots of reasons this happens, especially if there's a fair amount of sugar in the dough. But the long and short of it is that the edge is more prominent than the rest of the crust, and therefore it comes in more direct contact with the oven heat and is going to brown faster.

In some cases, this dark edge is just an occasional nuisance and not worth worrying about. But if it tends to be a chronic problem in your oven, here's one solution. Cut 4 strips of aluminum foil about 2 inches wide and 10 inches long, and then lay them right on top of the pie, as if you're making a box around it. Make sure to place the strips shiny side up to deflect the heat.

Don't do this when you first put the pie in the oven. Wait until about 30 minutes into the baking so that the edge has time to brown. I think you'll find that this does the trick nicely.

Sugarless Apple Pie

There are a lot of things you can't bake without sugar, but apple pie isn't one of them. I'm happy to tell you that, because over the years I've had a number of people ask me if I had a recipe for sugarless apple pie. One of the tricks to making a good sugarless pie is finding a sweet, juicy apple. There are any number of good choices, especially during the height of apple season. Honey Crisp apples are excellent; so are Fuji apples.

When they're fresh, Golden Delicious apples are also very good. Use any of them.

To help bring out the best in the apples, I recommend lots of lemon juice and lemon zest. Add a little bit of vanilla, a few pinches of spice, and—if your diet allows—a handful of dried fruit for a little extra natural sweetener. Dried pears and golden raisins are a couple of my favorites.

1 RECIPE ALL-AMERICAN DOUBLE CRUST
(PAGE 2), MADE WITHOUT SUGAR,
REFRIGERATED

FILLING:

8 CUPS PEELED, CORED, AND SLICED
APPLES (SEE HEADNOTE)

3 TABLESPOONS FRESH LEMON JUICE

½ TEASPOON PURE VANILLA EXTRACT

GRATED ZEST OF 1 LEMON OR ORANGE

½ CUP RAISINS OR CHOPPED DRIED PEARS

BIG PINCH EACH OF GROUND CINNAMON
AND NUTMEG

1 TABLESPOON CORNSTARCH

GLAZE:

MILK OR LIGHT CREAM

1. If you haven't already, prepare the pastry and refrigerate it until firm enough to roll, about 1 hour.

2. On a sheet of lightly floured waxed paper, roll the larger portion of the pastry into a 13½-inch circle with a floured rolling pin. Invert the pastry over a 9-inch deep-dish pie pan. Center it, then peel off the paper. Carefully tuck the pastry into the pan, without stretching it, and let the excess pastry drape over the side of the pan. Refrigerate.

3. While the pie shell chills, make the filling. Put the apples in a large mixing bowl. Blend the lemon juice and vanilla in a small mixing bowl. Pour the liquid over the apples, tossing well to mix. Mix in the lemon zest, raisins, and spices. Sprinkle the cornstarch over the filling and mix thoroughly. Set aside. Preheat the oven to 400 degrees.

4. On another sheet of lightly floured waxed paper, roll the other half of the pastry into an 11½-inch circle. Turn the filling into the pie shell, smoothing the filling with your hands to even it. Using a pastry brush or wet fingertip, moisten the edge of the pie shell. Invert the top pastry over the filling. Center it, then peel off the paper. Press the top and bottom pastries together along the moistened edge, then trim the pastry, leaving a ½-inch overhang. Sculpt the pastry into an upstanding ridge. Using a fork or paring knife, poke several steam vents in the top pastry; put a few of the vents near the edge, so you can check the juices there later.

Lightly brush the top of the pie with milk.

5. Put the pie directly on the center oven rack and bake for 30 minutes. Remove from the oven and place on a large, dark baking sheet covered with aluminum foil. Reduce the oven temperature to 375 degrees. Put the pie on the baking sheet back in the oven and bake until any juices—visible at the steam vents—bubble thickly, an additional 30 to 35 minutes.

6. Transfer the pie to a cooling rack and let cool for at least 1 hour before slicing.

Makes 8 to 10 servings

Here's Why You Need an 8-Cup Measure

It makes about as much sense measuring 8 or 10 cups of sliced apples in a 1-cup measure as it does weighing your arms, legs, head, torso, and butt separately to see how much you weigh. Even if you wanted to, you couldn't do an accurate job of measuring 8 cups of apples in a 1-cup measure since there's not enough room for the slices to lay flat and fit snugly in a small measuring cup.

So when I want to measure apples, I use my large 8-cup glass measure; it's perfect for the job because it's so big and I can see right through it. It's okay that there are no markings for 9 or 10 cups because I can eyeball it, when necessary, increasing the volume proportionately. Of course, there are times when my 8-cup measure is preoccupied. This has happened frequently enough that I've long since dumped 8 cups of apples into one of my plastic mixing bowls and marked the appropriate spot with a permanent magic marker. The mark has to be darkened from time to time, but so far my makeshift measure has worked swell, and I've managed to put off buying a second large measure.

Honey Apple Pie with Walnut Mosaic Crust

I think this is one of the most attractive things you can do to a pie crust—that is, rolling nuts directly into the top crust. The effect is arresting: a random mosaic of inlaid walnut pieces atop a golden crust, resting handsomely on a compact layer of thickly sliced apples. Better yet, it's one of those touches that looks hard, but you and I know otherwise: all you have to do is scatter a handful of nuts over the top pastry and gently roll them into the dough. If there's any trick at all, it's to make sure the nuts are chopped coarsely and are embedded in the pastry, rather than protruding from it, or they may scorch. Keep an eye on the crust during the last 15 minutes in the oven, and if that's happening, loosely cover the pie with tented foil. To help prevent the scorching, bake the pie on one of the lower oven racks; in most ovens, that will concentrate the heat below the pie, rather than above it, and alleviate top browning.

Almost any apple will do here; try Jonagold, Crispin, Granny Smith, or Northern Spy.

1 RECIPE ALL-AMERICAN DOUBLE CRUST
(PAGE 2), REFRIGERATED

FILLING:

8 CUPS PEELED, CORED, AND SLICED
APPLES (SEE HEADNOTE)

⅓ CUP HONEY

2 TABLESPOONS SUGAR

1½ TABLESPOONS FRESH LEMON JUICE

GRATED ZEST OF ½ LEMON

¾ CUP COARSELY CHOPPED WALNUTS

2 TABLESPOONS ALL-PURPOSE FLOUR

PINCH OF GROUND CLOVES

2 TABLESPOONS COLD UNSALTED BUTTER,
CUT INTO SMALL PIECES

GLAZE:

MILK

SUGAR

1. If you haven't already, prepare the pastry and refrigerate it until firm enough to roll, about 1 hour.

2. On a sheet of lightly floured waxed paper, roll the larger portion of the pastry into a 13½-inch circle with a floured rolling pin. Invert the pastry over a 9-inch deep-dish pie pan. Center it, then peel off the paper. Gently tuck the pastry into the pan, without stretching it, and let the edge of the pastry drape over the side of the pan. Refrigerate.

3. To make the filling, combine the apples, honey, sugar, lemon juice, and lemon zest in a large mixing bowl; toss well. Set aside for 10 minutes. Preheat the oven to 375 degrees.

4. On another sheet of lightly floured waxed paper, roll the other half of the pastry into an 11½-inch circle. Scatter the walnuts more or less evenly over the pastry and run your rolling pin gently over them to embed them in the pastry. Invert the pastry onto another sheet of waxed paper and peel off the paper. Keep the pastry handy.

5. Shake the flour and cloves over the filling and mix. Scrape the filling into the chilled pie shell, smoothing the top with your hands. Dot the top of the filling with the butter. Moisten the edge of the pie shell with a wet fingertip or pastry brush. Invert the nut-studded top pastry over the filling, center it, and peel off the paper. Press the pastries together along the dampened edge, then trim the excess dough with scissors or a paring knife to an even ½ inch all around. Sculpt the edge into an upstanding ridge. Using a fork or paring knife, poke several steam vents in the top pastry; put several vents near the edge of the pie, so you can check the juices there later. Lightly brush the pie with milk and sprinkle with sugar.

6. Put the pie on a dark baking sheet covered with aluminum foil and bake until the juices bubble thickly along the edge, about 70 minutes.

7. Transfer the pie to a cooling rack and let cool for at least 1 hour before slicing.

Makes 8 to 10 servings

Nittany Apple Pie with Molasses and Whole Wheat Streusel

I was shopping at the Fresh Fields store in Annapolis when I spotted a display of Nittany apples, a variety I had never seen before. The sign said that these apples had been grown in West Virginia, which I found notable because, to my knowledge, I had never eaten a West Virginia apple. I asked the produce stocker what she knew about them, which was very little, though she was kind enough to offer a taste. It was appealing: a very firm apple with a good texture and flavor—not a brilliant flavor, and not very tart, but sweet and appley, certainly worth trying in a pie.

As for how the molasses and apple butter ended up in the pie, my partner Bev's aunt lives in West Virginia, and Bev told me that she cooks with a lot of molasses, so I thought I'd include a little. Her aunt also makes apple butter by the ton every fall, so I decided to add that also. You can argue with that logic, but even so, the pie tastes very good, with a dark, strongly flavored filling. As for the whole wheat streusel, I wanted something earthy that would stand up to the filling, and this does the trick. This is a gutsy pie for adventurous eaters.

1 RECIPE BEST BUTTER PIE PASTRY
(PAGE 8) OR ½ RECIPE WHOLE WHEAT
DOUBLE CRUST (PAGE 6), REFRIGERATED

FILLING:

8 CUPS PEELED, CORED, AND SLICED
NITTANY, CORTLAND, OR OTHER APPLES

⅓ CUP SPICED APPLE BUTTER, HOMEMADE
(PAGE 101) OR STORE-BOUGHT

2 TABLESPOONS SUGAR OR HONEY

1½ TABLESPOONS UNSULFURED MOLASSES

1½ TABLESPOONS FRESH LEMON JUICE

WHOLE WHEAT STREUSEL TOPPING:

½ CUP ALL-PURPOSE FLOUR

½ CUP WHOLE WHEAT FLOUR

⅔ CUP SUGAR

¼ TEASPOON SALT

¼ TEASPOON GROUND CINNAMON

½ CUP (1 STICK) COLD UNSALTED BUTTER,
CUT INTO ¼-INCH PIECES

1. If you haven't already, prepare the pastry and refrigerate it until firm enough to roll, about 1 hour.

2. On a sheet of lightly floured waxed paper, roll the pastry into a 13½-inch circle with a floured rolling pin. Invert the pastry over a 9-inch deep-dish pie pan. Center it, then peel off the paper. Gently tuck the pastry into the pan, without stretching it, and sculpt the overhang into an upstanding ridge. Put the pie shell in the freezer for at least 30 minutes.

3. To make the filling, combine the apples, apple butter, sugar, molasses, and lemon juice in a large mixing bowl and toss well. Set aside for 10 minutes. Preheat the oven to 400 degrees.

4. Scrape the filling into the frozen pie shell, smoothing the surface of the apples with your hands. Put the pie directly on the center oven rack and bake for 25 minutes.

5. While the pie bakes, make the topping. Put the flours, sugar, salt, and cinnamon in a food processor and pulse several times to mix. Remove the lid and scatter the butter pieces over the dry ingredients. Pulse the machine repeatedly, until the mixture resembles fine crumbs. Dump the crumbs into a large mixing bowl and rub them between your fingers to make large, buttery crumbs. Refrigerate.

6. After 25 minutes, remove the pie from the oven and place on a large, dark baking sheet covered with aluminum foil. Carefully dump the streusel crumbs in the center of the pie, spreading them with your hands to cover the entire surface. Tamp the crumbs down gently. Put the pie on the baking sheet back in the oven and bake until the juices bubble thickly near the edge, an additional 25 to 30 minutes.

7. Transfer the pie to a cooling rack and let cool for at least 1 hour before slicing.

Makes 8 servings

Honeyed Apple Pear Pie in a Rosemary Semolina Crust

Here's a lemony, honey-sweetened apple pie with Mediterranean leanings. If you like a soft pie, you'll love this one. It has McIntosh apples and pears, both of which bake up very tender. The semolina (or cornmeal) in the pastry makes the crust fairly collapsible, so it falls onto the filling as the pie cools and results in a very neat slice. The rosemary-flecked crust is a delicious counterpoint to the honeyed sweetness of the pie.

One last touch: if you have some star anise on hand, bury two pieces right in the center of the pie (keeping them in the center makes them easy to find when you slice the pie). The flavor of the anise infuses the entire filling and smells lovely as the pie bakes.

1 RECIPE ROSEMARY SEMOLINA DOUBLE
   CRUST (PAGE 3), REFRIGERATED

FILLING:

6 CUPS PEELED, CORED, AND THINLY SLICED
   APPLES (SUCH AS NORTHERN SPY)

2 CUPS CORED AND THINLY SLICED RIPE
   PEARS

⅓ CUP HONEY

1 TABLESPOON FRESH LEMON JUICE

GRATED ZEST OF 1 LEMON

2 TABLESPOONS ALL-PURPOSE FLOUR

2 WHOLE PIECES STAR ANISE (OPTIONAL)

1. If you haven't already, prepare the pastry and refrigerate it until firm enough to roll, about 1½ hours (this pastry requires a somewhat longer chilling to roll well).

2. On a sheet of lightly floured waxed paper, roll the larger portion of the pastry into a 13½-inch circle with a floured rolling pin. Invert the pastry over a 9-inch deep-dish pie pan. Center it, then peel off the paper. Gently tuck the pastry into the pan, without stretching it, and let the excess pastry drape over the side of the pan. Refrigerate for at least 15 minutes. Preheat the oven to 400 degrees.

3. To make the filling, mix the apples, pears, honey, lemon juice, and lemon zest together in a large mixing bowl. Stir in the flour and set the filling aside while you roll the top pastry.

4. On another sheet of lightly floured waxed

paper, roll the top pastry into an 11½-inch circle. Turn the filling into the refrigerated pie shell and smooth with your hands. If you're using it, bury the anise in the center of the pie, covering it with a few apple slices. Lightly moisten the edge of the pie shell with a wet fingertip or pastry brush. Invert the top pastry over the filling, center it, and peel off the paper. Press the top and bottom pastries together along the dampened edge. Trim the pastry with scissors or a paring knife, leaving an even ½-inch overhang all around. Sculpt the overhang into an upstanding ridge. Poke several steam vents in the top of the pie with a fork or paring knife; put a couple of the vents near the edge of the crust, so you can check the juices there later.

5. Put the pie directly on the center oven rack and bake for 30 minutes. Remove from the oven and place on a large, dark baking sheet covered with aluminum foil. Reduce the oven temperature to 375 degrees. Put the pie on the baking sheet back in the oven and bake until any juices—visible at the steam vents—bubble thickly, another 30 to 40 minutes.

6. Transfer the pie to a cooling rack and let cool for at least 1 hour before slicing. Do remember to remove the whole star anise before you serve.

Makes 8 to 10 servings

APPLE PIE CAN BRING COMFORT

After the World Trade Center and Pentagon were devastated on September 11, 2001, the *Washington Post* asked readers to share how they were coping with the anxiety resulting from the attacks. This is what Valerie C. Walker wrote:

"The Sunday after the attacks, my family took a long drive through rural Fauquier County. We stopped at the orchard we visit every fall and picked up a bushel of Golden Delicious apples. For the past week and a half, I have made two pies every other day. The mixing and rolling of dough, slicing and peeling of apples, allows me the opportunity to exert energy on something creative while allowing my mind the freedom to run through its thoughts. The smell of baking apples filling the kitchen reminds me of the comfort of childhood and a time when everything seemed right, even though the reality was only hidden behind the grownups.

"So what am I doing with these pies? I donated one to a funeral reception for a woman at my church. Others I am freezing and I will use them as needed as gifts for people in my neighborhood who are bereaved, ill, or who have just brought home babies. This way I get comfort a few times over: once from the ritual of baking and again from the pleasure of sharing my labor with others who need support."

Maple Apple Pie with a Very Pecan Crumb Crust

In the shameless self-promotion department, I've written cookbooks on subjects other than apple pie—one of them being a book of my favorite maple syrup recipes called, oddly enough, *Maple Syrup Cookbook* (Storey Books, 2001). I started cooking with maple syrup fairly religiously since moving to New Hampshire from New Jersey 20 years ago, and my appreciation for maple syrup has only increased over the years. Since I love to bake, it's no surprise that I've found lots of ways to use maple syrup in my favorite baked goods, including apple pie. Maple syrup and apple have a special affinity for each other. Maple syrup can add excitement and flavor to apples that are a little lacking. It can italicize the regional experience of apple pie, because a maple and apple pie isn't something you're likely to be served in the South, Southwest, or California.

Of course, you might argue that adding pecans to the topping of this pie takes it on a southern detour. Point taken. But pecans, to my palate, are the quintessential maple match, even more so than walnuts. And I like to show them off here by pressing some pecan halves into the crumb topping so that the top is studded with them—a little tease that can create quite a stir among the assembled. The filling itself is uncomplicated, so the maple flavor can shine: just the basics, with a touch of amaretto, if you like, to emphasize the nutty goodness of this pie.

---

1 RECIPE BEST BUTTER PIE PASTRY
   (PAGE 8), REFRIGERATED

FILLING:

9 CUPS PEELED, CORED, AND SLICED
   APPLES

⅓ CUP PURE MAPLE SYRUP

1½ TABLESPOONS FRESH LEMON JUICE

1 TABLESPOON AMARETTO OR RUM
   (OPTIONAL)

2 TABLESPOONS SUGAR

2 TABLESPOONS CORNSTARCH

VERY PECAN CRUMB CRUST:

1¾ CUPS PECAN HALVES

⅔ CUP SUGAR

¼ TEASPOON SALT

¾ CUP ALL-PURPOSE FLOUR

½ CUP (1 STICK) COLD UNSALTED BUTTER,
   CUT INTO ¼-INCH PIECES

1. If you haven't already, prepare the pastry and refrigerate it until firm enough to roll, about 1 hour.

2. On a sheet of lightly floured waxed paper, roll the pastry into a 13½-inch circle with a floured rolling pin. Invert the pastry over a 9-inch deep-dish pie pan. Center it, then peel off the paper. Gently tuck the pastry into the pan, without stretching it, and sculpt the overhang into an upstanding ridge. Put the pie shell in the freezer for at least 30 minutes.

3. To make the filling, combine the apples, maple syrup, lemon juice, and amaretto, if using, in a large mixing bowl. Set aside for 10 minutes. Preheat the oven to 400 degrees.

4. Mix the sugar and cornstarch together in a small mixing bowl. Add to the apples and toss well. Turn the filling into the frozen pie shell. Smooth the top with your hands to even it out. Place the pie directly on the center oven rack and bake for 35 minutes.

5. While the pie bakes, make the crumb crust. Put 1 cup of the pecans in a food processor with the sugar and salt. Pulse several times to chop the nuts well. Add the flour and pulse again to mix. Remove the lid and scatter the butter pieces over the surface of the dry mixture. Pulse the machine repeatedly, until the

mixture resembles coarse crumbs. Dump the crumbs into a large mixing bowl and rub them gently between your fingers to make the topping a bit more gravelly in texture. Refrigerate.

6. After 35 minutes, remove the pie from the oven and place it on a large, dark baking sheet covered with aluminum foil. Carefully dump the crumbs in the center of the pie and spread them evenly over the surface with your hands; don't press down on them just yet. Take the remaining ¾ cup pecans and stick them here and there into the crumbs so the rounded sides face out. Now press gently on the topping, essentially "setting" the pecans into the crumbs. You should be able to see the pecan halves, but they shouldn't protrude, or they'll scorch in the oven.

7. Put the pie on the baking sheet back in the oven and bake until any visible juices bubble thickly, about 40 minutes more. You'll probably want to cover the pie loosely with tented aluminum foil during the last 20 minutes to keep the crust and nuts from getting too dark.

8. Transfer the pie to a cooling rack and let cool for at least 1 hour before slicing.

Makes 8 servings

Honey Whole Wheat Apple Pie

There are many among us who prefer to bake primarily with whole-grain flour rather than white, and if you are in this group, this is the pie for you. It begins with a whole wheat crust and ends with a whole wheat and oatmeal crumb topping. In between is something else you might like: a honey-sweetened (no sugar) apple filling, flavored with a heavy dose of lemon juice and zest. It tastes amazingly good, like the serious apple pie that it is, and not like some half-baked—if you'll pardon the pun—substitute for a real apple pie. This is excellent with all Granny Smith apples or a mixture of Granny Smith and Golden Delicious. Bake this pie for a health food–loving friend, and you'll make a lasting impression.

½ RECIPE WHOLE WHEAT DOUBLE CRUST (PAGE 6), REFRIGERATED

FILLING:

9 CUPS PEELED, CORED, AND SLICED APPLES (SEE HEADNOTE)

½ CUP MILD-TASTING HONEY (SUCH AS CLOVER HONEY)

JUICE AND GRATED ZEST OF 1½ LEMONS

¼ CUP ALL-PURPOSE FLOUR

WHOLE WHEAT OATMEAL CRUMB TOPPING:

1 CUP WHOLE WHEAT FLOUR

¾ CUP OLD-FASHIONED ROLLED OATS (NOT INSTANT)

⅔ CUP FIRMLY PACKED LIGHT BROWN SUGAR

¼ TEASPOON SALT

½ CUP (1 STICK) COLD UNSALTED BUTTER, CUT INTO ¼-INCH PIECES

ABOUT 1 TEASPOON MILK OR HEAVY CREAM, IF NEEDED

1. If you haven't already, prepare the pastry and refrigerate it until firm enough to roll, about 1 hour.

2. On a sheet of lightly floured waxed paper, roll the pastry into a 13½-inch circle with a floured pin. Invert the pastry over a 9-inch deep-dish pie pan. Center it, then peel off the paper. Gently tuck the pastry into the pan, without stretching it, and sculpt the edge into an upstanding ridge. Put the pie shell in the freezer for at least 30 minutes.

3. To make the filling, combine the apples, honey, lemon juice and zest, and flour in a large mixing bowl. Mix well, then set aside for 10 minutes. Preheat the oven to 400 degrees.

4. Turn the filling into the frozen pie shell. Smooth the filling with your hands to even it out. Place the pie directly on the center oven rack and bake for 35 minutes.

5. While the pie bakes, make the crumb topping. Put the flour, oats, brown sugar, and salt in a food processor and pulse the machine several times to mix. Remove the lid and scatter the butter pieces over the dry mixture. Pulse the machine repeatedly, until the mixture resembles fine crumbs. Empty the crumbs into a large mixing bowl and rub them between your fingers—adding a teaspoon or so of milk, if necessary, to help dampen them—until you have large, buttery crumbs. Refrigerate.

6. After 35 minutes, remove the pie from the oven and place it on a large, dark baking sheet covered with aluminum foil. Reduce the oven temperature to 375 degrees. Carefully dump the crumbs in the center of the pie and spread them over the entire surface with your hands. Tamp them down lightly. Return the pie on the baking sheet to the oven and bake until the juices bubble thickly around the edge, an additional 35 to 45 minutes. Loosely cover the pie with tented aluminum foil during the last 15 minutes of baking to keep the top from browning too much.

7. Transfer the pie to a cooling rack and let cool for at least 1 hour before slicing.

Makes 8 to 10 servings

WHY CHILL THAT PIE SHELL?

You'll notice that, with few exceptions, I tell you to chill the pie pastry once you've rolled it and tucked it into your pie pan. (When no top crust will be used, I put the shell in the freezer. If a top crust is to be added, I simply put the shell in the refrigerator so the pastry edge stays supple enough to mold into the top crust.) Why do I do this? For a couple of reasons.

The first is that a trip to the freezer quickly restabilizes the butter or fat in the pastry, keeping it in little bits and flakes. That makes for a flakier crust. If you left the pastry at room temperature, the butter would essentially start to melt into the crust, yielding a far less flaky pastry. The other reason is that a frozen pastry is more durable. There's a lot of movement getting your filling into your pie shell and many opportunities to accidentally knock the shell with a wooden spoon or bowl. Freezing makes the pastry almost accident-proof.

The only downside is relatively minor: pies take a little longer to bake this way, by about 10 minutes. But that's a small price to pay for what you gain.

CHAPTER 8

When Apple Pie Meets Pantry

I have a real soft spot for pantries, no doubt because I grew up in a big eighteen-room Victorian house whose pantry always contained a wealth of wonderful foods, cooking gear, mysterious bottles, and assorted odd items such as button boxes and spare-change jars. The pantry was the place where my mom would hide desserts she didn't want us to discover before dinner; where the infrequently used liquor bottles would materialize from when my parents threw a party; and where I would stand up on the counter and fetch the hand grinder when my mom would make roast beef hash on Sunday morning. As a kid, I could spend a lot of time happily poking around in the pantry.

As a pie maker, I haven't lost my enthusiasm for poking around in the pantry. More often than not, when I want to make an apple pie, I begin with a quick survey of my pantry. I'm checking my supply of staples, of course—flour, sugar, spices. But part of me is also on the alert for that little something extra, an ingredient that will distinguish this pie from others I've baked recently. This exercise engages my frugal nature: with a little soaking, those old dried apricots over in the corner would make a nice little addition to the filling. It also stimulates my creative side: I wonder how that pecan syrup would taste in this apple pie?

What you'll find in this chapter is a collection of apple pie recipes with strong ties to the pantry. Today's pantry looks a little different from the one you and I might have grown up with. For one, it's probably a lot smaller, since pantries don't play the important role they once did in households. My own certainly can't compare to the large room I mentioned earlier. But even the smallest pantry is likely to hold a few items that would taste wonderful in an apple pie: prunes and a bottle of port; a box of gingersnaps to make a spicy crumb topping; a jar of five-spice powder to give your pie an exotic flavor. All those ingredients and others can turn a plain apple pie into one with a little pizzazz.

Poke around your own pantry and see what you can turn up. Chances are you'll find something to make one of these good pies with.

Rum Raisin Apple Pie

I'm not a big drinker of rum, or any hard liquor for that matter, though I do like the flavor. Rum raisin ice cream is a favorite of mine, for instance, and I thought that flavor profile might work well in a pie. It does. What I do here is soak raisins in rum, overnight or a couple of hours, then add the raisins and some of the rum to the pie. It has a bit of kick because not all of the alcohol cooks off, so this probably isn't a pie kids will be crazy about. I think it's most appropriate served around the holidays, since that's the time of year when adults seem to enjoy spirited foods. It's great with rum raisin ice cream, maple ice cream, or maple syrup–flavored whipped cream. Use a top crust, if you prefer, instead of this walnut crumb topping.

1 CUP RAISINS

¾ CUP RUM

1 RECIPE BEST BUTTER PIE PASTRY (PAGE 8) OR THREE-GRAIN BUTTER PASTRY (PAGE 10), REFRIGERATED

FILLING:

10 CUPS PEELED, CORED, AND SLICED APPLES

½ CUP FIRMLY PACKED LIGHT BROWN SUGAR

2 TABLESPOONS FRESH LEMON JUICE

3 TABLESPOONS ALL-PURPOSE FLOUR

WALNUT CRUMB TOPPING:

1 CUP WALNUT HALVES OR PIECES

1 CUP ALL-PURPOSE FLOUR

½ CUP FIRMLY PACKED LIGHT BROWN SUGAR

¼ CUP GRANULATED SUGAR

¼ TEASPOON SALT

½ CUP (1 STICK) COLD UNSALTED BUTTER, CUT INTO ¼-INCH PIECES

1. Put the raisins in a small mixing bowl and pour the rum over them. Set aside for at least 2 hours or overnight.

2. If you haven't already, prepare the pastry and refrigerate it until firm enough to roll, about 1 hour.

3. On a sheet of lightly floured waxed paper, roll the pastry into a 13½-inch circle with a floured rolling pin. Invert the pastry over a 9-inch deep-dish pie pan. Center it, then peel off the paper. Gently tuck the pastry down into the pan, without stretching it, and sculpt the edge into an upstanding ridge. Put the pie shell in the freezer for at least 30 minutes.

4. To make the filling, mix the apples and brown sugar together in a large mixing bowl; set aside for 10 minutes. Preheat the oven to 400 degrees.

5. Drain the raisins, reserving the rum, and add the raisins to the apples. Add ¼ cup of the reserved rum and the lemon juice. Sprinkle the flour over everything, then mix the filling well.

Turn the filling into the frozen pie shell. Try to push most of the raisins under the apples, or they'll scorch in the oven heat, then even the top of the filling by smoothing it with your hands. Put the pie directly on the center oven rack and bake for 30 minutes.

6. While the pie bakes, make the crumb topping. Put the walnuts in a food processor and chop semi-coarsely. Add the flour, sugars, and salt and process again to mix. Remove the lid and scatter the butter pieces over the dry ingredients. Pulse the machine repeatedly, until the mixture resembles fine crumbs. Empty the crumbs into a large mixing bowl and rub them between your fingers to make large, buttery crumbs. Refrigerate.

7. After 30 minutes, remove the pie from the oven and place it on a large, dark baking sheet covered with aluminum foil. Reduce the oven temperature to 375 degrees. Carefully dump the crumbs in the center of the pie, spreading them evenly over the entire surface with your hands. Tamp them down lightly. Put the pie on the baking sheet back in the oven and bake until the juices bubble thickly near the edge, an additional 30 to 40 minutes, covering the pie with loosely tented aluminum foil for the last 15 minutes.

8. Transfer the pie to a cooling rack and let cool for at least 1 hour before slicing.

Makes 8 to 10 servings

THE WISDOM OF WAXED PAPER

You can roll a pie pastry on almost any surface, and over the years I've tried many of them. I recall that my father had a large hardwood chopping board, with a lip on the front to grab the counter; that was his favorite surface. In more recent years, manufacturers have added concentric circles to the surface, so you can see how large your pastry is. I think that's a thoughtful touch. Some pastry makers swear by their marble slabs, which they keep in the refrigerator and pull out when they're rolling dough.

Personally, I think waxed paper is without equal when it comes to rolling pie pastry. For one, it's virtually stick-proof. You don't have to worry about your pastry Becoming One with the Formica or your wooden counter. You just invert the waxed paper and pastry over your pie pan, peel off the paper, and throw it away. There's nothing to wash.

Also, waxed paper has a built-in ruler; you don't need those circles on the wooden board. Waxed paper is 12 inches wide, so you know that if you roll your pastry until it hangs off the edge by about ¾ inch on both edges, you have a pastry that's 13½ inches wide—the size you need for most of the pie shells in this book.

Whether you're rolling on waxed paper or any other surface, I find that the best height to work at is just below waist level, so you can exert downward pressure on your dough. If the counter is too high, your pin tends to slide across the surface; you can't use your upper body strength to help you roll.

Cardamom Apple Pie with Dried Tart Cherries

Cardamom, widely used in Middle Eastern and Indian cooking, is one of my favorite spices. I started using it many years ago in my bread baking, as it would show up occasionally in the breads of Scandinavia and Germany. Cardamom is a member of the ginger family. It has a robust, lemony flavor that can penetrate through other seasonings and leave no doubt as to its presence. I hadn't thought of using it in apple pie until I was thumbing through my tattered copy of *The New York Times Cookbook* by Craig Claiborne (HarperCollins, 1990) and noticed his version of an apple pie made with cardamom. Although he gives no introduction to his recipe, my guess is that such a pie must have originated with American immigrants of Scandinavian descent and probably isn't all that uncommon in some parts of the country, such as Minnesota, where there are large communities of Scandinavian Americans. When you make this pie, see how many people can recognize the spice—which seems the perfect match with the dried tart cherries. Not many are familiar with its exotic taste, and they'll be interested to hear what spice you've put in the pie.

1 RECIPE ALL-AMERICAN DOUBLE CRUST (PAGE 2) OR SHORTENING DOUBLE CRUST (PAGE 4), REFRIGERATED

FILLING:

8 CUPS PEELED, CORED, AND SLICED GRANNY SMITH OR OTHER TART, JUICY APPLES

½ CUP SUGAR

1 TABLESPOON FRESH LEMON JUICE

GRATED ZEST OF ½ LEMON

¾ CUP DRIED TART CHERRIES

1½ TABLESPOONS ALL-PURPOSE FLOUR (SEE FLOUR VS. CORNSTARCH, PAGE 231)

1 TEASPOON CARDAMOM

GLAZE:

MILK

SUGAR

1. If you haven't already, prepare the pastry and refrigerate it until firm enough to roll, about 1 hour.

2. On a sheet of lightly floured waxed paper, roll the larger portion of the pastry into a 13½-inch circle with a floured rolling pin. Invert the pastry over a 9-inch deep-dish pie pan. Center it, then peel off the paper. Gently tuck the pastry down into the pan, without stretching it, and let the excess pastry drape over the side of the pan. Refrigerate.

3. To make the filling, combine the apples, sugar, lemon juice, lemon zest, and dried cherries in a large mixing bowl; toss well to mix. Set aside for 10 minutes. Preheat the oven to 400 degrees.

4. On another sheet of lightly floured waxed paper, roll the top pastry into an 11½-inch circle. Combine the flour and cardamom in a small bowl, shake over the filling, and mix. Turn the filling into the pie shell, smoothing the top of the filling with your hands. Lightly moisten the edge of the pie shell with a finger or pastry brush. Invert the top pastry over the filling, then press the pastries together along the dampened edge. Trim the pastry, leaving an even ½ inch all around. Sculpt the overhang into an upstanding ridge. Poke several steam vents in the top of the pie with a fork or paring knife; put a couple of the vents near the edge, so you can check the juices later. Lightly brush the top with milk and sprinkle with sugar.

5. Put the pie directly on the center oven rack and bake for 30 minutes. Remove the pie from the oven and place it on a large, dark baking sheet lined with aluminum foil. Reduce the oven temperature to 375 degrees. Put the pie on the baking sheet back in the oven and bake until any juices—visible at the steam vents—bubble thickly, another 30 to 35 minutes.

6. Transfer the pie to a cooling rack and let cool for at least 1 hour before slicing.

Makes 8 to 10 servings

Jonagold Apple Pie with Gingersnap Crumb Topping

In recent years, the Jonagold apple—a cross between a Jonathan and a Golden Delicious—has gained popularity at farm stands and larger markets. At their best, Jonagold apples are firm-textured, crisp, and juicy. Here's one pie you might want to try with them. Please note that you'll have to use your best cook's intuition when you're making this topping, since not all store-bought gingersnaps are the same. Some are sweeter or drier than others. So make the topping as instructed, then, if it seems to need it, work in just a bit more sugar or a teaspoon or so of milk to moisten it. Keep an eye on it in the oven, too. You may find that after 10 minutes, it's starting to get dark. If so, cover the top of the pie with a circle of aluminum foil.

1 RECIPE THREE-GRAIN BUTTER PASTRY (PAGE 10) OR BEST BUTTER PIE PASTRY (PAGE 8), REFRIGERATED

FILLING:

9 CUPS PEELED, CORED, AND SLICED JONAGOLD APPLES

⅔ CUP SUGAR

1½ TABLESPOONS FRESH LEMON JUICE

¼ CUP APPLESAUCE, HOMEMADE (PAGE 97) OR STORE-BOUGHT

2½ TABLESPOONS ALL-PURPOSE FLOUR

GINGERSNAP TOPPING:

2½ CUPS COARSELY BROKEN-UP STORE-BOUGHT GINGERSNAPS

¼ CUP ALL-PURPOSE FLOUR

¼ CUP SUGAR

½ CUP (1 STICK) COLD UNSALTED BUTTER, CUT INTO ¼-INCH PIECES

1. If you haven't already, prepare the pastry and refrigerate it until firm enough to roll, about 1 hour.

2. On a sheet of lightly floured waxed paper, roll the pastry into a 13½-inch circle with a floured rolling pin. Invert the pastry over a 9-inch deep-dish pie pan. Center it, then peel off the paper. Tuck the pastry into the pan, without stretching it, and sculpt the edge into an upstanding ridge. Place the pie shell in the freezer for at least 30 minutes.

3. To make the filling, combine the apples, sugar, and lemon juice in a large mixing bowl and toss well to mix. Set aside for 10 minutes. Preheat the oven to 400 degrees.

4. Stir the applesauce and flour into the apples. Turn the filling into the frozen pie shell. Place the pie directly on the center oven rack and bake for 30 minutes. Reduce the oven temperature to 375 degrees and bake for 10 minutes longer.

5. While the pie bakes, make the topping. Put the gingersnaps, flour, and sugar in a food processor and process—pulsing the machine at first—long enough to make fine crumbs. Remove the lid and scatter the butter pieces over the dry ingredients. Pulse the machine repeatedly, until the mixture forms coarse, buttery crumbs. Refrigerate.

6. Remove the pie from the oven and place it on a large, dark baking sheet covered with aluminum foil. Carefully dump the crumbs in the center of the pie, spreading them evenly over the surface with your hands. Tamp them down gently. Put the pie on the baking sheet back in the oven and bake until the juices bubble thickly near the edge, 20 to 25 minutes longer. Check the pie after 10 minutes to make sure the top isn't getting too dark. If it is, cover with aluminum foil.

7. Transfer the pie to a cooling rack and let cool for at least 1 hour before slicing.

Makes 8 to 10 servings

Apple Pie with Graham Cracker Streusel

Graham cracker crusts—bottom crusts, at least—don't work all that well with apple pie. That's because apple pie has to cook at a relatively high temperature, making the crust too dark. And the filling is generally too juicy, so the crust ends up sodden. Still, I wanted an apple pie with a graham cracker crust because I just love graham crackers. Indeed, one of my favorite breakfasts in the world is graham cracker mush: a big bowl of crushed graham crackers doused with milk. So what I've done here, essentially, is put a fairly traditional graham cracker crust on top of the pie, instead of on the bottom. To give it extra moisture and help make it clump together nicely, I've added 1½ ounces—half of a small package—of cream cheese to the topping, which also gives it a subtle tang. The topping is relatively soft when the pie comes out of the oven, firming up somewhat as it cools. I like it somewhere in between, while the pie is still a little warm.

1 RECIPE BEST BUTTER PIE PASTRY
 (PAGE 8), REFRIGERATED

FILLING:

8 TO 9 CUPS PEELED, CORED, AND SLICED
 FIRM-TEXTURED APPLES (SUCH AS GRANNY
 SMITH OR GOLDEN DELICIOUS)

½ CUP FIRMLY PACKED LIGHT BROWN SUGAR

1 TABLESPOON FRESH LEMON JUICE

GRATED ZEST OF 1 LEMON

2½ TABLESPOONS ALL-PURPOSE FLOUR

**GRAHAM CRACKER STREUSEL
TOPPING:**

8 WHOLE GRAHAM CRACKERS

½ CUP FIRMLY PACKED LIGHT BROWN SUGAR

¼ CUP ALL-PURPOSE FLOUR

½ TEASPOON GROUND CINNAMON

PINCH OF SALT

6 TABLESPOONS (¾ STICK) UNSALTED
 BUTTER, MELTED

1½ OUNCES COLD CREAM CHEESE, BROKEN
 INTO PIECES

1. If you haven't already, make the pastry and refrigerate it until firm enough to roll, about 1 hour.

2. On a sheet of lightly floured waxed paper, roll the pastry into a 13½-inch circle with a floured rolling pin. Invert the pastry over a 9-inch deep-dish pie pan. Center it, then peel off the paper. Tuck the pastry into the pan, without stretching it, and sculpt the edge into an upstanding ridge. Place the pie shell in the freezer for at least 30 minutes.

3. To make the filling, mix the apples, brown sugar, lemon juice, and lemon zest together in a large mixing bowl. Set aside for 10 minutes. Preheat the oven to 400 degrees.

4. Sprinkle the flour over the apples and toss well to mix. Turn the filling into the chilled crust, smoothing the top with your hands. Put the pie directly on the center oven rack and bake for 30 minutes.

5. While the pie bakes, make the topping. Put the graham crackers and brown sugar in a food processor and pulse to make fine crumbs. Add the flour, cinnamon, and salt; pulse again

to mix. Remove the lid and add the melted butter; pulse again to mix evenly. Remove the lid again, add the cream cheese, and pulse again repeatedly, until you have a clumpy, crumbly mixture. Refrigerate.

6. After 30 minutes, remove the pie from the oven. Place on a large, dark baking sheet covered with aluminum foil. Cover the filling with a round piece of foil the same size as the pie. Reduce the oven temperature to 375 degrees. Put the pie on the baking sheet back in the oven and bake for 15 minutes more.

7. After 15 minutes, remove the pie from the oven. Take off the foil and carefully dump the topping in the center of the pie, gently spreading it toward the edge with your hands. Tamp it down lightly. Put the pie on the baking sheet back in the oven and bake until the juices bubble thickly at the edge, another 15 to 20 minutes.

8. Transfer the pie to a cooling rack and let cool for at least 1 hour before slicing.

Makes 8 to 10 servings

Susan Jasse's Five-Spice Powder Peekaboo Pie

I wish I could take credit for this great idea—seasoning an apple pie with five-spice powder—but the actual credit goes to Susan Jasse, proprietor of Alyson's Apple Orchard. Like so many apple pie bakers I spoke to, Susan makes pies intuitively. She seldom measures ingredients, very often adds five-spice powder, and doesn't use a top crust. To keep the upper layer of apples from drying out, she brushes them with melted apple jelly partway through the baking. Susan recommends any tart-sweet, firm-textured apple. This is an excellent pie I know you'll enjoy. Read step 1 below before you make the pastry.

1 RECIPE ALL-AMERICAN DOUBLE CRUST
(PAGE 2), REFRIGERATED

FILLING:

8 CUPS PEELED, CORED, AND SLICED
APPLES (SEE HEADNOTE)

½ CUP SUGAR

1½ TEASPOONS FIVE-SPICE POWDER

2 TEASPOONS FRESH LEMON JUICE

1 TABLESPOON ALL-PURPOSE FLOUR

1 TABLESPOON COLD UNSALTED BUTTER,
CUT INTO SMALL PIECES

¼ CUP APPLE JELLY, WARMED UNTIL
MELTED

1. If you haven't already, prepare the pastry and refrigerate it until firm enough to roll, about 1 hour. The larger portion—the part you'll be using—should constitute about two-thirds of the total amount of dough. (Save the smaller piece to make a peekaboo pie, as on page 110.)

2. To make the filling, combine the apples, sugar, five-spice powder, and lemon juice in a large mixing bowl. Set aside for 10 minutes. Preheat the oven to 400 degrees.

3. On a sheet of lightly floured waxed paper, roll the larger portion of the pastry into a large circle, about 15 inches in diameter, with a floured rolling pin. Invert the pastry over a 9-inch deep-dish pie pan. Center it, then peel off the paper. Gently tuck the pastry into the pan, without stretching it, and let the excess pastry drape over the side of the pan.

4. Shake the flour over the apples and mix well. Scrape the filling into the pie shell and smooth the top with your hands. Dot the apples with the butter, then fold the pastry over the filling. The pastry will self-pleat as you fold it, making an approximate 2-inch border covering the apples. Place the pie directly on the center oven rack and bake for 30 minutes.

5. When the time is almost up, remove the pie from the oven and reduce the oven temperature to 375 degrees. Either spoon the melted jelly over the apples or brush it on with a pastry brush. Put the pie back in the oven and bake for about another 25 minutes. When the pie is done, the juices will likely be bubbling up in the middle and the exposed pastry will be golden brown.

6. Transfer the pie to a cooling rack and let cool for at least 1 hour before slicing.

Makes 8 to 10 servings

ALYSON'S APPLE ORCHARD

Bob Jasse has the sort of past that would suggest a number of eventual careers, though growing apples is not one of them. He flunked out of high school in the tenth grade, and had a few run-ins with the law. After Jasse turned 17, the local police chief gave him a choice of reform school or the service. Jasse opted for the Navy, where he spent more than three years as a corpsman. He went on to receive a degree in biology from Boston College. At the urging of Father Michael Walsh, he went to business school for his MBA, and later co-founded a specialty chemical company, Chomerics, which he sold to W. R. Grace in 1985.

Early in life, Jasse had fallen in love with orchards; he'd seen many during his frequent hunting, fishing, and mushrooming trips with his Uncle John. This love of the land had much to do with his decision to buy a large parcel in Walpole, New Hampshire, in which he would invest heavily with a 25,000 fruit tree planting, "going with the grain of nature" using ecologically sound strategies.

Today, Alyson's Apple Orchard has blossomed into quite the enterprise. Run by Jasse and his wife, Susan (a former professional chef), Alyson's grows more than 60 varieties of apples, from regionally common varieties—McIntosh, Cortland, Paula Red, and Northern Spy—to hard-to-find antique varieties like the Roxbury Russet, Esopus Spitzenberg, and Cox's Orange Pippin (see page 56). In addition to the business of growing apples and raising plums, peaches, pears, and berries, the Jasses run an event center and maintain lodging for weddings, business retreats, and family gatherings on their bucolic grounds in Walpole.

Jasse, who takes great pride in the environmentally responsible way his orchard is run, is a staunch steward of the land. He points to his own trout pond as a measure of his resolve to do things right: "Trout and amphibians are the orchard's equivalent of canaries in a coal mine: if we mess with their environment, they—and the birds that nest in our fruit trees and the mushrooms that grow on our orchard floor—will not survive."

You can reach Alyson's Apple Orchard at (800) 856-0549 or online at www.alysonsorchard.com.

Southern Apple Pie with Pecan Syrup

My better half, Bev, lived for much of her life in Charleston, South Carolina, a geographical circumstance that's had some influence on my diet over the past several years. She introduced me to peach cider, which I had never even heard of until I met her. And she's a real fan of pecan syrup, something she picks up from a certain farm stand whenever she heads south. If you've never seen it, pecan syrup is a blend of corn syrup, sugar, toasted pecans, and vanilla extract. We use it on pancakes and waffles, but along the way it occurred to me that it would make an excellent sweet-ener for apple pie. If you're not planning a trip south anytime soon, don't worry: this recipe assumes as much and calls for ingredients you can get your hands on easily. (If you do have pecan syrup, substitute ½ cup of it for the corn syrup and vanilla.) How does the pie taste? It's excellent—lots of southern charm with a sort of north-meets-south flavor tucked between a Shortening Double Crust.

For an extra-special touch, roll some finely chopped pecans into the top crust, as described with walnuts in the recipe on page 158.

1 RECIPE SHORTENING DOUBLE CRUST (PAGE 4), REFRIGERATED

FILLING:

8 CUPS PEELED, CORED, AND THINLY SLICED FIRM-TEXTURED COOKING APPLES (SUCH AS NORTHERN SPY OR GOLDEN DELICIOUS)

½ CUP DARK CORN SYRUP

½ CUP WHOLE PECANS, TOASTED (SEE PAGE 181) AND COARSELY CHOPPED

1 TABLESPOON FRESH LEMON JUICE

½ TEASPOON PURE VANILLA EXTRACT

2½ TABLESPOONS ALL-PURPOSE FLOUR

2 TABLESPOONS COLD UNSALTED BUTTER, CUT INTO SMALL PIECES

1. If you haven't already, prepare the pastry and refrigerate it until firm enough to roll, about 1 hour.

2. On a sheet of lightly floured waxed paper, roll the larger portion of the pastry into a 13½-inch circle with a floured rolling pin. Invert the pastry over a 9-inch deep-dish pie pan. Center it, then peel off the paper. Gently tuck the pastry into the pan, without stretching it, and let the excess pastry drape over the side of the pan. Refrigerate.

3. While the pie shell chills, make the filling. Combine the apples, corn syrup, pecans, lemon juice, and vanilla in a large mixing bowl. Toss well to mix. Shake the flour over the filling and toss again. Set aside. Preheat the oven to 400 degrees.

4. On another sheet of lightly floured waxed paper, roll the top pastry into an 11½-inch circle. Turn the filling into the pie shell, smoothing the top with your hands. Dot the apples with the butter. Moisten the edge of the pie shell with a wet finger or pastry brush. Invert the pastry over the filling, center it, and peel off the paper. Press the top and bottom pastries together along the dampened edge. Trim the pastry with scissors or a paring knife, leaving an even ½-inch overhang all around, then sculpt the overhang into an upstanding ridge. Poke several steam vents in the top of the pie with a fork or paring knife; put a couple of the steam vents near the edge of the crust, so you can check the juices there later.

5. Put the pie directly on the center oven rack and bake for 30 minutes. Remove the pie from the oven and place it on a large, dark baking sheet covered with aluminum foil. Reduce the oven temperature to 375 degrees. Put the pie on the baking sheet back in the oven and bake until the juices bubble thickly at the edge, an additional 30 to 35 minutes.

6. Transfer the pie to a cooling rack and let cool for at least 2 hours, preferably 4 to 5 hours, before slicing and serving.

Makes 8 to 10 servings

HOW TO TOAST NUTS

If you're a regular baker of pies or anything else, you'll often be instructed to use toasted nuts, which have a deeper, richer flavor than untoasted nuts. Here's how it's done.

Preheat the oven to 350 degrees. Spread the nuts in a single, uncrowded layer on an ungreased baking sheet. Place the sheet on the center oven rack and set the timer for 8 minutes. When the timer goes off, you should be getting the first whiff of toasted nuts. Remove the sheet from the oven, then tilt the nuts off the sheet and onto a large plate to cool.

The method for toasting hazelnuts is a little different, since you have to remove the skins. Proceed as directed above, but toast them a little longer—10 to 12 minutes—until the skins are well blistered. Tilt the nuts off the sheet onto a clean tea towel. Fold the towel over the nuts, wait 1 minute, and rub the nuts vigorously through the towel to remove the skins. You don't need to get every last bit of skin off.

In all cases, cool the nuts thoroughly before you chop them—especially if you're using a food processor—or they'll turn very pasty.

Apple Pie with Prunes and Port

Prunes have perhaps the least sexy reputation among dried fruits, but I think precious few others can match it for apple compatibility. I had made several versions of apple prune pie over the years, and they were very good, but then I stumbled upon the idea of adding port wine to the filling, which turned out to be the bridge between flavors that really sealed the deal. I thoroughly soak the prunes in port, which helps prevent them from soaking up all the juices the pie creates,

then I reduce the port and add it to the filling. (Since this addition makes the pie juicier than most apple pies, I use cornstarch instead of flour for optimum thickening.) The port gives the apples a gorgeous mahogany hue and winy-sweet flavor that is wonderful with the prunes. I'll be honest: kids may not place this at the top of the list, but everyone else probably will. I like a walnut crumb topping, but you can use a top crust, if you prefer.

1 ½ CUPS MOIST PITTED PRUNES, CUT INTO
LARGE PIECES

ABOUT 2 CUPS RUBY PORT

1 RECIPE BEST BUTTER PIE PASTRY
(PAGE 8) OR THREE-GRAIN BUTTER
PASTRY (PAGE 10), REFRIGERATED

FILLING:

9 TO 10 CUPS PEELED, CORED, AND SLICED
APPLES

2 TABLESPOONS FRESH LEMON JUICE

GRATED ZEST OF 1 LEMON

½ CUP GRANULATED SUGAR

3 TABLESPOONS CORNSTARCH

TOPPING:

1 CUP WALNUT HALVES OR PIECES

1 CUP ALL-PURPOSE FLOUR

½ CUP FIRMLY PACKED LIGHT BROWN SUGAR

½ CUP GRANULATED SUGAR

¼ TEASPOON SALT

½ CUP (1 STICK) COLD UNSALTED BUTTER,
CUT INTO ¼-INCH PIECES

1. A few hours before you bake the pie, put the prunes in a medium-size mixing bowl and add enough port to cover them by ¼ to ½ inch. Set aside at room temperature to soak.

2. If you haven't already, prepare the pastry and refrigerate it until firm enough to roll, about 1 hour.

3. On a sheet of lightly floured waxed paper, roll the pastry into a 13½-inch circle with a floured rolling pin. Invert the pastry over a 9-inch deep-dish pie pan. Center it, then peel off the paper. Gently tuck the pastry down into the pan, without stretching it, and sculpt the edge into an upstanding ridge. Place the pie shell in the freezer for at least 30 minutes.

4. While the shell chills, drain the prunes, transferring the port to a small saucepan. Bring the port to a boil and reduce to about ⅓ cup. Pour it directly into a heatproof measuring cup to check the amount, then set aside. Preheat the oven to 400 degrees.

5. To make the filling, mix the apples, lemon juice, and lemon zest together in a large mixing bowl. Stir in the prunes and reduced port. Mix the sugar and cornstarch together in a small mixing bowl, then add to the apples and mix well. Turn the filling into the frozen pie shell, patting the filling with your hands to even it out. Try to bury any exposed prunes under the apple slices so they don't scorch during baking, but you need not be obsessive about it. Place the pie directly on the center oven rack and bake for 30 minutes.

6. While the pie bakes, make the topping. Put the walnuts in a food processor and pulse several times to chop them coarsely. Add the flour, sugars, and salt and pulse again to mix. Add the butter pieces, scattering them over the dry mixture. Pulse the machine repeatedly, until the mixture resembles fine crumbs. Empty the crumbs into a large mixing bowl and rub them between your fingers to make large, buttery crumbs. Refrigerate.

7. After 30 minutes, remove the pie from the oven and place it on a large, dark baking sheet covered with aluminum foil. Reduce the oven temperature to 375 degrees. Carefully dump the crumbs in the center of the pie, spreading them evenly over the surface with your hands. Tamp down lightly to smooth the top. Put the pie on the baking sheet back in the oven and bake until the juices bubble thickly around the edge, an additional 35 to 40 minutes. Loosely cover the pie with tented aluminum foil during the last 15 minutes of baking to keep the top from browning too much.

8. Transfer the pie to a cooling rack and let cool for at least 1 hour before slicing.

Makes 8 to 10 servings

Apple Apricot Pie

Apples and apricots are regular pie soul mates, though with vastly different market lives: good fresh apples are available essentially all year round, but good fresh apricots—at least in New England—aren't easy to find even during their peak season. At some point in my pie-making career, I started experimenting with canned apricots, with better results than I expected. Canned apricots weren't nearly as dry and mealy as the fresh market apricots I'd been using, in large part thanks to the syrup they're packed in. And canned apricots seem to be processed at the peak of their ripeness, so the flavor is nice and apricoty. I also found that I could get even more apricot flavor by reducing the syrup they're packed in and adding it to the filling. Which is to say I'm very happy with this pie made from fresh apples and canned apricots. If you can find good fresh apricots, use them (you don't have to peel them). Since the pie won't be as juicy as with canned fruit, use 3 tablespoons flour instead of the tapioca. This is also nice with a top crust, if you prefer.

1 RECIPE BEST BUTTER PIE PASTRY (PAGE 8), REFRIGERATED

FILLING:

THREE 15-OUNCE CANS APRICOTS, DRAINED (RESERVE THE SYRUP) AND SLICED, OR 3 CUPS PITTED AND SLICED FRESH APRICOTS

4 LARGE GRANNY SMITH OR OTHER APPLES, PEELED, CORED, AND SLICED

⅓ CUP GRANULATED SUGAR

JUICE AND GRATED ZEST OF 1 LEMON

3 TABLESPOONS INSTANT TAPIOCA

¼ TEASPOON GROUND NUTMEG

OATMEAL CRUMB TOPPING:

1 CUP ALL-PURPOSE FLOUR

¾ CUP OLD-FASHIONED ROLLED OATS (NOT INSTANT)

⅔ CUP FIRMLY PACKED LIGHT BROWN SUGAR

½ TEASPOON GROUND CINNAMON

¼ TEASPOON SALT

½ CUP (1 STICK) COLD UNSALTED BUTTER, CUT INTO ¼-INCH PIECES

1. If you haven't already, make the pastry and refrigerate it until firm enough to roll, about 1 hour.

2. On a sheet of lightly floured waxed paper, roll the pastry into a 13½-inch circle with a floured rolling pin. Invert the pastry over a 9-inch deep-dish pie pan. Center it, then peel off the paper. Gently tuck the pastry down into the pan, without stretching it, and sculpt the edge into an upstanding ridge. Place the pie shell in the freezer for at least 30 minutes.

3. If using canned apricots, pour 1 cup of the reserved apricot syrup into a small saucepan and bring to a boil. Continue to boil the liquid, reducing it to about ½ cup. Keep a heatproof measuring cup close by and pour the syrup directly into the cup to check the amount. Set aside.

4. Combine the apricots, apples, granulated sugar, lemon juice and zest, and reduced syrup in a large mixing bowl. Set aside for 10 minutes. Preheat the oven to 400 degrees.

5. Sprinkle the tapioca and nutmeg over the filling and mix well. Turn the filling into the frozen pie shell. Smooth the filling with your hands to even it out. Place the pie on a large,

dark baking sheet covered with aluminum foil and bake on the center rack for 35 minutes.

6. While the pie bakes, make the crumb topping. Put the flour, oats, brown sugar, cinnamon, and salt in a food processor and pulse several times to mix. Remove the lid and scatter the butter pieces over the dry mixture. Pulse the machine repeatedly, until the mixture resembles fine crumbs. Dump the crumbs into a large mixing bowl and rub between your fingers to make large, buttery crumbs. Refrigerate.

7. After 35 minutes, remove the pie from the oven. Reduce the oven temperature to 375 degrees. Carefully dump the crumbs in the center of the pie, spreading them evenly over the surface with your hands. Tamp them down lightly. Return the pie on the baking sheet to the oven and bake until the juices bubble thickly around the edge, an additional 35 to 40 minutes. Loosely cover the pie with aluminum foil during the last 15 minutes of baking to keep the top from browning too much.

8. Transfer the pie to a cooling rack and let cool for at least 1 hour before slicing.

Makes 8 to 10 servings

Dried Apple and Walnut Pie

This recipe is based on a favorite gooey bar cookie of mine made with walnuts and dates. Instead of the dates, I use finely chopped dried apples here. The apples and nuts go into a baked pie shell, then the sweet-gooey mixture gets poured over the top. The pie has a short baking time, just 20 minutes. I like to eat this pie at room temperature, not warm. If you chill it, it's easy to slice. If you'd like, you can wrap the slices in plastic, refrigerate, and serve for snacks and in lunches.

1 RECIPE THREE-GRAIN BUTTER PASTRY
   (PAGE 10), REFRIGERATED

FILLING:

⅓ CUP HONEY

⅓ CUP APPLE JELLY

2 TABLESPOONS UNSALTED BUTTER

¼ CUP FIRMLY PACKED LIGHT BROWN SUGAR

2 TABLESPOONS ALL-PURPOSE FLOUR

¼ TEASPOON BAKING POWDER

⅛ TEASPOON SALT

2 LARGE EGGS

½ TEASPOON PURE VANILLA EXTRACT

1 CUP FINELY CHOPPED DRIED APPLES

½ CUP CHOPPED WALNUTS

1. If you haven't already, prepare the pastry and refrigerate it until firm enough to roll, about 1 hour.

2. On a sheet of lightly floured waxed paper, roll the pastry into a 13½-inch circle (to get the correct thickness), then trim the pastry to 11 inches before you line the pan with it. Because this is a shallow pie, you can use a standard 9-inch pie pan, if you'd rather, instead of a deep-dish one. The edge of the pie shell should come only about two-thirds up the side of the pan. Put the pie shell in the freezer for at least 30 minutes, then partially prebake it according to the directions on page 19. Let the pastry cool for at least 30 minutes on a cooling rack before you fill it. Set the oven temperature to 350 degrees.

3. While you're waiting for the pastry to cool, make the filling. Combine the honey, apple jelly, and butter in a small saucepan. Heat gently over medium-low heat, whisking occasionally, for about 5 minutes, until the jelly melts and the mixture is smooth. Remove from the heat and let cool along with the pastry.

4. In a medium-size mixing bowl, combine the brown sugar, flour, baking powder, and salt. Mix together with your hands, then add the eggs and vanilla to the bowl, whisking until the mixture is smooth. Add the warm jelly mixture and whisk again until smooth.

5. Evenly scatter the dried apples and walnuts in the prebaked pastry. Slowly and evenly, pour the liquid over the apples and nuts, smoothing the filling with the back of a spoon so the liquid goes between all of the nuts and apples. Place the pie directly on the center oven rack and bake until the top is slightly puffed and the liquid is set, about 20 minutes. You can check by inserting a paring knife into the center. The filling shouldn't seem loose or runny.

6. Transfer the pie to a cooling rack and let cool to room temperature before slicing.

Makes 8 to 10 servings

OF THE APPLE BEE AND PIE PASTRIES FROM HELL

In her 1901 book *Old Time Gardens*, Alice Morse Earle tells us that the wassailing of apple trees (see page 207) gave way in America to a more jovial fall celebration known as the apple paring or apple bee. The apple bee was a daylong gathering to process the apple harvest by hand, interspersed with apple fun and games. Barrels full of apples were arranged around the kitchen to be deftly sliced by skillful hands. Many of the apples were dried by hanging quarter sections of them by homemade linen thread.

"When thoroughly dried in sun and wind, these sliced apples were stored for the winter by being hung from rafter to rafter of various living rooms, and remained thus for months [gathering vast accumulations of dust and germs for our blissfully ignorant and unsqueamish grandparents] until the early days of spring, when Apple sauce, Apple butter, and the stores of Apple bin and Apple pit were exhausted, and they then afforded, after proper baths and soakings, the wherewithal for that domestic comestible—dried Apple pie."

She goes on to write that one Swedish parson, in a letter home, was apparently less than smitten with these pies. His letter states that "Apple pie is used throughout the whole year, and when fresh Apples are no longer to be had, dried ones are used. It is the evening meal of children. House pie, in country places, is made of Apples neither peeled nor freed from their cores, and its crust is not broken if a wagon wheel goes over it."

One suspects that the maker of this particular pie was not swamped with requests for her recipe.

Ginger Gold Apple Pie with Golden Raisins

Recently, I've been noticing a relatively new apple in the market, the Ginger Gold, which comes highly recommended from a number of fans and apple growers. I heard that it makes a good pie, and after trying it, I have to agree. The story goes that the Ginger Gold was discovered as a seedling in Virginia after Hurricane Camille hit the southern states in 1969—something I noted with interest since I was stationed in Gulfport, Mississippi, the area hardest hit by Camille, in the early 1970s. The hurricane destroyed much of the orchard of Clyde and Ginger Harvey, who several years later discovered a tree that had grown from a seed that had likely blown in with the storm. The naming rights went to Mrs. Harvey. Researchers think that the Ginger Gold might be an offspring of the Albemarle Pippin, and like other Pippins I've baked with, it makes a good pie. It seems to be better for baking just after being picked, when the flavor is more tart than sweet; as the apple matures, the taste gets sweeter. I like the name of the apple, and the golden images it conjures up, so in this pie I play on the gold theme by adding golden raisins. If you can find Ginger Gold apples at your farm stand or market, I think you'll be very pleased with this pie.

1 RECIPE ALL-AMERICAN DOUBLE CRUST (PAGE 2), MADE WITH ½ TEASPOON GROUND GINGER ADDED TO THE DRY INGREDIENTS

FILLING:

8 CUPS PEELED, CORED, AND SLICED GINGER GOLD APPLES

¼ CUP SUGAR

1 TABLESPOON FRESH LEMON JUICE

1 TEASPOON GRATED LEMON ZEST

½ CUP GOLDEN RAISINS

1 ½ TABLESPOONS ALL-PURPOSE FLOUR

GLAZE:

MILK

SUGAR

1. If you haven't already, prepare the pastry and refrigerate it until firm enough to roll, about 1 hour.

2. On a sheet of floured waxed paper, roll the larger portion of the pastry into a 13½-inch circle with a floured rolling pin. Invert the pastry over a 9-inch deep-dish pie pan. Center it, then peel off the paper. Tuck the pastry into the pan, without stretching it, and let the excess drape over the side. Refrigerate for at least 15 minutes. Preheat the oven to 400 degrees.

3. To make the filling, mix the apples, sugar, lemon juice, lemon zest, and raisins together in a large mixing bowl. Set aside for 10 minutes.

4. On another sheet of lightly floured waxed paper, roll the top pastry into an 11½-inch circle. Sprinkle the flour over the filling and mix well. Turn the filling into the refrigerated pie shell and smooth with your hands. Lightly moisten the edge of the pie shell with a wet fingertip or pastry brush. Invert the top pastry over the filling, center it, and peel off the paper.

Press the top and bottom pastries together along the dampened edge. Trim the pastry with scissors or a paring knife, leaving an even ½-inch overhang all around, then sculpt the overhang into an upstanding ridge. Poke several steam vents in the top of the pie with a fork or paring knife; put a couple of the vents near the edge of the crust, so you can check the juices there later. Brush the top of the pie with a little milk and sprinkle lightly with sugar.

5. Put the pie directly on the center oven rack and bake for 30 minutes. Remove from the oven and place on a large, dark baking sheet covered with aluminum foil. Reduce the oven temperature to 375 degrees. Return the pie on the baking sheet to the oven and bake until any juices—visible at the steam vents—bubble thickly, another 30 to 40 minutes.

6. Transfer the pie to a cooling rack and let cool for at least 1 hour before slicing.

Makes 8 to 10 servings

DRIED FRUIT: A NATURAL THICKENER

When you use raisins or other dried fruit in an apple pie, consider using less thickener than you otherwise might. The reason is simple: dried fruit absorbs juice like a sponge, reducing the need for a thickening agent. There are no hard and fast rules about this; just use your judgment. However, if a recipe directs you to soak the dried fruit in liquid ahead, be aware that it will absorb less liquid in the pie. My favorite dried fruits for apple pies are raisins, of course, dried tart and sweet cherries, sweetened dried cranberries (also known as Craisins), dried pears, dried figs, and prunes.

Apple and Poached Fig Pie with Hazelnut Crumb Crust

I don't know where the rest of the food world shops, but what I read in so many cookbooks would lead me to believe that fresh figs can be had at just about any corner grocery or convenience store. Well, that's not the case where I live in New Hampshire. Yes, occasionally I will see a flat of fresh figs at the supermarket, but they usually look like I feel after a nonstop flight, in coach, from the East Coast to Hawaii—exhausted would be putting it kindly—and they cost about as much as the ticket. Thus over the years I've become a great fan of dried figs, which I love to cook with. The first step with dried figs is to poach them, which I do here in red wine. Then I reduce the sweetened poaching liquid and use it to sweeten and flavor the pie, whose apple fig filling takes on a beautiful wine red cast. The finishing touch is a hazelnut crumb topping, because they have a real affinity for figs—a combination I've seen in several books on Mediterranean cooking. This adds up to a stunning winter pie you'll want to serve with a fresh pot of hot coffee.

1 CUP WHOLE HAZELNUTS

8 OUNCES WHOLE DRIED FIGS (ABOUT 1 ½ CUPS), STEMS REMOVED

2 CUPS DRY RED WINE

½ CUP SUGAR

1 RECIPE BEST BUTTER PIE PASTRY (PAGE 8), REFRIGERATED

FILLING:

6 LARGE APPLES, PEELED, CORED, AND SLICED

JUICE OF 1 LEMON

GRATED ZEST OF 1 ORANGE

¼ TEASPOON GROUND CINNAMON

3 TABLESPOONS INSTANT TAPIOCA

HAZELNUT CRUMB TOPPING:

⅔ CUP SUGAR

¾ CUP ALL-PURPOSE FLOUR

¼ TEASPOON SALT

½ CUP (1 STICK) COLD UNSALTED BUTTER, CUT INTO ¼-INCH PIECES

1. Preheat the oven to 350 degrees. Spread the hazelnuts on a large baking sheet and place the sheet on the center oven rack. Toast until the skins look blistered, about 10 minutes. Place a clean tea towel on your counter and tilt the nuts out of the pan and onto the towel. Fold the towel over the nuts, wait 1 minute, and rub the nuts vigorously through the towel to remove the skins. Don't worry if you can't get every last bit of skin off. Transfer the nuts to a plate and let cool to room temperature.

2. Halve the figs, unless they're very large, in which case you can even cut them into quarters. In a small saucepan, bring the wine and sugar nearly to a boil; add the figs. Cover the pan partially, reduce the heat to low, and simmer gently for about 30 minutes. Using a slotted spoon, transfer the figs to a small bowl. Return the wine to a boil and reduce the remaining liquid to about ½ cup; keep a heatproof measuring cup nearby to check the amount. Set aside.

3. If you haven't already, make the pastry and refrigerate it until firm enough to roll, about 1 hour.

4. On a sheet of lightly floured waxed paper, roll the pastry into a 13½-inch circle with a floured rolling pin. Invert the pastry over a 9-inch deep-dish pie pan. Center it, then peel off the paper. Gently tuck the pastry down into the pan, without stretching it, and sculpt the edge into an upstanding ridge. Place the pie shell in the freezer for at least 30 minutes.

5. To make the filling, mix together the apples, lemon juice, orange zest, and cinnamon in a large mixing bowl. Add the figs and reduced wine and toss well. Sprinkle the tapioca over the top, then stir it into the filling. Turn the filling into the frozen pie shell and smooth with your hands to even it out. Place the pie on a large, dark baking sheet covered with aluminum foil and bake on the center oven rack for 35 minutes.

6. While the pie bakes, make the hazelnut crumb topping. Put the toasted hazelnuts and sugar in a food processor and pulse until the nuts are well chopped but not overly so. Add the flour and salt and pulse again to mix. Remove the lid and scatter the butter pieces over the surface of the dry ingredients. Pulse until the mixture resembles medium-fine crumbs. Empty the crumbs into a large mixing bowl and rub between your fingers to make large, buttery crumbs. Refrigerate.

7. After 35 minutes, remove the pie from the oven. Reduce the oven temperature to 375 degrees. Carefully dump the crumbs in the center of the pie, spreading them evenly over the surface with your hands. Tamp them down lightly. Put the pie on the baking sheet back in the oven and bake until the juices bubble thickly around the edge, an additional 35 to 45 minutes. Loosely cover the pie with aluminum foil during the last 15 minutes of baking to keep the top from browning too much.

8. Transfer the pie to a cooling rack and let cool for at least 1 hour before slicing.

Makes 8 to 10 servings

CHAPTER 9

Apple Pie on the Fringes

When we think of apple pie, we imagine a dish with a bottom crust, filling, and either a top crust or crumb topping. Correct? For the most part. But there are apple pies whose architecture doesn't quite travel along traditional lines. Those are the apple pies you will find in this section—the renegades who thumb their collective nose at tradition in the service of a good idea that doesn't fit the standard mold.

This group ranges from fairly traditional non-traditionalists, such as apple pear hand pies made with a delicate cream cheese pastry, to extremists like apple pizza made with a yeasted pastry and apple burritos made with flour tortillas. Some, like the hand pies, are quite sturdy and eminently portable. Others, like the apple burritos, should be eaten right away, lest their warm, crisp appeal vanish.

So whether you're searching for an apple pie that suits your own renegade style or you're just looking for an alternative to the apple pies you're accustomed to, poke around here. You're bound to find something that speaks to your taste buds.

Apple Cheesecake Burritos

When you think about it, a burrito is actually a kind of pie—a hand pie. So I have no qualms about offering you this excellent recipe for a sort of warm apple cheesecake pie with a tortilla "crust." It tastes like a cheesecake because there is a sweetened cream cheese layer in the filling, but it also has another layer of sautéed diced apples tossed with brown sugar and graham cracker crumbs. These layers are wrapped in a warm flour tortilla, slathered with softened butter, and dusted with sugar, then briefly broiled to give the outside a crispy texture.

The kids will love these hand pies, and they're great for fall parties. The recipe can be easily multiplied to make more servings.

One 3-ounce package cold cream cheese

1 tablespoon granulated sugar

1 teaspoon fresh lemon juice

2 whole graham crackers

2 tablespoons firmly packed light brown sugar

⅛ teaspoon ground cinnamon

1 tablespoon unsalted butter

1 Golden Delicious or other firm-textured baking apple, peeled, cored, and cut into ½-inch chunks

Two 8- or 9-inch flour tortillas

GLAZE:

1 tablespoon unsalted butter, softened

Granulated sugar

1. Put the cream cheese on a small plate and mash well with a fork. Add the granulated sugar and lemon juice and mash again. Refrigerate.

2. Break the graham crackers up coarsely and put them in a zipper-topped plastic storage bag. Using a rolling pin, crush the crackers to make fine crumbs. Put the crumbs in a medium-size mixing bowl. Add the brown sugar and cinnamon and toss well to mix. Set aside.

3. Melt the butter in a medium-size skillet. Add the apples and cook, stirring, over medium heat until heated through but still crunchy, about 2 minutes. Remove from the heat and scrape into the crumb mixture, tossing well to mix with the crumbs. Set aside. Preheat the broiler.

4. To assemble the burritos, warm one of the tortillas just until it's flexible in a skillet over low heat. Place the tortilla on the counter and spread half of the cream cheese mixture in the center of it, in a rectangle about 1¼ inches wide and 4 inches across. Spoon half of the apple crumb mixture on top of the cheese, then fold the sides over the filling as if you were making the first 2 folds of a regular burrito. Next fold the edge closest to you over the filling, then roll up the burrito to seal. Repeat for the other tortilla and the rest of the cream cheese and apple mixtures.

5. Place the burritos in a shallow, buttered baking dish, seam side down. Smear the softened butter over the surface and sprinkle with sugar. Run the burritos under the broiler—6 to 8 inches from the heat—until the tops are golden brown, 1 to 2 minutes. Watch them like a hawk, so they don't burn.

6. Transfer to a cutting board and cut in half diagonally before serving.

Makes 2 regular or 4 modest dessert- or snack-size servings

Apple and Brie Hand Pies

Elsewhere in this collection, I've talked about the tasty tradition of eating cheese with apple pie (see page 46). Alas, I've tried baking cheese into apple pie on more than a few occasions, and the result has never been very pretty. Inevitably, the intense heat of the oven breaks the cheese down, leaving the filling an oily, salty mess. But if the cheese doesn't do well in the oven, I reasoned, perhaps it would do much better on top of the stove, with only a brief encounter with the heat. That's how I came up with this hand pie—essentially a sort of grilled cheese and apple sandwich made in a tortilla. There are only three ingredients in the filling—sliced apples, Brie cheese, and apple butter—and a dusting of rosemary-and-cinnamon sugar. The pie can be thrown together in minutes, and it makes a great lunch or an unusual sweet-and-savory dessert. The recipe makes 1 or 2 servings, but it can be easily multiplied to feed a number of people.

1 TABLESPOON SUGAR

½ TEASPOON CRUSHED DRIED ROSEMARY

¼ TEASPOON GROUND CINNAMON

1 TO 2 TEASPOONS UNSALTED BUTTER, SOFTENED

ONE 8- OR 9-INCH FLOUR TORTILLA

1 TABLESPOON SPICED APPLE BUTTER, HOMEMADE (PAGE 101) OR STORE-BOUGHT

1 GRANNY SMITH OR OTHER CRISP, TART APPLE, PEELED, CORED, AND THINLY SLICED

3 OR 4 SLICES BRIE CHEESE NOT QUITE ¼ INCH THICK

1. Mix the sugar, rosemary, and cinnamon together in a ramekin or small bowl; set aside.

2. Spread the butter on one side of the tortilla and place buttered side down in a large, heavy skillet over medium heat. Spread the apple butter over the tortilla with the back of the spoon.

3. Arrange the apple slices over half of the tortilla, overlapping a little if you like; you may not need them all. Place the cheese on top of the apples, then fold the uncovered half of the tortilla over the filling, pressing down gently with a metal spatula. Heat for 30 to 45 seconds.

4. Flip the hand pie over and heat for about the same amount of time on the other side to melt the cheese. Brush the top with a bit of the melted butter in the skillet and sprinkle generously with the sugar mixture.

5. Transfer the hand pie to a chopping board and cut in half. Serve hot.

Makes 1 or 2 servings

NOW HERE'S A GAL WITH A PEEL

In 1976, at the ripe old age of 16, Kathy Wafler Madison of Wolcott, New York, took horticultural knife in hand and pared her way into the history books by peeling the longest apple peel on record. According to the *Guinness Book of World Records*, the peel measured 2,068 inches, or roughly 172 feet, long—slightly longer than half a football field. I caught up with Kathy at her place of business, Wafler Nursery in Wolcott, to ask her about her incredible feat.

Ken Haedrich (KH): So how did this whole thing start?

Kathy Wafler Madison (KWM): A local mall was opening, and as part of their promotion they decided to have an apple-peeling contest. I'd entered peeling contests before this, at a local apple festival, so I thought I'd give it a shot.

KH: What sort of peeler did you use?

KWM: I had a special knife that we use in this business for grafting and budding. My dad adjusted the angle on the tip of the blade so I had two angles, one for scoring the apple and one for peeling it.

KH: It must make for a pretty thin peel, to get that long.

KWM: The average width of the peel was about one-thirty-second of an inch.

KH: And the apple you used?

KWM: As far as I know, there are no restrictions on the apple you can use. Mine was a processing apple named a twenty-ouncer, and I believe it weighed about that much.

KH: How long did it take to peel the apple?

KWM: It took about eleven hours, and I don't know if I could do that today, stand on my feet for that long. I would take short breaks, but you can't stop for too long because the longer the peel sits there, the more fragile it becomes. So you want to keep peeling.

KH: What advice do you have for someone who might want to try and break your record?

KWM: Get a big apple. And have a lot of patience.

KH: By the way, what happened to the record-setting peel and apple?

KWM: As for the peel, I dried it, then had it framed. Now I keep it in a safe. I'm not sure about the apple. I think I ate a little of it and threw the rest away.

Apple Hand Pies with Apricot Preserves

Apple hand pies, also known as turnovers, are a pleasant departure from traditional apple pie. They're more delicate—especially these, with their soft, flaky cream cheese pastry—and there's a higher proportion of crust to filling.

Be aware that the cream cheese makes this a fairly soft dough. If it becomes a little too soft while you're working it, simply slide the dough, waxed paper and all, onto a small baking sheet and refrigerate it for a few minutes before continuing.

1 RECIPE FLAKY CREAM CHEESE PASTRY (PAGE 14), DIVIDED AS INSTRUCTED IN STEP 1 AND REFRIGERATED

FILLING:

1 TABLESPOON GRANULATED SUGAR

2 TEASPOONS ALL-PURPOSE FLOUR

¼ TEASPOON GROUND CINNAMON

2 APPLES, PEELED

ABOUT 3 TABLESPOONS APRICOT PRESERVES

GLAZE AND DUSTING:

MILK OR LIGHT CREAM

GRANULATED SUGAR

CONFECTIONERS' SUGAR (OPTIONAL)

1. When you prepare the pastry, divide it into 4 equal-size balls. Flatten the balls into ½-inch-thick disks and wrap the disks in plastic wrap. Refrigerate until firm, 1 to 1½ hours, but not overly so, or it will be difficult to roll.

2. To assemble the filling, mix the granulated sugar, flour, and cinnamon together in a small bowl; set aside. Halve the apples lengthwise and core them. Place each half on a cutting board, flat side down, and cut straight down through it, making even ⅛-inch-thick slices. Set aside.

3. Working with one piece of dough at a time, roll it into an 8-inch circle on a sheet of lightly floured waxed paper with a floured rolling pin. Dot with about 2 teaspoons of the preserves, spreading it around the center of the circle. Sprinkle lightly with some of the sugar mixture. Arrange a single row of overlapping apples slices over one half of the dough. Leave a good ¾-inch border around the slices, more or less following the curve of the pastry. Sprinkle a little more of the sugar mixture over the apples.

4. Moisten the edge of the pastry with a finger, then fold the empty half over the apples. Fold up the border and pinch the edges together, rolling them between your fingers into a sort of rope edge. Place the turnover on a large, lightly buttered baking sheet. Refrigerate while you make the remaining hand pies, putting each on the sheet as it is assembled. Preheat the oven to 400 degrees.

5. Remove the sheet from the refrigerator and brush each hand pie with a little milk. Sprinkle with granulated sugar, then poke the surface 2 or 3 times with a fork to make steam vents. Place on the center oven rack and bake for 10 minutes. Reduce the oven temperature to 375 degrees and bake for 20 minutes longer, until golden brown. You may see steam coming from the vents.

6. Transfer the pies to a cooling rack and let cool slightly. While they are still warm, dust them with a little confectioners' sugar, if you like. I just put a couple of tablespoons of sugar in a sieve and shake it right over the pies. I think these are best eaten warm.

Makes 4 hand pies

Apple and Pear Hand Pies with Raisins and Walnuts

The previous hand pie recipe uses sliced apples on a bed of apricot preserves. This one uses chopped apples and pears mixed with walnuts, raisins, cinnamon, coconut, and brown sugar. The first is a little more refined; this is more informal, something you might take on a picnic or tuck into a youngster's lunch bag.

1 RECIPE FLAKY CREAM CHEESE PASTRY (PAGE 14), DIVIDED AS INSTRUCTED IN STEP 1 AND REFRIGERATED

FILLING:

⅓ CUP RAISINS

⅓ CUP WALNUT HALVES OR PIECES

¼ CUP FIRMLY PACKED LIGHT BROWN SUGAR

¼ CUP SWEETENED FLAKED COCONUT

¼ TEASPOON GROUND CINNAMON

1 APPLE, PEELED, CORED, AND CUT INTO BITE-SIZE CHUNKS

1 RIPE PEAR, QUARTERED, CORED, AND CUT INTO BITE-SIZE CHUNKS

1 TABLESPOON FRESH LEMON JUICE

GLAZE AND DUSTING:

MILK

GRANULATED SUGAR

CONFECTIONERS' SUGAR (OPTIONAL)

1. When you make the pastry, divide the dough into 4 equal-size balls. Flatten the balls into ½-inch-thick disks and wrap the disks in plastic wrap. Refrigerate until fairly firm, 1 to 1½ hours, but not overly so, or it will be difficult to roll.

2. To make the filling, put the raisins, walnuts, brown sugar, coconut, and cinnamon in a food processor and pulse repeatedly, until the nuts are finely chopped—but not too finely; you want some larger pieces, too. Transfer to a medium-size mixing bowl and add the apple, pear, and lemon juice. Mix well and set aside.

3. Working with one piece of dough at a time, roll it into an 8-inch circle on a sheet of lightly floured waxed paper with a floured rolling pin. Spoon about one-quarter of the filling over half of the dough, leaving a ¾-inch border along the edge.

4. Moisten the edge of the pastry with a finger, then fold the empty half over the filling.

Fold up the border and pinch the edges together, rolling them between your fingers into a sort of rope edge. Place the turnover on a large, lightly buttered baking sheet. Refrigerate while you make the remaining hand pies, putting each on the sheet as it is assembled. Preheat the oven to 400 degrees.

5. Remove the sheet from the refrigerator and brush each hand pie with a little milk. Sprinkle them with granulated sugar, then poke the surface 2 or 3 times with a fork to make steam vents. Place on the center oven rack and bake for 10 minutes. Reduce the oven temperature to 375 degrees and bake for 20 minutes longer, until golden brown. You may see steam coming from the vents.

6. Transfer the pies to a cooling rack and let cool slightly. While they're still warm, dust them with a little confectioners' sugar, if you like. I just put a tablespoon or two of sugar in a sieve and shake it right over the pies. I think these are best eaten warm.

Makes 4 servings

A SLICE OF PIE HISTORY

We Americans—always quick to embrace a good idea—have adopted apple pie as our own. But pie, even apple pie, has a rather long and rich history that predates the founding of our country.

The first published pie recipe—for a fairly contemporary-sounding goat cheese and honey pie in a rye crust—reportedly dates back to the early Romans, who may have learned to make pie from the Greeks. These earliest pies were baked in inedible reeds, whose sole purpose was to contain the filling.

This tradition of baking pies in inedible crusts would continue for hundreds of years. When "pyes" originally appeared in England, as early as the 12th century, the crust was a series of thick, straight walls known as a "coffyn." Fowl and other meats were the pies of the day. Often the legs of the bird were left dangling off the side of the dish, providing a handle for transporting it.

Fruit fillings emerged around the 16th century and followed settlers from Britain to the New World. The pie-in-a-box concept had yet to die off: the earliest colonists baked thick-crusted pies in long, rectangular pans they called—you guessed it—coffins. In time, though, pie baking would evolve from essentially a survival skill to a domestic art, as evidenced in the first American cookbook, by Amelia Simmons (1796), which includes 14 pie recipes and a variety of crusts. More reliable ovens would allow for thinner, edible crusts whose function did not disregard flavor. The abundance and variety of early American apple orchards would give our ancestor cooks the opportunity to bring a certain degree of nuance and sophistication to the baking of apple pies.

So, American as apple pie? Certainly. But with acknowledgment and gratitude to the tradition from whence we came.

"Assembled" Apple Pie

There are those who believe that the best apple pie is cooked not as a single unit but as separate entities—pastry, filling, top crust—then assembled just before serving. The thinking is that a pie whose components are cooked separately will have more distinct layers and be less inclined to develop a damp crust. Frankly, I hadn't thought too much about it until one of my editors mentioned that a respected cookbook author and food scientist, Shirley Corriher, included a recipe for just such a pie in her book *Cookwise* (Morrow, 1997). Rather than consult her recipe, I thought it would be an interesting exercise to try to invent one of my own, based on some of the broad strokes my editor relayed to me. Thus I came up with what I call an assembled apple pie. In a nutshell, here's what happens: The pie shell is baked separately until golden brown. Then the top pastry is rolled out and cut into wedges, which are also baked separately. The filling—sliced apples, brown sugar, confectioners' sugar, and applesauce—is simmered in a saucepan, then poured into the crust, and the wedges are placed on top. The applesauce, I find, is an important touch because it fills in between the apple slices and gives the pie a long-baked taste and texture. Without it, the filling is a little lacking.

So is this a better apple pie? I'll let you be the judge of that. This is a great choice for those who like to eat their apple pie hot.

1 RECIPE ALL-AMERICAN DOUBLE CRUST (PAGE 2), REFRIGERATED

FILLING:

2 TABLESPOONS UNSALTED BUTTER

6 CUPS PEELED, CORED, AND SLICED FIRM-TEXTURED APPLES (SUCH AS GALA OR GOLDEN DELICIOUS)

PINCH OF SALT

2 TABLESPOONS FIRMLY PACKED LIGHT BROWN SUGAR

⅓ CUP CONFECTIONERS' SUGAR

1 TABLESPOON FRESH LEMON JUICE

⅛ TEASPOON GROUND CINNAMON

1 CUP APPLESAUCE, HOMEMADE (PAGE 97) OR STORE-BOUGHT

1. If you haven't already, prepare the pastry and refrigerate it until firm enough to roll, about 1 hour.

2. On a sheet of lightly floured waxed paper, roll the larger portion of the pastry into a 13½-inch circle with a floured rolling pin. Invert the pastry over a 9-inch deep-dish pie pan. Center it, then peel off the paper. Gently tuck the pastry into the pan, without stretching it, and sculpt the edge into an upstanding ridge. Place the pie shell in the freezer for 30 minutes, then fully prebake it according to the directions on page 19. Transfer the pie shell to a cooling rack and let cool. Preheat the oven to 375 degrees.

3. While the pie shell is baking, prepare the top pastry. On a sheet of lightly floured waxed paper, roll the pastry into a 10-inch circle, trimming the edges with a paring knife or pizza cutter to make it nice and even. Cut the pastry into 8 wedges, as you would a pie, and place the wedges on a lightly buttered baking sheet.

Refrigerate for 5 to 10 minutes, then place the sheet on the center oven rack and bake until the wedges are golden brown, about 15 minutes. With a metal spatula, transfer the wedges from the sheet to a cooling rack.

4. To make the filling, melt the butter in a large, nonreactive sauté pan or Dutch oven. Stir in the apples, salt, and brown sugar. Cook, partially covered, over medium heat for about 5 minutes, stirring often. Stir in the confectioners' sugar, lemon juice, and cinnamon and continue to cook, partially covered, until the apples are tender, 5 to 8 minutes. Stir in the applesauce, cook another minute or so, and remove from the heat.

5. Scrape the filling into the pie shell, smoothing the top with a fork. Assemble the pastry wedges on top of the pie. Bring the pie to the table and slice.

Makes 8 servings

Apple "Calzone" Pie

The yeasted butter pastry I use to make the apple pizza on page 206 makes the perfect wrapper for this sweet version of a calzone filled with sautéed apple slices and ricotta cheese. This one is put together in essentially the same way as a true calzone: a yeast dough is rolled into a large circle, the filling goes on half, and the dough is folded over. Since the apples are precooked, the calzone bakes relatively quickly—in just about 20 minutes—and it emerges crusty, brown, and perhaps somewhat inflated. Rather than eat it right away, I like to wait about an hour, after the dough softens to a strudel-like texture and collapses to hug the filling. Cut it into narrow strips and serve it with coffee or tea for a special Sunday morning treat.

1 RECIPE YEASTED BUTTER PASTRY
   (PAGE 12), RISEN

FINE CORNMEAL OR SEMOLINA

FILLING:

2 TABLESPOONS UNSALTED BUTTER

2 GOLDEN DELICIOUS OR OTHER FIRM-
   TEXTURED APPLES, PEELED, CORED, AND
   THICKLY SLICED

2 TABLESPOONS PLUS ⅓ CUP GRANULATED
   SUGAR

1 ¼ CUPS RICOTTA CHEESE

½ TEASPOON PURE VANILLA EXTRACT

2 TEASPOONS FRESH LEMON JUICE

2 TEASPOONS GRATED LEMON ZEST

1 TABLESPOON PLAIN YOGURT, SOUR
   CREAM, OR HEAVY CREAM

PINCH OF GROUND NUTMEG

GLAZE AND DUSTING:

MILK

GRANULATED SUGAR

CONFECTIONERS' SUGAR

1. If you haven't already, prepare the pastry and set it aside to rise at room temperature for 1 hour. Meanwhile, lightly oil a large baking sheet and dust it with the cornmeal.

2. After an hour, punch the dough down gently and knead for 30 seconds on a lightly floured work surface. Put the dough back in the same bowl, cover with plastic, and refrigerate while you prepare the filling.

3. Melt the butter in a large nonreactive skillet over medium heat. Stir in the apples and 2 tablespoons of the granulated sugar. Cook the apples, stirring often, until tender, about 8 minutes, then remove from the heat and set aside to cool. Preheat the oven to 400 degrees.

4. Put the ricotta cheese, remaining ⅓ cup granulated sugar, vanilla, lemon juice, lemon zest, yogurt, and nutmeg in a food processor. Pulse several times to puree; it needn't be a perfectly smooth puree, however. Set aside.

5. Flour your work surface, then put the dough in the center of it, without punching it down. Dust the dough and your rolling pin with flour and gently roll the dough into a 15-inch circle. Lift the dough onto the prepared baking sheet, letting a little of it drape over the edge.

6. Draw an imaginary line down the center of the dough. Scrape the cheese mixture onto the dough, spreading it over one half but leaving a 2-inch border around the edge. Spoon the apples over the cheese. Lightly moisten the edge of the pastry with a pastry brush, then fold the uncovered dough over the filling. Pinch the edges together, then roll the edge up slightly tohelp prevent leakage. Using a fork, poke a few steam vents in the top of the dough. Brush with a little milk and sprinkle with granulated sugar. Place the baking sheet on the center oven rack and bake until nicely browned, 20 to 22 minutes.

7. Remove from the oven and slide the calzone onto a large cooling rack. Let cool for about 10 minutes, then dust the top generously with confectioners' sugar. Let cool for 1 hour more, then cut into roughly 1½-inch-wide slices and serve.

Makes 9 or 10 servings

Apple Pizza Pie

If you like bready things, you'll love this pastry—and this pizza pie. It's a yeasted pastry, based on the French pastry used for *galettes*—thin tarts made with all sorts of different toppings. It can be mixed easily right in your food processor. (Don't be surprised if you start using it for regular pizza—that's how good it is.) Like any yeasted dough, it rises for about an hour, then it's rolled out and covered with a layer of very thinly sliced apples. It's baked just like that for about 10 minutes, then covered with Gruyère or cheddar cheese and baked for about 5 minutes more. I sometimes spread a layer of sauerkraut over the apples just before I sprinkle on the cheese. The combination of the apples, cheese, bready crust, and kraut is sensational. This is best eaten warm, but it can be cooled on a rack and gently reheated later. But do eat it the same day you make it; the crust is not a great keeper. Unusual and delicious, it makes a great party dish.

1 RECIPE YEASTED BUTTER PASTRY
(PAGE 12), RISEN

FINE CORNMEAL OR SEMOLINA

FILLING:

2 TABLESPOONS COLD UNSALTED BUTTER,
CUT INTO SMALL PIECES

2 GOLDEN DELICIOUS OR OTHER FIRM-
TEXTURED COOKING APPLES, PEELED AND
CORED

1 TABLESPOON SUGAR

PINCH OF GROUND CINNAMON

BIG PINCH OF FINELY CHOPPED FRESH
ROSEMARY LEAVES

2 CUPS SAUERKRAUT (OPTIONAL), DRAINED
AND WARMED

2 CUPS GRATED GRUYÈRE OR EXTRA-SHARP
CHEDDAR CHEESE

1. If you haven't already, prepare the pastry and set it aside to rise for 1 hour. Meanwhile, lightly oil a large baking sheet and dust it with the cornmeal.

2. When the dough has risen, without punching it down, turn it out onto the center of the baking sheet. Using oiled fingers, press the dough out into a 13-inch circle, smoothing it, if you like, with a floured rolling pin. Try to keep it of even thickness; you want to avoid making thin spots you can see through. Pinch the dough around the edge, forming an upstanding rim. Refrigerate the dough for 10 minutes. Preheat the oven to 425 degrees.

3. Dot the surface of the dough with the butter. Halve the apples lengthwise. Place each half cut side down on a cutting board and cut into very thin slices. Arrange the slices on the crust, overlapping them slightly. Mix the sugar, cinnamon, and rosemary together in a small mixing bowl and sprinkle evenly over the apples.

4. Place the baking sheet on the center oven rack and bake for 8 minutes. Reduce the oven temperature to 375 degrees. Remove the pizza from the oven and sprinkle with the sauerkraut, if using. Sprinkle evenly with the cheese.

5. Bake the pizza for another 5 minutes, until the cheese has melted nicely; it shouldn't bubble. Do not overbake; since this is a buttery, porous dough, it tends to get fairly brown after about 15 minutes. Slice into wedges and serve as soon as possible.

Makes 10 servings

OF APPLE PIES AND TAILGATE PARTIES

I'm a big fan of tailgate parties—so much so that I've actually written a handy laminated guide to throwing your own tailgate party, complete with recipes and tips. (You can read more about it at my Web site, www.duraguides.com.)

Shameless self-promotion aside, an apple outing really is a great venue for a tailgate party. I'm thinking specifically about a day trip to a local orchard, where you can pick your own apples and perhaps join in the festivities if the orchard is sponsoring a special day of events, which orchards often do in the fall.

Tailgate parties are all about friends and food, so invite other families to join you. Come up with a menu, divvy up the cooking duties, and don't forget the essentials, such as bagged ice, cutting boards, plastic forks and knives, and garbage bags. If the weather promises to be cool, hot soup is one good course. Sandwiches—wraps or regular—are easy to make and portable. Everyone likes a good old American potato salad. And serve apple pie for dessert, of course, along with plenty of hot spiced cider to drink (see Mulled Cider, page 37).

To keep the kids busy and happy, bring along stuff they can do. Disposable cameras are a hit. Face paints are fun, too. And don't forget the Frisbees, mitts and softball, blankets, and lawn chairs for when Mom and Pop need a break.

CHAPTER 10

A Few for the Kids

My kids are in their teens and twenties now, with little room on their social calendars to be baking with the old man. But when they were younger, it was much different. I couldn't bake anything, pie or otherwise, without the kids swarming around me like a cloud of locusts. There were times when I would have one of the kids in a backpack, two more sitting on my baker's bench, and another around the corner, cracking eggs into the toaster. This was a typical day at the Haedrich house for many years. And the toaster has never been the same since.

Apple pie was often the center of attention at these baking sessions, so my kids learned at a very early age what was involved in making an apple pie: you make a crust, roll it out, slice up the apples, and mix them with good stuff such as brown sugar, cinnamon, and raisins. As adults, it's easy for us to take the process—and the ingredients—for granted. But to our kids, this is all in the spirit of great fun, and it's quite captivating as well, seeing firsthand this transformation from raw ingredients to a great-smelling, bubbling-hot baked pie.

So if you have kids, be sure to bake with them. They'll thank you if you do—though perhaps not until they're 45 and have their own kids and can understand what a mess kids can make in the kitchen.

Here are a few recipes you can turn to when you start making apple pies with your kids—these being pies I've made with my kids or ones they've made on their own, with little or no help from me. All will engage your kids on some level, either because they're made with caramel, because they make individual kid-size pies, or because—in the case of the hand pie made with a tortilla—they include marshmallows and chocolate chips.

Remember, kids will make a mess in the kitchen: flour will fly, eggs will drop, and chaos will reign. Learn to accept a certain amount of mess, and you'll have more fun. Consider doing what a friend of mine used to do. She would spread a tarp on the floor, under the counter, then not worry about the mess. After each baking session, she'd hose down the tarp and hang it out to dry. In the summer, she'd hose down the kids, too.

Individual Double-Crust Apple Pear Pies

Just about everyone loves an individual apple pie, particularly kids, who also love to make them. I've tried all sorts of small pie pans over the years, with varying outcomes. The standard mini pie tins aren't really the best because they're too small and too shallow to make a pie of any consequence, although they do make an okay open-faced pie. What I've finally settled on are the standard, old-fashioned 10-ounce Pyrex custard cups. You can find these at almost any housewares store; the last time I bought some, I think I paid about five bucks for a set of four. The best feature of these cups is their depth: you can fit a generous amount of filling in each one.

If you're looking for a fun project with the kids, consider these pies. The recipe could easily be doubled for a Halloween or other party. Give each child a portion of dough to roll, some waxed paper to roll it on, and some flour. Use the basic filling below, then give each kid the option of customizing his or her pie. One might want to add a few raisins or nuts, a different spice. These extras can be arranged in the center of the work table in little bowls.

1 RECIPE ALL-AMERICAN DOUBLE CRUST
(PAGE 2) OR SHORTENING DOUBLE CRUST
(PAGE 4), DIVIDED AS INSTRUCTED IN STEP
1 AND REFRIGERATED

FILLING:

2½ LARGE APPLES, PEELED, QUARTERED,
AND CORED

1 LARGE RIPE PEAR, QUARTERED AND CORED

⅓ CUP SUGAR

1 TABLESPOON FRESH LEMON JUICE

2 TABLESPOONS PEACH OR APRICOT
PRESERVES

1½ TABLESPOONS ALL-PURPOSE FLOUR

¼ TEASPOON GROUND CINNAMON

GLAZE:

MILK

SUGAR

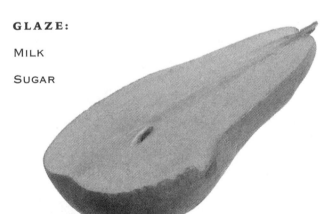

1. Prepare the pastry as directed, dividing it as follows. Lift the pastry out of the bowl onto a sheet of lightly floured waxed paper. Press it into a large, thickish rectangle and divide the rectangle in half, making half of the rectangle slightly larger than the other. Divide the larger half into 4 equal pieces; these will be the bottom crusts. Divide the other half of the dough into 4 equal pieces; these will be the top crusts. Shape each piece into a thick disk and place them on a small baking sheet lined with plastic wrap. Cover with plastic wrap and refrigerate for at least 1 hour.

2. When you're almost ready to start the assembly, prepare the filling. Slice the apples and pears crosswise into thin slices. Combine the fruit, sugar, lemon juice, and preserves in a large mixing bowl and mix well. Shake the flour and cinnamon over the fruit and mix again. Set the filling aside while you roll the pastry. Preheat the oven to 400 degrees.

3. Working with one of the larger pieces of dough at a time, roll the dough into a 7½- to 8-inch circle on a sheet of lightly floured waxed paper with a floured rolling pin. Before you lift the dough into the custard cup, make four 1½-inch slits at the 12, 3, 6, and 9 o'clock positions. The slits will allow the dough to neatly self-pleat when you tuck it into the cup. Invert the dough onto your hand and carefully lower the pastry into the cup. Tuck it into the bottom and sides of the cup, letting the dough hang over the edge. Refrigerate while you repeat this operation for the remaining dough cups.

4. Spoon an equal amount of the apple filling into each cup; set aside. On fresh sheets of lightly floured waxed paper, roll the remaining pieces of dough into 5½-inch circles. Moisten the edge of each pie shell and lift the top pastry into place, pressing the top and bottom pastries together at the dampened edge. As you do so, push the pastry down into the pan slightly, then trim the overhanging dough with a paring knife. With the knife, poke several steam vents in the top pastry. Brush lightly with milk and sprinkle with sugar.

5. Put the cups on a large, dark baking sheet covered with aluminum foil and place on the center oven rack. Bake for 25 minutes, then reduce the oven temperature to 375 degrees and bake for an additional 20 to 25 minutes. When the pies are done, you may or may not see thick juices bubbling up onto the crust; it will depend on the amount of juices and the level of the pastry. Nonetheless, 50 minutes should be more than enough time.

6. Transfer the pies to a cooling rack and let cool for at least 30 minutes before serving.

Makes 4 servings

Apple, Marshmallow, and Chocolate Chip Hand Pies

This and the next recipe may or may not be apple pies in your book, but I think they're close enough—especially since they are such a big hit with kids, who can make them with a minimum of adult supervision. Nor will the kids have to wait long to enjoy these hand pies, because they're cooked in a skillet, not the oven. The trick? Flour tortillas instead of any sort of traditional pastry. You make these essentially the same way you make a quesadilla, with the marshmallows providing the gooeyness—like cheese in a real quesadilla—to help hold the thing together. The tortilla is folded in half to enclose the filling. Butter is brushed on the surface, then the pie is flipped, brushed with more butter, and dusted with cinnamon sugar. And that's all there is to it. This recipe is written for a single serving, which, depending on the size of the tortilla, will serve one or two people. You can easily multiply the recipe if you're feeding a crowd.

1 TABLESPOON SUGAR, PLUS MORE TO TASTE

½ TEASPOON GROUND CINNAMON

1 TABLESPOON UNSALTED BUTTER, SOFTENED

1 APPLE, PEELED, CORED, AND SLICED

ONE 8- OR 9-INCH FLOUR TORTILLA

SMALL HANDFUL OF MINI MARSHMALLOWS

2 TABLESPOONS SEMISWEET CHOCOLATE CHIPS

1. Mix the sugar and cinnamon together in a small mixing bowl; set aside.

2. Melt about half of the butter in a medium-size skillet. Add the apple slices and cook over medium heat, turning them over until they're almost tender, 2 to 3 minutes. Sprinkle with a little cinnamon sugar during the last 30 seconds of cooking. Remove the skillet from the heat and set aside.

3. In a large, heavy skillet, warm the flour tortilla over medium-low heat. Arrange the apple slices in a single random layer over half of the tortilla; you may not need them all. Scatter the marshmallows over the apples, followed by the chocolate chips. Fold the uncovered half of the tortilla over the filling, pressing down on it to make a neat fold.

4. Using a pastry brush, brush the exposed half of the tortilla with the remaining softened butter. Sprinkle with some of the cinnamon sugar. Heat for 30 to 45 seconds, then flip the pie over and repeat the process—brushing with melted butter from the skillet and sprinkling with the cinnamon sugar. Heat for another 30 seconds. When the marshmallows are gooey and the chocolate is melted, slide the pie out of the skillet and onto a cooling rack.

5. Let the hand pie cool for a couple of minutes. Slide it onto a cutting board, cut it in half, and serve. Try to get your kids to wait for a couple of extra minutes so they don't burn themselves on the very hot filling.

Note: If you're going to make another hand pie, immediately grab the still-hot skillet and run it under water. Any cinnamon sugar that's stuck to the pan should boil right off. Dump the rinse water into the sink, wipe the pan with paper towels, and put it back on the heat.

Makes 1 or 2 servings

PIE SAFES

Before iceboxes and more reliable means of food storage were the norm, most homes had at least one pie safe in the house. Pie safes came into regular use during the 1700s and remained an important feature of American households through the 1800s.

The pie safe was a place to keep pies, meats, breads, and other perishable foods safe from flies, other insects, rodents, and other unwanted intruders. About the size of a large bureau and perhaps eighteen inches deep, pie safes were made from both softwoods and hardwoods. They had a pair of hinged doors on the front, typically covered with punched-tin panels—or in some cases simple screens—for ventilation. Sims Rogers—an antique dealer in Cambridge, Maryland, who often trades in pie safes—tells me that the punched-tin panels were often quite intricate and may have had special meaning for an owner. The punches might represent a church scene, a Masonic emblem, or eagles and stars. Often they were simply attractive shapes.

Freestanding pie safes generally had long legs to keep them well off the floor, but some were suspended from the ceiling or mounted on the wall. This being a less disposable era of American history, they were commonly made from packing crates or discarded pieces of wood. Markings on the wood, says Rogers, will sometimes give you a clue as to a pie safe's place of origin.

Frozen Apple and Peanut Butter Cloud Pie

When people tick off their personal lists of things they like to eat with apples, peanut butter often comes out near the top. Thus it was an easy—and indeed correct—assumption that apples would work well as a bottom layer in this, one of my all-time-favorite peanut butter pies.

There are three layers here: a graham cracker crust; sautéed apples on top of that; and then a sort of peanut butter mousse, made with whipped cream, cream cheese, peanut butter, sugar, and beaten egg whites. Once the pie is assembled, it goes into the freezer for at least four to five hours to get it good and firm—so you'll need to make this in the morning if you want to serve it for dinner. For a special touch, drizzle a little chocolate dessert topping over each slice. Kids are crazy about this pie.

1 RECIPE GRAHAM CRACKER CRUST (PAGE 20) OR 1 LARGE STORE-BOUGHT GRAHAM CRACKER CRUST

APPLE LAYER:

2 TABLESPOONS UNSALTED BUTTER

3 FIRM-TEXTURED COOKING APPLES (SUCH AS GOLDEN DELICIOUS OR NORTHERN SPY), PEELED, CORED, AND SLICED

¼ CUP GRANULATED SUGAR

1 TEASPOON FRESH LEMON JUICE

2 TABLESPOONS CONFECTIONERS' SUGAR

PEANUT BUTTER CLOUD LAYER:

1 CUP HEAVY CREAM

ONE 8-OUNCE PACKAGE CREAM CHEESE, SOFTENED

1 CUP SMOOTH PEANUT BUTTER

¾ CUP GRANULATED SUGAR

½ CUP FIRMLY PACKED LIGHT BROWN SUGAR

2 TEASPOONS PURE VANILLA EXTRACT

2 LARGE EGG WHITES

½ CUP FINELY CHOPPED SALTED DRY-ROASTED PEANUTS

1. Prepare the crust and press it into a 9-inch deep-dish pie pan, then fully prebake according to the directions on page 19. Or simply use a store-bought crust, prebaking it according to the package directions, if necessary. In either case, set the crust aside on a cooling rack and let cool thoroughly.

2. To prepare the apple layer, melt the butter in a large sauté pan. Stir in the apples and granulated sugar and cook over medium heat, stirring often, until almost tender, about 5 minutes. Stir in the lemon juice and confectioners' sugar and cook, stirring, for 1 minute longer. Remove from the heat, scrape the apples onto a plate, and let cool thoroughly.

3. When the apples have cooled, spoon them into the crust. If there's a fair amount of juice, use a slotted spoon and don't add all the juice with the apples; reserve the remaining juice. Put the pie shell in the freezer. If you have reserved some of the juice, wait until the apples have been in the freezer for 20 minutes or so, then pour on the juice.

4. To make the peanut butter cloud layer, use an electric mixer to whip the heavy cream until it holds semi-firm peaks. Cover and refrigerate.

5. Using the mixer, beat the cream cheese and peanut butter together until smooth. Gradually beat in the sugars, then the vanilla. The mixture will be lumpy, like cookie dough. Add the whipped cream to the peanut butter mixture, slowly blending them together with the electric mixer until smooth.

6. Clean and dry the beaters. Using a clean bowl, beat the egg whites until they hold stiff peaks. Fold the whites into the peanut butter mixture with a rubber spatula until evenly blended. Scrape the mixture over the apples and smooth with a spoon. Sprinkle the chopped nuts over the pie. Loosely cover with aluminum foil and place in the freezer for at least 5 hours, until firm. Remove the pie from the freezer about 15 minutes before you plan to slice it.

Makes 10 servings

No-Bake Apple Ice Cream Pie

Well, almost no bake, because the graham cracker crust you buy for this might need to be prebaked. Here again is a pie the kids can make—and I've gone out of my way to keep it as simple as possible, so they can proceed without Mom or Dad needing to hover too much. This concept grew out of one of my many meetings with some of my pie consultants—my kids Sam and Ali and their friends. There was unanimous agreement that an apple and ice cream pie was a neat idea; we simply had to iron out the particulars. Not surprisingly, caramel topping was voted in. We settled on a jar of Smucker's Dulce de Leche—not only because it sounded delicious but also because the lid said we might instantly win one of 10,000 great prizes. Alas, we didn't. But we still made one heck of a pie: layers of sautéed apple slices, caramel, lots of vanilla ice cream, more caramel, and nuts in a graham cracker crust. Depending on the ages of your pie crew, you might sauté the apples or have them do it. If the latter, work with them at the stove to guard against mishaps. This would make a good party pie for a birthday, Halloween, or another special event.

1 LARGE STORE-BOUGHT GRAHAM CRACKER CRUST

2 TABLESPOONS UNSALTED BUTTER

3 GOLDEN DELICIOUS APPLES, PEELED, CORED, AND CUT INTO 1-INCH CHUNKS

¼ CUP CONFECTIONERS' SUGAR, SIFTED

1½ TABLESPOONS FRESH LEMON JUICE

ONE 12-OUNCE JAR DULCE DE LECHE CARAMEL TOPPING (SEE HEADNOTE)

1 QUART VANILLA ICE CREAM

½ CUP CHOPPED WALNUTS OR PECANS, TOASTED (SEE PAGE 181)

1. Read the package directions on the graham cracker crust and prebake if necessary. You can, of course, use your favorite homemade crust recipe, pressed into a 9-inch pie pan and prebaked. In either case, let the crust cool on a cooling rack while you prepare the apples.

2. Melt the butter in a large nonreactive skillet or sauté pan. Add the apples and cook, stirring, over medium heat until they're just about tender, 5 to 6 minutes. Stir in the confectioners' sugar and lemon juice, cook for another minute or so, and remove from the heat. Scrape the apples and their juice onto a large plate and let cool.

3. When the apples are almost cool, scrape them and their juice into the pie shell, spreading them evenly in the crust. Without measuring— that's the fun part, not measuring—slowly pour a little less than half of the bottle of caramel evenly over the apples. Put the pie shell in the freezer for 30 minutes to firm up the apples and caramel. When you do this, put the ice cream in the refrigerator to soften it.

4. After 30 minutes, spoon the softened ice cream over the apples, pressing it down and smoothing it out with the back of a fork. Now pour as much of the remaining caramel over the ice cream as you like. You can pour it in a spiral, a zigzag, or any decorative fashion you like. (Note to kids: You probably won't need to use all of the remaining topping, but you don't have to tell your parents I said that, if you don't want to.) Sprinkle the nuts over the top of the pie, then put the pie back in the freezer for 1 hour to firm it up. No cheating and taking it out before an hour is up. Slice and serve.

Makes 8 to 10 servings

Sam and Jim's Butterscotch Apple Pie for Kids

Kids like to bake apple pies; mine certainly do. But they don't like a long list of ingredients. And most prefer to do things by hand, rather than by machine, because getting your hands into your work and making a bit of a mess is at least half the fun. So here is a pie I created—with the help of my 13-year-old son, Sam, and his friend Jim—mainly for kids, no machines needed. We began with the premise that kids love caramel apples and almost all things caramel, so we would stay in that approximate flavor range. A jar of butterscotch dessert topping seemed like a good bet because it would both flavor and sweeten the pie in one swoop. Beyond that, we would need just a little flour, for thickening, and a squeeze of lemon, to perk things up. Remember that this recipe is written for kids, in language they can follow. Don't be alarmed if it reads a little differently than most of the other recipes in this book.

1 STORE-BOUGHT FROZEN 9-INCH DEEP-DISH
  PIE SHELL

FILLING:

6 APPLES

½ LEMON OR 1 TABLESPOON FRESH LEMON
  JUICE

2 TABLESPOONS ALL-PURPOSE FLOUR

⅔ CUP STORE-BOUGHT BUTTERSCOTCH
  DESSERT TOPPING

NUT TOPPING:

1 CUP ALL-PURPOSE FLOUR

⅔ CUP FIRMLY PACKED LIGHT BROWN SUGAR

¼ TEASPOON SALT

¼ TEASPOON GROUND CINNAMON

½ CUP (1 STICK) COLD UNSALTED BUTTER,
  CUT INTO LITTLE PIECES

½ CUP CHOPPED WALNUTS OR PECANS

1. Remove the frozen crust from the package but keep it in the freezer until you're ready to use it.

2. About 10 minutes before you plan to bake the pie, preheat the oven to 400 degrees, then start making the filling. First, peel all the apples, then core them using an apple corer. Cut the apples in half, from top to bottom. Working with one-half apple at a time, put it on a cutting board—flat side down, so it doesn't wobble—and slice straight down through the apple, cutting it into 7 or 8 slices. As you cut each apple, slide it into a big mixing bowl.

3. When you're done with all of the apples, put a fine-mesh sieve in the apple bowl and squeeze the lemon into it, to catch the seeds. (Or just measure out 1 tablespoon lemon juice.) Using a wooden spoon, mix the apples with the lemon juice. Shake the flour over the apples and mix again. Finally, measure out the butterscotch sauce, pour it over the apples, and mix well.

4. Take the pie shell out of the freezer and scrape the filling into it. Even the top of the apples with your hands, so the apple slices aren't sticking up all over the place. Wearing oven mitts, put the pie on the center rack of the oven—ask an adult for help if you haven't put things in the oven before—and close the door. Set the timer for 35 minutes.

5. While you're waiting for the timer, make the nut topping. Measure out the flour, sugar, salt, and cinnamon and put them in a large mixing bowl. Mix them together with your hands. Put the butter pieces on top of the flour. Mix them up with the flour, then start rubbing the flour and butter together with your hands. The mixture will get all damp and buttery and feel a little like damp sand. Stop rubbing when it is still sandy; it shouldn't all pack together. Add the nuts and mix them in just a little with your hands.

6. When the timer goes off after 35 minutes, reduce the oven temperature to 375 degrees. Then put a large, dark baking sheet covered with aluminum foil on top of the stove or on a counter right next to it. Using oven mitts—or an adult—take the pie out of the oven and put it on top of the baking sheet. Now reach into the bowl and take out a big handful of the nut topping. Place it on top of the pie, taking care not to burn yourself. Do this several more times, to get all the topping, then spread it around so it's even all over the top of the pie. Press down lightly to compact the topping.

7. Put the baking sheet and pie back in the oven and bake for another 35 to 40 minutes, until the pie is done. You can tell it's done when any juices that you can see are bubbling quite a bit. The top of the pie will be a dark golden brown. If you look at the pie while it is still in the oven and the top is getting really dark, put a piece of aluminum foil over it.

8. When the pie is done, take it out of the oven and put it on a cooling rack. Let cool for at least 1 hour before slicing.

Makes 8 to 10 servings

Caramel-Apple Nut Pie

The flavors of caramel and apples together are wonderful—witness our nation's love affair with caramel apples. Pulling off this flavor combination in a pie, however, is not so simple. One can't simply pour store-bought caramel sauce over a piece of pie—too tacky, to say the least. Here's a better idea: pouring heavy cream into a brown sugar–sweetened pie. The combination of the heavy cream, brown sugar, and extra flour in the pie conspire to create a thick caramel sauce that bakes all around the apples—though you must wait until the pie is nearly cool for this "sauce" to achieve the proper body.

I like to give a sneak preview of the contents by coating the top pastry with a simple caramel sauce. As you might imagine, it changes the texture of the pastry. Rather than remaining crisp and flaky, the pastry becomes quite soft and tends to collapse and press down on the filling, making for a compact slice. It all adds up to an interesting pie any caramel fan will adore.

1 RECIPE ALL-AMERICAN DOUBLE CRUST
(PAGE 2) OR SHORTENING DOUBLE CRUST
(PAGE 4), REFRIGERATED

FILLING:

6 LARGE APPLES, PEELED, CORED, AND
SLICED

¾ CUP FIRMLY PACKED LIGHT BROWN SUGAR

5 TABLESPOONS ALL-PURPOSE FLOUR

1 CUP CHOPPED WALNUTS

½ TEASPOON GROUND CINNAMON

PINCH OF SALT

¼ CUP HEAVY CREAM

GLAZE:

½ CUP HEAVY CREAM

¼ CUP FIRMLY PACKED LIGHT BROWN SUGAR

1 TABLESPOON UNSALTED BUTTER

1. If you haven't already, prepare the pastry and refrigerate it until firm enough to roll, about 1 hour.

2. On a sheet of lightly floured waxed paper, roll the larger portion of pastry into a 13½-inch circle with a floured rolling pin. Invert the pastry over a 9-inch deep-dish pie pan. Center it, then peel off the paper. Gently tuck the pastry down into the pan, without stretching it, and let the excess pastry drape over the side of the pan. Cover loosely with plastic wrap and refrigerate for 15 minutes. Preheat the oven to 400 degrees.

3. To make the filling, mix the apples, brown sugar, flour, walnuts, cinnamon, and salt together in a large mixing bowl. Set aside.

4. On another sheet of lightly floured waxed paper, roll the top pastry into an 11½-inch circle. Using the lid of a jar or another small (1- to

1½-inch) circle, cut a hole in the very center of the pastry. Remove and discard the center circle.

5. Turn the filling into the pie shell and smooth the top with your hands. Lightly moisten the edge of the shell with a wet fingertip or brush. Invert the top pastry over the filling, center it, and peel off the paper. Press the top and bottom pastries together along the dampened edge. Trim the pastry, leaving an even ½ inch all around, then sculpt the overhang into an upstanding ridge. Place the pie on a large, dark baking sheet covered with aluminum foil. Bake on the center rack for 30 minutes.

6. Near the end of the 30 minutes, put the heavy cream in a small saucepan and bring nearly to a boil over medium heat. Transfer to a heatproof measuring cup. Remove the pie from the oven and pour the hot cream through the hole in the center of the pie. Reduce the oven temperature to 375 degrees, then put the pie on the baking sheet back in the oven and bake for 25 minutes longer.

7. When the 25 minutes are nearly up, combine the glaze ingredients in a small saucepan. Bring to a boil, then remove from the heat. Remove the pie and baking sheet from the oven. Spoon and spread the glaze over the entire top crust, then bake for about 3 minutes more.

8. Transfer the pie to a cooling rack and let cool to room temperature before serving.

Makes 8 to 10 servings

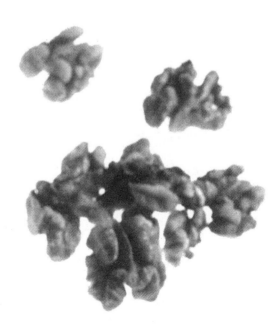

Apple Pie in a Jiffy

Everyone—even a dedicated pie guy like myself—has moments when an apple pie and crust, both made from scratch, are out of the question. Perhaps you're heading out to a tailgate party or potluck supper, and time is running short. Or you've overslept and there's no time to make a pastry. Maybe you're just plain feeling lazy. Or homemade pastry just isn't your thing: you came, you rolled, you were conquered.

Whatever the case, you needn't feel that you're washed up as an apple pie maker. There are lots of good apple pies you can make, unashamedly, with someone else's pie shell—and here are eight of them to prove my point. These pies will save you time not only because you're using frozen pastry. I've incorporated other shortcuts as well to streamline the process further. First, these pies tend to use fewer apples because frozen pie shells even deep-dish ones—hold less fruit than a typical deep-dish pie shell. Also, almost all these pies finished with an easy-to-mix crumb topping, which can be made in just five minutes after the pie

is already in the oven, so there's no top crust to roll and attach. And where I've been able to, I've used shortcut ingredients such as lemonade concentrate, whose flavor packs so much lemon punch that you needn't add lemon juice and lemon zest.

Of course, a frozen pie pastry isn't going to taste quite as good as your own. But I think most of us would say that given the choice between homemade apple pie with someone else's crust and no apple pie at all, someone else's crust is just fine. Try a few of these and see if you agree.

The Easiest Apple Pie of All

Some cooks are happy to make an apple pie that's just sort of homemade. My girlfriend, Bev, happens to be one them, and one of a number of people who told me that I simply had to include a recipe based on a canned apple pie filling, which—pie purist that I am—I had never bought until this past year, at the age of 46. Anyway, Bev belongs to this significant group of home pie makers who will empty a can of apple pie filling into a frozen store-bought pie shell, add a crumb topping, and suffer not an ounce of guilt or a moment of equivocation when asked if the pie is homemade. Bev asserts that when this happens to her, she doesn't actually lie. She simply affects a bashful, aw-shucks pose, steps back, and collects the compliments. I tell her that's a lie of omission. She tells me I'm an old fuddy-duddy, a killjoy, and a snob—in light of which I started playing around with canned apple filling. To my surprise, I found that some of these fillings aren't without merit—enough so that, with a couple of homey touches and a somewhat broadened definition of homemade, one could make a respectable homemade pie with canned apple pie filling. The touches are simple: a tart apple, a bit of lemon juice to counter the sweetness of the filling, cinnamon, a few raisins, and a homemade oatmeal topping. Does the pie taste good? Let's just say much better than I would have thought—this, don't forget, coming from an old pie fuddy-duddy and snob.

1 STORE-BOUGHT FROZEN 9-INCH DEEP-DISH PIE SHELL

FILLING:

TWO 21-OUNCE CANS APPLE PIE FILLING

1 GRANNY SMITH OR OTHER TART, JUICY APPLE, PEELED, CORED, AND FINELY CHOPPED

1½ TABLESPOONS FRESH LEMON JUICE

½ CUP RAISINS OR DRIED CURRANTS

½ TEASPOON GROUND CINNAMON

OATMEAL CRUMB TOPPING:

1 CUP ALL-PURPOSE FLOUR

½ CUP OLD-FASHIONED ROLLED OATS (NOT INSTANT)

⅔ CUP FIRMLY PACKED LIGHT BROWN SUGAR

½ TEASPOON GROUND CINNAMON

¼ TEASPOON SALT

½ CUP (1 STICK) COLD UNSALTED BUTTER, CUT INTO ¼-INCH PIECES

1. Remove the pie shell from the box but leave in the freezer. Preheat the oven to 400 degrees.

2. Mix the apple pie filling, apple, lemon juice, raisins, and cinnamon in a medium-size mixing bowl. Turn it into the frozen pie shell and smooth the top with your hands. Put the pie directly on the center oven rack and bake for 25 minutes.

3. While the pie bakes, make the topping. Put the flour, oats, brown sugar, cinnamon, and salt in a food processor and pulse several times to mix. Remove the lid and scatter the butter pieces over the dry mixture. Pulse the machine repeatedly, until the mixture resembles fine crumbs. Empty the crumbs into a large mixing bowl and rub between your fingers to make large, buttery crumbs. Refrigerate.

4. After 25 minutes, slip a large metal spatula or small rimless cookie sheet under the pie and slide it onto a large, dark baking sheet covered with aluminum foil. Reduce the oven temperature to 375 degrees. Carefully dump the crumbs in the center of the pie, spreading them evenly over the surface with your hands. Tamp them down lightly. Return the pie on the baking sheet to the oven and bake until the juices bubble thickly around the edge, an additional 20 to 25 minutes.

5. Slip the metal spatula or cookie sheet under the pie and slide the pie onto a cooling rack. Let cool at least 1 hour before slicing.

Makes 8 servings

THOSE FROZEN PIE SHELLS

Do I use them? Sure I do. Do I recommend them? Certainly. They're irreplaceable when time is short or you want to make a pie that's more or less homemade. Are they without their drawbacks? Well, I have a couple of little beefs.

The first is flavor. I find frozen pie crusts rather bland, but I suppose that's a fair tradeoff for the time you save not having to bake your own. And some brands do seem to have more to offer, flavor-wise, than others. I tested half a dozen, both big-name and store-brand pastries, and the one standout was made by Marie Callender's. At least some of the difference, I believe, is due to the fact that this one has a heavier aluminum pan, which seems to do a better job of browning the bottom crust. (Heavy enough that the package encourages you to reuse it; you can.) Some of the brands I tried barely browned at all on the bottom.

The other problem with these pans—and again, the reason I like the brand I mention above—is their flexible nature. If you've ever tried to lift a hot pie that's been baked in one of these pans out of the oven, you know that the pan can buckle dangerously by the time the pie is fully baked. What I recommend, therefore, is sliding these pies onto and off of your baking sheet with either a large metal spatula or a small rimless cookie sheet, so you don't actually have to lift the pan.

Your Basic Great Apple Pie with Northern Spies

It might seem obvious, but I'll say it anyway: one of the easiest ways to make an extraordinary apple pie, even with a pie crust that's not homemade, is to use the very best apples you can. Short of seeking out antique apples, the best—in many pie makers' books—is the Northern Spy, which comes along late in the season. "Spies are for pies," the old saying goes, and this pie—a model for building almost any 9-inch apple pie with a frozen pastry—is a fine showcase for that timeless sentiment.

As I pointed out in the introduction to this section, what's called a 9-inch deep-dish pie shell in the freezer section actually holds 1 to 2 cups fewer apples than the standard 9-inch deep-dish Pyrex pie pans I used to test most of the recipes in this book. So this pie calls for 7 cups of apples, which still makes for a generous pie. (If you'd like to scale this up to fit the larger pan with your own crust, use 9 cups of apples and ½ cup sugar, add the grated zest of the entire lemon, and increase the flour to 2 tablespoons.)

If you can't find Northern Spy apples, look for Rhode Island Greening, Pippin, or even Granny Smith apples, if your options are limited to the standard supermarket varieties, as is often the case.

1 STORE-BOUGHT FROZEN 9-INCH DEEP-DISH PIE SHELL

FILLING:

7 CUPS PEELED, CORED, AND SLICED APPLES (SEE HEADNOTE)

⅓ CUP GRANULATED SUGAR

1½ TABLESPOONS FRESH LEMON JUICE

GRATED ZEST OF ½ LEMON

1½ TABLESPOONS ALL-PURPOSE FLOUR

OATMEAL CRUMB TOPPING:

1 CUP ALL-PURPOSE FLOUR

½ CUP OLD-FASHIONED ROLLED OATS (NOT INSTANT)

⅔ CUP FIRMLY PACKED LIGHT BROWN SUGAR

¼ TEASPOON SALT

¼ TEASPOON GROUND CINNAMON

½ CUP (1 STICK) COLD UNSALTED BUTTER, CUT INTO ¼-INCH PIECES

1. Remove the pie shell from the package but leave it in the freezer until you're ready to fill it.

2. In a large mixing bowl, combine the apples, granulated sugar, lemon juice, and lemon zest. Mix well, then set aside for 10 minutes. Preheat the oven to 400 degrees.

3. Shake the flour over the apples and mix. Scrape the filling into the frozen pie shell, smoothing the top with your hands. Place the pie directly on the center oven rack and bake for 25 minutes.

4. While the pie bakes, make the topping. Put the flour, oats, brown sugar, salt, and cinnamon in a food processor and pulse to mix. Remove the lid and scatter the butter pieces over the dry ingredients. Pulse the machine repeatedly, until the mixture resembles fine crumbs. Dump the crumbs into a large mixing bowl and rub them between your fingers to make large, buttery crumbs. Refrigerate.

5. After 25 minutes, slip a large metal spatula or small rimless cookie sheet under the pie and slide it onto a large, dark baking sheet covered with aluminum foil. Reduce the oven temperature to 375 degrees. Carefully dump the crumb topping in the center of the pie, spreading it evenly over the surface with your hands. Tamp down lightly to compact the crumbs. Return the pie on the baking sheet to the oven and bake until the juices bubble thickly around the edge, 25 to 30 minutes longer.

6. Slip the metal spatula or cookie sheet under the pie and slide the pie onto a cooling rack. Let cool for at least 1 hour before slicing.

Makes 8 servings

Crispin Apple Lemonade Pie

Here's another way to throw an apple pie together in a snap, without a lot of ingredients. This pie came together one morning when I needed to get to a Navy football game and an ensuing tailgate party, for which I was supposed to bring the dessert. A quick inventory of the pantry and fridge turned up a fresh batch of Crispin apples, a can of lemonade concentrate, and a frozen pie shell. The lemonade was the real stroke of luck: so concentrated is the flavor that you don't need to squeeze fresh lemon juice or grate lemon zest, as I do for so many of my apple pies. And it's sweet enough that very little additional sugar is needed—just a few tablespoons. While the pie started baking, I mixed the streusel topping in the food processor. Especially when time is tight, I'll choose a streusel topping such as this one because it's so simple and wildly popular. Said Stu, my good friend who attended the party, "This topping is so good you ought to patent it." As for the Crispin, it's a late-ripening apple you find in the fall, usually after the first or second week of October. Also known as the Mutsu and a relative of the Golden Delicious, it's a green-skinned apple with very juicy, white, crisp flesh. The ones you find in the market tend to be huge; you could make a whole pie from two or three of them. I think they make a very good pie.

1 STORE-BOUGHT FROZEN 9-INCH DEEP-DISH PIE SHELL

FILLING:

6 CUPS PEELED, CORED, AND SLICED CRISPIN OR OTHER APPLES

⅓ CUP FROZEN LEMONADE CONCENTRATE, THAWED

3 TABLESPOONS SUGAR

1 TABLESPOON CORNSTARCH

STREUSEL TOPPING:

1 CUP ALL-PURPOSE FLOUR

⅔ CUP SUGAR

¼ TEASPOON SALT

¼ TEASPOON GROUND CINNAMON

½ CUP (1 STICK) COLD UNSALTED BUTTER, CUT INTO ¼-INCH PIECES

1. Remove the pie shell from the package but leave it in the freezer until you're ready to fill it. Preheat the oven to 400 degrees.

2. To make the filling, combine the apples and lemonade concentrate in a large mixing bowl; mix well. In a small mixing bowl, combine the sugar and cornstarch; mix well. Shake the dry mixture over the fruit, then toss well to combine. Scrape the filling into the frozen pie shell and smooth the top with your hands. Place the pie directly on the center oven rack and bake for 25 minutes.

3. While the pie bakes, make the topping. Put the flour, sugar, salt, and cinnamon in a food processor. Pulse several times to mix. Remove the lid and scatter the butter pieces over the dry mixture. Pulse the machine repeatedly, until the mixture resembles fine crumbs. Empty the crumbs into a large mixing bowl and rub them with your fingers to make large, buttery crumbs. Refrigerate.

4. After 25 minutes, slip a large metal spatula or small rimless cookie sheet under the pie and slide it onto a large, dark baking sheet covered with aluminum foil. Reduce the oven temperature to 375 degrees. Carefully dump the topping in the center of the pie, spreading it evenly with your hands over the surface. Tamp down gently to compact the crumbs. Put the pie on the baking sheet back in the oven and bake until the juices bubble thickly around the edge, 30 to 35 minutes longer.

5. Slip the metal spatula or cookie sheet under the pie and slide it onto a cooling rack. Let cool for at least 1 hour before slicing.

Makes 8 servings

Quick Apple Cherry Pie

My first choice for an apple cherry pie is almost always fresh cherries, but there are a lot of times when I want a cherry pie without the hassle of rinsing cherries, removing the stems, and pitting them. When that's the case, I use frozen. In truth, the quality of the frozen cherries I buy is quite good—often better than fresh cherries, which may be bruised or not at the correct stage of ripeness. Those frozen cherries, a handful of apples, and a store-bought pastry will make for a fine pie that you can prepare in about 10 minutes, plus a minute or two to mix up the streusel topping in your food processor. If you'd like to get a little fancier, you can use the almond crumb topping from the apple cherry pie on page 76.

1 STORE-BOUGHT FROZEN 9-INCH DEEP-DISH
   PIE SHELL

FILLING:

4 CUPS PEELED, CORED, AND SLICED
   APPLES

ONE 1-POUND BAG FROZEN PITTED SWEET
   CHERRIES

½ CUP SUGAR

1 TABLESPOON FRESH LEMON JUICE OR
   CIDER VINEGAR

2½ TABLESPOONS ALL-PURPOSE FLOUR

STREUSEL TOPPING:

1 CUP ALL-PURPOSE FLOUR

⅔ CUP SUGAR

¼ TEASPOON SALT

¼ TEASPOON GROUND CINNAMON

½ CUP (1 STICK) COLD UNSALTED BUTTER,
   CUT INTO ¼-INCH PIECES

1. Remove the pie shell from the package but leave it in the freezer until you're ready to fill it.

2. To make the filling, combine the apples, cherries (leaving them whole), sugar, and lemon juice in a large mixing bowl; toss well to mix. Set aside for 15 minutes. Preheat the oven to 400 degrees.

3. Shake the flour over the filling and mix well. Turn the filling into the frozen pie shell, smoothing the top with your hands. Place the pie directly on the center oven rack and bake for 30 minutes.

4. While the pie bakes, make the streusel topping. Combine the flour, sugar, salt, and cinnamon in a food processor, pulsing several times to mix. Remove the lid and scatter the butter pieces over the dry ingredients. Pulse the machine repeatedly, until the mixture resembles fine crumbs. Dump the crumbs into a large mixing bowl and rub with your fingers to make large, buttery crumbs. Refrigerate.

5. After 30 minutes, slip a large metal spatula or small rimless cookie sheet under the pie and slide it onto a large, dark baking sheet covered with aluminum foil. Reduce the oven temperature to 375 degrees. Carefully dump the streusel crumbs in the center of the pie, spreading them evenly over the surface with your hands. Tamp them down lightly. Put the pie on the baking sheet back in the oven and bake until the juices bubble thickly around the edge, an additional 25 to 30 minutes.

6. Slip the metal spatula or cookie sheet under the pie and slide the pie onto a cooling rack. Let cool for at least 1 hour before slicing.

Makes 8 servings

FLOUR VS. CORNSTARCH: IT'S ENOUGH TO MAKE YOU THICK

Perhaps you've observed that some of the recipes here use cornstarch for thickening, but many more use flour. Some even use quick-cooking tapioca. (And a few use no thickener at all.) Does it really matter which kind of thickener you use?

To my taste, there's little difference between the results you achieve with cornstarch or flour. I have read complaints from serious cooks who prefer cornstarch over flour, maintaining that flour clouds the finished color of the pie, leaving the filling somewhat opaque. Cornstarch, they say, cooks up clear and glossy. These people have a point, but I think any opaqueness you get with flour is minor to the point of niggling. You can bet almost no one will notice.

Flour or cornstarch, I find the most important thing is to cook the pie long enough to make the juices boil so the thickener can "take," meaning that the starch has reached the swelling point and thickened the juices. I've seen many a pie get close to this point but not reach it. You can spot a pie like this because its juices run very thin. For this reason, I'll always err on the side of baking a pie a little too long. It's also why almost all of my recipes admonish you to bake the pie until the juices bubble thickly.

Flour, incidentally, can be sprinkled right on the fruit and mixed in. Cornstarch tends to clump up if you mix it in this way, so always blend it with some of the sugar before adding it to an apple pie.

As for instant tapioca, most apple pies don't make enough juice to require tapioca, which I normally use for a very juicy peach or berry pie. I will occasionally use it when I mix apples with these fruits because it does such an efficient job of thickening. Be aware that tapioca leaves a somewhat noticeable network of little bubbles, which some people consider less than attractive in pie. Personally, I don't mind it.

Gravenstein Apple and Pear Pie with Cornmeal Streusel

Here's an excellent pie, and one that's easy and quick to assemble if you're heading off to a fall event and don't have time to make pastry from scratch. I agree with my friend Marion Cunningham (see page 139): Gravenstein apples make a great pie—and this is your chance to find out. They're agreeably tart, juicy, and firm-textured, which makes them a perfect match for soft, sweet pears. To top things off, I use a thick layer of cornmeal streusel. The crunch and flavor of the cornmeal work very well with this delicious pie.

1 STORE-BOUGHT FROZEN 9-INCH DEEP-DISH PIE SHELL

FILLING:

4 CUPS PEELED, CORED, AND SLICED GRAVENSTEIN OR GRANNY SMITH APPLES

3 CUPS PEELED, CORED, AND SLICED RIPE PEARS

⅓ CUP SUGAR

1 TABLESPOON FRESH LEMON JUICE

GRATED ZEST OF ½ LEMON

⅓ CUP RAISINS

1 TO 2 TABLESPOONS ALL-PURPOSE FLOUR

CORNMEAL STREUSEL TOPPING:

⅔ CUP ALL-PURPOSE FLOUR

⅓ CUP FINE YELLOW CORNMEAL

⅔ CUP SUGAR

¼ TEASPOON GROUND CINNAMON

¼ TEASPOON SALT

½ CUP (1 STICK) COLD UNSALTED BUTTER, CUT INTO ¼-INCH PIECES

1. Remove the pie shell from the package but leave in the freezer until you're ready to use it.

2. To make the filling, mix the apples, pears, sugar, lemon juice, lemon zest, and raisins together in a large mixing bowl. Set aside for 10 minutes. Preheat the oven to 400 degrees.

3. Check the juice in the bottom of the bowl. If there's quite a bit, sprinkle on 2 tablespoons flour and mix it into the fruit. If there's not too much juice, stir in only 1 tablespoon flour. Scrape the filling into the frozen pie shell. Smooth the top of the fruit with your hands and, as much as reasonably possible, bury the raisins under the fruit so they don't scorch in the oven. Place the pie directly on the center oven rack and bake for 30 minutes.

4. While the pie bakes, prepare the streusel topping. Put the flour, cornmeal, sugar, cinnamon, and salt in a food processor and pulse several times to mix. Remove the lid and scatter the butter pieces over the dry ingredients. Pulse the machine repeatedly, until the mixture resembles fine crumbs. Empty the crumbs into a large mixing bowl and rub them between your fingers to make large, buttery crumbs. Refrigerate.

5. After 30 minutes, slide a large metal spatula or small rimless cookie sheet under the pie and slide the pie onto a large, dark baking sheet covered with aluminum foil. Carefully dump the streusel in the center of the pie, spreading the crumbs evenly over the surface with your hands. Tamp down lightly to compact. Put the pie on the baking sheet back in the oven and bake until the juices bubble thickly around the edge, about another 25 minutes.

6. Slide the metal spatula or cookie sheet under the pie and slide it onto a cooling rack. Let cool for at least 1 hour, preferably longer, before slicing.

Makes 8 servings

Cortland Apple Pie with Granola Crumb Crust

Cortland apples are a major presence in northeastern and New England markets during the fall. The early crop is small, firm, juicy, and tart; later ones are sweeter, with a whiter, more tender flesh. The Cortland is often touted as being a great salad apple—not only because it has great off-the-tree flavor but also because it's less prone to browning. Wonderful as it is fresh, I think the early Cortland makes a good pie as well—baking up not too soft, not too firm—and I offer this pie as proof. A little sugar, a bit of lemon juice—nothing too out of the ordinary in the filling here. But I do like to use this special granola crust for a change of pace. A couple of hints: Don't use granola with raisins in it; the raisins will burn on top of the pie. And if your granola is rather coarse—homemade granola, for instance, often is—quickly run it through the food processor to chop it up a little before you work it into the rest of the topping.

1 STORE-BOUGHT FROZEN 9-INCH DEEP-DISH PIE SHELL

FILLING:

8 CUPS PEELED, CORED, AND SLICED EARLY OR OTHER CORTLAND APPLES

½ CUP GRANULATED SUGAR

1 ½ TABLESPOONS FRESH LEMON JUICE

¼ TEASPOON GROUND CINNAMON

PINCH OF SALT

1 ½ TABLESPOONS ALL-PURPOSE FLOUR

GRANOLA TOPPING:

½ CUP ALL-PURPOSE FLOUR

⅓ CUP FIRMLY PACKED LIGHT BROWN SUGAR

PINCH OF SALT

5 TABLESPOONS COLD UNSALTED BUTTER, CUT INTO ¼-INCH PIECES

1 CUP GRANOLA CEREAL WITHOUT RAISINS

1. Remove the pie shell from its package but leave it in the freezer until you're ready to fill it.

2. To make the filling, mix the apples, granulated sugar, lemon juice, cinnamon, and salt together in a large mixing bowl. Set aside for 10 minutes. Preheat the oven to 400 degrees.

3. Shake the flour over the filling and mix well. Scrape the filling into the frozen pie shell. Put the pie directly on the center oven rack and bake for 25 minutes. Reduce the oven temperature to 375 degrees and bake 10 minutes more.

4. While the pie bakes, make the granola topping. Put the flour, brown sugar, and salt in a food processor and pulse to mix. Remove the lid and scatter the butter pieces over the dry ingredients. Pulse the machine repeatedly, until the mixture resembles fine crumbs. Dump the crumbs into a large mixing bowl and rub between your fingers to make large, buttery crumbs. Add the granola and rub it into the crumbs. Refrigerate.

5. After the pie has baked for 10 minutes at 375 degrees, slip a large metal spatula or small rimless cookie sheet under it and slide it onto a large, dark baking sheet covered with aluminum foil. Carefully dump the crumbs in the center of the pie, spreading them evenly over the surface with your hands. Press down to compact. Return the pie on the baking sheet to the oven and bake until the juices bubble thickly at the edge, roughly 15 minutes longer.

6. Slip the metal spatula or cookie sheet under the pie and slide it onto a cooling rack. Let cool for at least 1 hour before slicing.

Makes 8 servings

Four-Apple Pie

When I have a lot of different apples on hand I often find myself with an odds-and-ends assortment of apples, one or two to a bag. That's when I like to make a pie like this, combining a variety of apples to create a balanced flavor. That's the way, in fact, cider makers create the perfect blend of cider, so it stands to reason the same approach would make for a superior pie.

If you like this idea, you don't have to use these particular apples, but do go for a mix of tastes and textures.

For example, I like a Granny Smith for tartness; a Golden Delicious or Ginger Gold for sweetness; a McIntosh for softness (it sort of cooks around the other apples and fills in the gaps); and a Northern Spy for firmness and great flavor. And because four apples aren't quite enough to fill a pie—you will need 7 cups to fill the store-bought pie shell—you can either choose a fifth type of apple or double up on one or two of the others, depending on the size of the apples.

1 STORE-BOUGHT FROZEN 9-INCH DEEP-DISH PIE SHELL

FILLING:

1 GRANNY SMITH APPLE

1 GOLDEN DELICIOUS APPLE

1 MCINTOSH APPLE

1 NORTHERN SPY APPLE

ENOUGH ADDITIONAL APPLES TO MAKE 7 CUPS SLICED (SEE HEADNOTE)

⅓ CUP SUGAR

1½ TABLESPOONS FRESH LEMON JUICE

PINCH OF GROUND NUTMEG OR CINNAMON

1½ TABLESPOONS ALL-PURPOSE FLOUR

STREUSEL TOPPING:

1 CUP ALL-PURPOSE FLOUR

½ CUP SUGAR

⅛ TEASPOON SALT

PINCH OF GROUND CINNAMON

½ CUP (1 STICK) COLD UNSALTED BUTTER, CUT INTO ¼-INCH PIECES

1. Remove the pie shell from its package but leave it in the freezer until you're ready to fill it.

2. To make the filling, peel, core, and slice the apples, using enough to make 7 cups total. Put the apples in a large mixing bowl and add the sugar, lemon juice, and nutmeg. Mix well, then set aside for 10 minutes. Preheat the oven to 400 degrees.

3. Shake the flour over the apples and mix. Scrape the filling into the frozen pie shell, smoothing the apples with your hands. Place the pie directly on the center oven rack and bake for 25 minutes.

4. While the pie bakes, make the streusel topping. Put the flour, sugar, salt, and cinnamon in a food processor and pulse several times to mix. Remove the lid and scatter the butter pieces over the dry ingredients. Pulse the machine repeatedly, until the mixture resembles fine crumbs. Dump the crumbs into a large mixing bowl and rub them with your fingers to make large, buttery crumbs. Refrigerate.

5. After 25 minutes, slip a large metal spatula or small rimless cookie sheet under the pie and slide it onto a large, dark baking sheet covered with aluminum foil. Remove from the oven. Reduce the oven temperature to 375 degrees. Carefully dump the topping in the center of the pie, spreading it evenly with your hands. Tamp down gently to compact. Put the pie on the baking sheet back in the oven and bake until the juices bubble thickly around the edge, an additional 25 to 30 minutes.

6. Slip the metal spatula or cookie sheet under the pie and slide it onto a cooling rack. Let cool for at least 1 hour before slicing.

Makes 8 servings

New York State's Official Apple Pie

Peter Gregg, the New York State Apple Commission's spokesperson, feels that pie apples are a matter of personal preference—like chili, he says—and he recommends New York State (of course) Crispin, Golden Delicious, or Jonagold apples for a sweet apple pie. For a tarter pie, he'd try Ida Red, Rhode Island Greening, Rome Beauty, or Northern Spy. But New York's real soft spot is for the McIntosh—its official state apple.

Peter was kind enough to provide me with this, New York's prize pie recipe. I decided, since this is meant to go between two crusts, to use the pie to demonstrate a little trick of mine: putting a homemade top pastry on top of a store-bought frozen pie shell. There are advantages to doing this. The first is that you may have only enough pastry on hand for a top or bottom crust—but you really want to make a double-crust pie. Or you might want the look of a homemade crust with the convenience of a store-bought bottom pastry. In any event, it's really a simple procedure: you turn the filling into the frozen pie shell and smooth it out, then roll out the top pastry, drape it over the pie, trim, and bake. Even if the pie shell is frozen hard, the top pastry will mold right to it.

The state's recipe calls for more rapid baking than I am accustomed to: 45 minutes at 425 degrees, which yields a pretty toasty crust. I suggest that you keep an eye on the crust and, if it's looking rather brown after 25 minutes, turn the oven temperature down to 375 degrees and continue to bake for another 25 to 30 minutes. Since the Mac is the official state apple, I use it here, and the result is a very soft filling. If you'd rather, use one of the apples listed above.

1 RECIPE BEST BUTTER PIE PASTRY (PAGE 8) OR OTHER SINGLE-CRUST PASTRY, REFRIGERATED

1 STORE-BOUGHT FROZEN 9-INCH DEEP-DISH PIE SHELL

FILLING:

6 CUPS PEELED, CORED, AND THINLY SLICED McINTOSH APPLES

¾ CUP SUGAR

2 TABLESPOONS ALL-PURPOSE FLOUR

¾ TEASPOON GROUND CINNAMON

¼ TEASPOON SALT

⅛ TEASPOON GROUND NUTMEG

1 TABLESPOON FRESH LEMON JUICE

1. If you haven't already, prepare the pastry and refrigerate it until firm enough to roll, about 1 hour. Take the frozen pie shell out of the package but leave it in the freezer until you're ready to assemble the pie.

2. Combine all of the filling ingredients in a large mixing bowl. Mix well. Preheat the oven to 425 degrees.

3. On a sheet of lightly floured waxed paper, roll the pastry into an 11-inch circle with a floured rolling pin. Remove the pie shell from the freezer and scrape the filling into it, smoothing the apples with your hands. Moisten the rim of the pie shell with a wet fingertip or pastry brush. Invert the pastry over the filling, center it, and peel off the paper. Press the edge of the top pastry into the rim of the pie shell, sealing the two as best as you can. Using scissors or a paring knife, trim the overhang to a reasonably uniform ½ inch, then sculpt the edge into an upstanding ridge. Poke several steam vents in the top of the pie with a fork or paring knife; put a couple of the vents near the edge of the crust, so you can check the juices there later.

4. Put the pie on a large baking sheet covered with aluminum foil. Place on the center oven rack and bake for about 45 minutes (see headnote), until any juices—visible at the steam vents—bubble thickly.

5. Transfer the pie to a cooling rack and let cool for at least 1 hour before slicing.

Makes 8 servings

Index